The Case for Repatriating China's Cultural Objects

Zuozhen Liu

The Case for Repatriating China's Cultural Objects

Springer

Zuozhen Liu
Jinan University
Guangzhou, Guangdong
China

This study is financed by the Oversea Study Program of Guangzhou Elite Project.

ISBN 978-981-10-0595-4 ISBN 978-981-10-0597-8 (eBook)
DOI 10.1007/978-981-10-0597-8

Library of Congress Control Number: 2016932349

Printed on acid-free paper

This Springer imprint is published by SpringerNature
The registered company is Springer Science+Business Media Singapore Pte Ltd.

Foreword

This book explores the topic of restitution of cultural objects. The objects at stake were illegally removed from China a very long time ago and are now housed in Europe. From a legal point of view, should a new owner by obligated to return the objects illegally taken from the original owners? Many answers come to mind. If the law mandates a return of the objects, the new owner has to comply. If the rule of law is silent, new questions arise. For example: How do parties deal with each other outside the scope of the rule of law? The answers to these questions encompass many complex issues: the lapse of time; the knowledge of the new owner about the provenance; the knowledge of the interim owners; the activities of the original owner to seek its return; the significance of the object to both owners; can nonlegal entities, i.e., a specified group of people, qualify as owner; is cultural identity important; do universal museums need protection?

Although UNESCO has set up various treaties to protect cultural heritage, they do not work retroactively. Disputes with regard to looting of cultural objects or pillage of world heritage sites during an international armed conflict cannot be solved under the rule of the Convention for the Protection of Cultural Property in the Event of Armed Conflict. It was issued in 1954 and it has effect only if states are party to it. All other conventions in this area are from a later date.

The question of restitution or return therefore is open to debate.

The issue of ownership of cultural objects is not settled between the Western world on the one side and Africa, the Middle East, China, and many other countries on the other side. What is of more significance: a cultural object's original context or its power to impress when compared to other objects from elsewhere? The seemingly neutral issue is affected by history. Some want to avoid the shadows and endeavor not to mingle with the past. They want to maintain the status quo, while others want to balance the injustices of the past. A better outcome can be reached by publishing the history and shedding light on the provenance.

Dr. Zuozhen Liu has done just that. She discusses all of these topics in a clear way, disentangling them and offering a clear analysis. By giving examples in various cases that she explores in detail, she makes the issues accessible for everyone. Her focus is on China, from where her examples are derived. You will never forget the history of the Dunhuang manuscripts and the legal implications after reading her description of the legal route followed. She sheds light from the legal perspective on the sale of the manuscripts by a monk to the British explorer who was better informed about the market value. The relationship of the explorer and the British Museum is still under a veil of secrecy.

This book offers a framework of the way these problems can be studied step by step. Each step offers new particularities and different legal issues. The author guides the reader through all steps. The story does not end at the conclusion of the book. Finding the right place for cultural objects will take a long time and is partly dependent on the issue of cultural identity. How society thinks about cultural identity is changing. Determination of the right place for a cultural object will follow new insights into the values of cultural identity.

The style of the book is very clear due to the help of William Fearnow. I highly recommend it.

Amsterdam Prof. Dr. Inge van der Vlies

Preface

Related to history, law, culture, and international politics, the allocation of cultural heritage is both controversial and complicated. Beginning in the mid-twentieth century, an international legal regime was developed to protect cultural heritage against military operations and illicit trafficking. Subsequent international campaigns seeking the return of cultural heritage to their respective countries of origin have drawn public attention. My interest in this topic arose 5 years ago while studying law in China from reading the numerous press reports in mainland China, as well as attending numerous lectures, regarding the auction of Yves Saint-Laurent's bronze heads from the Old Summer Palace. My master's dissertation treated private international law applicable to the recovering of stolen cultural property. Upon completing my master's dissertation, the Guangzhou Municipality provided me funding for further research.

This book comprises the findings of my 3 years of research into the issues surrounding the repatriation of cultural objects, particularly Chinese cultural relics 'lost' in modern Chinese history, conducted under the guidance of Profs. Inge Van der Vlies and Arthur Salomons, both members of the Faculty of Law at the University of Amsterdam. Following an introduction, I study a number of specific losses of Chinese cultural relics and the legal regimes regarding the protection of cultural heritage applicable to such losses. These case studies first assess the possibility of seeking legal remedies of restitution under the contemporary legal regime. Next, they examine the cultural and ethical issues underpinning the international conventions protecting cultural heritage as well as the claims being made for the return of cultural heritage. The related issues of cultural identity, right to cultural heritage, multiculturalism, the politics of recognition, human rights, and cosmopolitanism are also studied. In the concluding chapter, I answer the research questions and suggest areas warranting future research.

This study has required knowledge in public international law, private international law, common law, ancient Chinese law, Chinese history and culture, and art theory, among other disciplines. In addition to the inherent difficulty of translating Chinese terms into English, terms such as 'unequal treaties,' 'century of humiliation' and 'patriotism,' which are commonly used in China, are criticized in the West as ideological CPC propaganda. Although I appreciate the comments of Westerners alerting me to cultural and ideological differences and I readily admit such comments have helped me become more objective and view my topic from various perspectives, such comments have made me acutely aware of the chasm of misunderstanding between China and the West regarding this topic. I sincerely hope this book will, to some extent, lay a foundation for bridging that chasm and resolving our respective cultures' disputes over cultural heritage.

Summer 2015 Zuozhen Liu

Acknowledgments

One month before my doctoral promotion in April 2015, I had a call from a Chinese reporter, who told me that there was a Buddha statue containing a mummified monk being exhibited in a Hungarian museum. This statue was believed to be stolen from a village temple in Fujian province in the end of 1995, and then smuggled to Hong Kong. Its present possessor turned out to be a Dutch collector. This case was widely reported in China, and raised huge public interest in and attention to this mummified statue. It has been reported that some local villagers wept tears of joy, set off fireworks, offered sacrifices to the ancestors to celebrate that their God was found. It was the local villagers that make this mummified statue known over China and even the world, because they used all means to make their restitution claims heard and reported. The SACH was requested to make an official claim of the restitution of the statue on behalf of the local villagers. This case also indicates that the disputes over cultural objects are going to resonate in our world, as the illicit trade of cultural objects across borders is sustained by the demands from the art market.

I am so grateful for the opportunity of doing my Ph.D. on this topic in the law faculty of the University of Amsterdam. Before April of 2011, I would not have expected to do a Ph.D. outside of China, as studying abroad is fashionable but unaffordable for most Chinese students. One day, Prof. Yuan, who supervised my master's dissertation in China, informed me about the project launched by the Guangzhou Municipality funding students to do Ph.D. programs abroad. She encouraged me to seize this opportunity to broaden my horizons, which, in her words, might change my life. After the frustrating preparation and applications, finally I got the admission to the law faculty of the University of Amsterdam in May of 2011. Then I came to the Netherlands in the autumn of 2011. At the beginning, everything was so fresh and exciting to my eyes. Compared with the large cities in China, the skyline of Amsterdam is much lower; old-fashioned bicycles are seen everywhere; everything moves at a slower pace. However, my excitement and romantic imagination was quickly converted to frustration and disappointment. Lack of fluency in English, gaps in knowledge, cultural differences, and homesickness all presented unexpected difficulties. Apart from that, living in Amsterdam still has not been easy. I had two bikes stolen and moved three times in the first 2 years. Fortunately, I am not alone while being faced with all these difficulties during my adventures in the Netherlands. I would take this opportunity to express my gratitude to the people who have helped me out and made my life colorful along the way.

First of all, I would like to thank my parents for their unreserved love, for their continuous belief in me, and for their disobedience of the One-Child policy by giving births to me and my younger brother. In a culture where boys are preferred, my parents love me as much as they love my two brothers. After being laid off from collective enterprises in the 1990s, they have done many low-paid jobs to pay our living expenses and support our grandparents. Growing up in the chaos of the Cultural Revolution, they did not go to university, but they saw their three children through universities. Although they believe that girls need family protection, they have supported me to live alone on the other end of the earth. Compared with the European way of life, my parents have lived a very ascetic life. The word 'luxury' does not exist in their vocabulary. They are just like many ordinary Chinese people: tolerant, hardworking, humble, firm, and content. These qualities help them to cope with all kinds of difficulties in a rapidly transforming society, which has also taught me to be strong and optimistic.

I also owe a debt of gratitude to my supervisors, Profs. Inge Van der Vlies and Arthur Salomons. Without their inspiring encouragement and professional guidance, I do not think I could have finished this book as scheduled. Apart from that, I am very grateful to Inge for her help and care in my expat life in Amsterdam. She did a lot to teach me how to enjoy the Dutch experience, by taking me to museums, concerts, and movies, by lending me a real Dutch bike, and introducing me new friends…The experts of my promotion committee also provided helpful suggestions to the completion of this book. Another debt of gratitude is due to my English teachers, particularly Bill. I feel so lucky to know Bill and Betsy. Bill is unbelievably kind-hearted to help me with the English of this book for free, and polish my daily English so patiently. He is a maximal help in the editing of this book. Also by communicating to the people with different cultural background, it helps to broaden my horizon and know the world.

I would like to thank so many kind and friendly people I have met in the Netherlands, as well as my colleagues of the Department of Constitutional and Administrative Law and other staff members in the Faculty of Law. They all made my Dutch experience joyful and fruitful. Last but not least, I would like to express my gratitude to the municipality of Guangzhou for funding my study in the Netherlands.

July 2015 Dr. Zuozhen Liu

Contents

A Note About Chinese Dynasties and Names

Timeline of Chinese History

Xia dynasty: 2100–1600 BC
Shang dynasty: 1600–1050 BC
Zhou dynasty: 1046–256 BC
Qin dynasty: 221–206 BC
Han dynasty: 206 BC–220 AD
Three Kingdoms: 220–265 AD
Jin dynasty: 265–420 AD
Period of the Northern and Southern dynasties: 386–589 AD
Sui dynasty: 581–618 AD
Tang dynasty: 618–906 AD
Period of the Five dynasties: 907–960 AD
Song dynasty: 960–1279 AD
Yuan dynasty: 1279–1368 AD
Ming dynasty: 1368–1644 AD
Qing dynasty: 1644–1912 AD
Republic of China: 1912–1949 AD
People's Republic of China: 1949 AD–present

Chinese Names and Romanization

In Chinese, the family name, stated first, is followed by the given name. For example: Wang Yuanlu—Wang is the family name and Yuanlu is the given name. Except when spelling names already well known outside China such as Sun Yat-sen for Sun Zhongshan, and except for a few old spellings of some Chinese place names such as Canton for Guangzhou, I have used the pinyin system, the official Chinese phonetic system for transcribing the Mandarin pronunciation of Chinese characters into the Latin alphabet, throughout.

Abbreviations

CPC	Communist Party of China
ICJ	International Court of Justice
ICOM	International Council of Museums
ICPRCP	Intergovernmental Committee for Promoting the Return of Cultural Property to its Countries of origin or its Restitution in Case of Illicit Appropriation
ILC	International Law Commission
PRC	People's Republic of China
ROC	Republic of China
SACH	State Administration of Cultural Heritage (of the PRC)
UN	United Nations
UNESCO	United Nations Educational, Scientific and Cultural Organization
US	The United States
UK	The United Kingdom
WWI	The First World War
WWII	The Second World War
Lieber Code	Instructions for the Government of Armies of the United States in the Field (April 24, 1863)
Brussels Declaration	Project of an International Declaration concerning the Laws and Customs of War (Brussels, August 27, 1874)
Oxford Manual	The Laws of War on Land (Oxford, September 9, 1880)
The 1899 Hague Convention (II)	Convention (II) with respect to the Laws and Customs of War on Land and its annex: Regulations concerning the Laws and Customs of War on Land (The Hague, July 29, 1899)
The 1907 Hague Convention (IV)	Convention (IV) Respecting the Laws and Customs of War on Land and its annex: Regulations concerning the Laws and Customs of War on Land (The Hague, October 18, 1907)

Roerich Pact	Treaty on the Protection of Artistic and Scientific Institutions and Historic Monuments (Washington, April 15, 1935)
The 1954 Hague Convention	Convention for the Protection of Cultural Property in the Event of Armed Conflict (The Hague, May 14, 1954)
The 1970 UNESCO Convention	Convention on the Means of Prohibiting and Preventing the Illicit Import, Export and Transfer of Ownership of Cultural Property (Paris, November 14, 1970)
The 1995 UNIDROIT Convention	Convention on Stolen or Illegally Exported Cultural Object (Rome, June 24, 1995)
The ICTY Statute	Statute for the International Criminal Tribunal for Yugoslavia (United Nations Security Council, May 25, 1993)
The Rome Statute of ICC	Rome Statute for the International Criminal Court (Rome, July 17, 1998)

Terminology

Cultural Heritage, Cultural Property, Cultural Objects, Cultural Relics, and Art

Twentieth Century international legal conventions have variously used terms such as 'cultural heritage,' 'cultural objects,' and 'cultural property' when referring to an item of cultural value.[1] 'Cultural object' is used in The 1995 UNIDROIT Convention. The 1954 Hague Convention and the 1970 UNESCO Convention use 'cultural property.' More recently, the 1972 UNESCO Convention concerning the Protection of World Cultural and Natural Heritage, the 2001 UNESCO Convention for the Protection of Underwater Cultural Heritage, and the 2003 UNESCO Convention for the Safeguarding of the Intangible Cultural Heritage use 'cultural heritage.' According to cultural rights expert Farida Shaheed, from a human rights perspective 'cultural heritage is to be understood as resources enabling the cultural identification and development processes of individuals and communities which they, implicitly or explicitly, wish to transmit to future generations.'[2] Although the existing international conventions use 'cultural heritage' to encompass both tangible and intangible cultural heritage, this study discusses only tangible cultural heritage.

At the previous stage, the term 'antiquities' (古物) was more widely used, but the term 'cultural relics' (文物) is more commonly used in the contemporary Chinese legal documents. Beginning with the Tang dynasty, 'cultural relics' referred to historical remains of previous dynasties and their celebrities. Coming into use with the Republic of China, 'cultural relics' and 'antiquities' refer to the

[1]There is a disagreement over 'cultural property' versus 'cultural heritage.' To Prott and O'Keefe, 'property' connotes ownership, while 'heritage' creates a perception of something handed down, cared for and cherished. Because 'cultural heritage' connotes the interconnection between people and the items, some argue that 'cultural heritage' rightfully supersedes 'cultural property.' For more information, see Prott and O'Keefe (1992).

[2]Shaheed (2011).

tangible legacy of valuable historical, artistic, and scientific items.[3] Contemporary PRC legal documents use 'cultural relics' more widely than 'antiquities.'[4] In the PRC Law on Protection of Cultural Relics of 2002, 'cultural relics' are items of historical, artistic, or scientific value dating from various historical periods, together with significant items related to more recent or contemporary major events, revolutionary movements or famous individuals (Article 2). Immovable cultural relics are protected at the national, provincial, and municipal or county level depending on their importance and value. Movable cultural relics are divided into valuable cultural relics and ordinary cultural relics, and valuable cultural relics are further divided into three grades (Article 3). Administrative departments at or above the county level authenticate and grade cultural relics.

'Art' and 'works of art' are also used. According to Canadian legal theorist Rosemary J. Coombe, in the eighteenth century, 'art' referred primarily to 'skill and industry;' not until the nineteenth century was 'art as imaginative expression distinguished from 'art' as industry and utilitarianism.[5] In *The Predicament of Culture*, James Clifford posits that 'the capacity of art to transcend its cultural and historical context is asserted repeatedly.'[6] According to Clifford, the 'art-culture system' developed in the nineteenth century recognizes two categories of expressive works of esthetic value in the context of European colonialism and imperialism: first, 'authentic masterpieces' are created by individual geniuses, the second are 'authentic artifacts' created by cultures imagined as collectivities.[7] Because I agree with Coombe that although Clifford's 'art-culture system' continues to inform property law, his categories may no longer be appropriate in a post-colonial context,[8] the cultural objects discussed herein include both 'authentic masterpieces' and 'authentic artifacts,' unless otherwise specifically noted. As Craig Clunas observes, the term 'Chinese art' was created in the nineteenth century in Europe and North America. Before the nineteenth century, no one in China considered textiles, calligraphy, paintings, sculptures, ceramics, and other works as parts of a single field of enquiry, despite the long and sophisticated tradition of writing about, collecting, showing, and consuming such works by successive Chinese elites.[9]

---

[3]The Chinese term for 'cultural relics,' '*wenwu*' (文物) first appeared in the first Chinese narrative history, *Chronicle of Zuo* (*Zuozhuan*, covering 722–468 BC), and referred to objects used in the ritual and ceremonial systems originated during the West Zhou dynasty. See Lei (2012), at 4–5.

[4]In today's Chinese museum community, cultural relics can be divided into two categories: antiquities and modern cultural relics. Antiquities are cultural relics from before 1840, while modern cultural relics are objects of historical importance related to modern Chinese history. See Zhang Song, 'Legal History of Protecting Cultural Heritage in China' (in Chinese), *China Ancient City* (2009), no. 3, pp. 27–33.

[5]Coombe (1993), at 255.

[6]Clifford (1988), at 195.

[7]*Ibid.*, at 215–251.

[8]Coombe, *supra* note 5, at 255.

[9]See C. Clunas, *Art in China*, Oxford: Oxford University Press 1997, at 9, 12, 125.

Because 'cultural property,' 'cultural objects,' 'cultural heritage,' 'cultural relics,' and 'art' have been used in various legal documents and writings, their precise meaning when used herein depends on the context in which they appear.

Return, Restitution, Recovery, and Repatriation

'Return' and 'recovery' are both value-free, focusing on the interest or action of the requesting party.[10] Wojciech Kowalski claims that 'restitution' arose in Roman private law as 'restoration of the previous state' pursuant to the maxim '*restitutio in integrum*'[11] so that in a general sense, restitution is connected with responsibility and depends on a given legal system and time of origin.[12] Because 'restitution' invariably denotes an unlawful situation such as theft or pillage, the use of 'restitution' when discussing the relocation of cultural objects is contentious.[13]

The twentieth session of UNESCO's General Conference in 1978 makes a clear distinction between 'restitution' and 'return.'[14] The *Guideline for the Use of the 'Standard Form concerning Requests for Return or Restitution'* issued by UNESCO in 1986 provides: "The term 'restitution' should be used 'in case of illicit appropriation,' i.e., when objects have left their counties of origin illegally, according to the relevant national legislation and with particular reference to UNESCO's 1970 Convention on the subject."[15] 'Return' "should apply to cases 'where cultural objects left their countries of origin prior to the crystallization of national and international law on the protection of cultural property. Such transfers of ownership were often made from a colonized territory to the territory of the colonial power or from a territory under foreign occupation. In many cases, they were the result of an exchange, gift, or sale and did not therefore infringe on any laws existing at the time. In some cases, however, the legitimacy of the transfer can

[10]L.V. Prott, 'Note on Terminology,' in L.V. Prott (ed.), *Witnesess to History: A Compendium of Documents and Writings on the Return of Cultural Objects*, Paris: UNESCO 2009, at xxi.

[11]See W.W. Kowalski, *Restitution of Works of Art pursuant to Private and Public International Law* (Receuil des Cours 288), Leiden: Nijhoff Online 2001, at 24.

[12]*Ibid.*, at 24–25. Along with compensation and satisfaction, restitution is a form of reparation provided in the Draft Articles on Responsibility of States for Internationally Wrongful Acts wherein restitution is intended 'to re-establish the situation which existed before the wrongful act was committed.' There are two exceptions to the foregoing rule of restitution: when restitution is not materially possible, and when the duty of restitution would involve a much heavier burden than compensation. The first exception relates to the circumstance of the wrongful act. For example, a destroyed cultural object cannot be the subject of a restitution for the simple reason it no longer exists. The second exception relates to the capacity or capability of the wrong-doing state (Article 35).

[13]Prott, *supra* note 10, at xxi–xxiii.

[14]UNESCO, Guidelines for the Use of the 'Standard Forum concerning Request for Return or Restitution', CC-86/WS/3, (April 30, 1986), at 11.

[15]*Ibid.*

be questioned. Among the many variants of such a process is the removal of objects from a colonial territory by people who were not nationals of the colonial power. There may have also been cases of political or economic dependence which made it possible to effect transfer of ownership from one territory to another which would not be envisaged today."[16] 'Restitution' and 'return' are used herein in accordance with the foregoing.

'Repatriation' is used herein in accordance with the definition provided by Lyndel Prott, a leading authority on cultural heritage law. According to Prott, 'repatriation' applies not only to returns from one country to another, but also to returns from an institution to a tribal or indigenous community within the same country.[17] Similarly, according to Kowalski, the destination of repatriation can be either the location or country where the cultural property belongs or the ethnic group that was its original owner.[18] Repatriation aims to protect the integrity of cultural heritage in the event of cession of territory or the breakup of states. The principal objective of repatriation is attaining and maintaining a heritage's territorial attachment.[19] 'Repatriation' is used herein because in addition to the property law aspects of cultural objects, this study explores the interconnection between cultural objects and not only states but cultural groups.

---

[16] *Ibid.*

[17] Prott, *supra* note 10, at xxiii.

[18] W.W. Kowalski, 'Types of Claim for Recovery of Lost Cultural Property', *Museum International* 57 (2005), no. 4, at 95.

[19] *Ibid.*, at 97.

Introduction

The bronze heads from the Old Summer Palace were part of the water clock designed by the Italian Jesuit missionary priest Giuseppe Castiglione for the European-styled palaces of the Old Summer Palace at the Qing Court.[20] Missing from the Old Summer Palace after it was ransacked and destroyed in 1860 by Anglo-French troops, the bronze heads began to appear on the international art market in the 1980s.[21] The 2000 auction of the bronze heads of the monkey, ox, and tiger by Christie's and Sotheby's in Hong Kong drew both local and international media attention.[22] Although the SACH urged the auction houses not to sell the looted treasures, relying on the 'one country, two systems' principle, Christies's and Southeby's decided they could proceed with impunity under the laws of

[20]The fountain featured a large, clam shell-shaped basin surrounded by 12 carved, stone statues of clothed, seated humans, each with head of one of the Chinese zodiac animals representing a 2 h period in the Chinese horary cycle. Each statue spouted water through its mouth for 2 h of the day, and all twelve spouted water simultaneously at noon.

[21]An American antiques dealer reportedly discovered another three bronze heads (ox, tiger, and horse) in Palm Springs, California, in 1985 and purchased them for US$1500 each. The bronze heads of the monkey and the boar, exhibited in the Metropolitan Museum of Art from 1980 through 1981, were auctioned by Sotheby's in New York in 1987. The bronze head of the monkey was purchased by an American collector for US$165,000, and the bronze head of the boar was purchased by a Taiwanese entrepreneur for US$150,000. In 1989, the bronze heads of the ox, the tiger, and the horse were auctioned by Sotheby's in London. A telephone buyer paid £148,500 for the ox, £137,500 for the tiger, and £181,500 for the horse. The telephone buyer was Wang Dingqian, director of My Humble House Corporation, an antiques dealer in Taiwan, which subsequently exhibited the three bronzes in Taiwan, thereby bringing them to the attention of the public. See Wu Shu, *Who is Collecting China* (in Chinese), Taiyuan: Shanxi Renmin Chubanshe 2008, at 76–82.

[22]See Tuyet Nguyet, 'Editorials', *Arts of Asia,* April 30, 2000; Erik Eckholm, Mark Landler, State Bidder Buys Relics For China, *The New York Times*, May 3, 2000, viewed June 5, 2013, http://www.nytimes.com/2000/05/03/arts/state-bidder-buys-relics-for-china.html.

Hong Kong.[23] Ultimately, the bronze heads of the monkey, ox, and tiger were purchased by China Poly Group Corporation and brought back to Beijing.[24] In 2003 and 2007, respectively, Macao casino tycoon Stanley Ho purchased, and donated to China, the bronze heads of the boar and horse.[25]

In October, 2008, Christie's announced the bronze heads of the rat and the rabbit, part of Yves Saint-Laurent's collection, would be auctioned in Paris in February, 2009. The announcement unleashed a fury in China. Chinese scholars launched a fierce attack, claiming China's treasures were being plundered for the second time. The SACH condemned the public auction of looted cultural relics and opposed buying back such relics. A group of lawyers and the Association for the Protection of Chinese Art in Europe filed suit in Paris seeking to enjoin the auction. The injunction was denied[26] and despite the vociferous objections from China, the auction proceeded and the two bronzes were purchased by an anonymous telephone bidder for a total of €28 million. Hours after the sale, the SACH officially condemned the auction and tightened controls on Christie's activities in China.[27]

---

[23]*Ibid.* Pursuant to the 'one country, two systems' principle, is the Chinese constitutional provision pursuant to which Hong Kong and Macau retain their capitalist economic and democratic political systems while the rest of China uses its socialist system.

[24]*Ibid.* The Poly Group stated that because their attempts to halt the auction or bring the relics back by means of persuasion had failed, 'we had to resort to commercial means.' The bronze heads of the monkey, the ox, and the tiger were purchased by The Poly Group for HK$8.185 million, HK $7.745 million and over HK$15 million, respectively.

[25]In the summer of 2003, the bronze head of the boar was found in the possession of an American collector in New York. After lengthy negotiations, the collector agreed to cede the bronze head to China. Stanley Ho made a donation of approximately 6 million yuan to the Fund under the Chinese Social and Cultural Development Foundation and the bronze was returned to China. In 2007, Stanley Ho purchased the bronze head of the horse HK$69.1 million (£4.42 million) prior to its scheduled public auction by Sotheby's in Hong Kong. The bronze head of the boar and the bronze head of the horse are housed in the Poly Art Museum. See 'Dr. Stanley Ho Donates to China the Bronze Horse Head of the Summer Palace Purchased at Sotheby's Hong Kong', Sotheby's Hong Kong Press Release, 20 September 2007.

[26]The court found: it did not have jurisdiction over the French Cultural Ministry; the Association did not have standing to file the motion because it did not have a direct relationship with the bronze heads; and the motion was not timely filed. The court ordered the Association to pay €1000 in fines to both Christie's and to the firm of Pierre Berge. See 'French Court Throws out Appeal over Yves St Laurent Chinese Bronzes as Christie's Sale Begins', The Telegraph, 23 February 2009, viewed July 12, 2012, http://www.telegraph.co.uk/culture/art/artsales/4788662/French-court-throws-out-appeal-over-Yves-St-Laurent-Chinese-bronzes-as-Christies-sale-begins.html.

[27]The SACH statement focused on three points: (a) Although The SACH had repeatedly urged Christie's to halt the sale of the bronzes, Christie's had insisted on auctioning looted relics in contravention of the spirit of relevant international conventions and the common consensus regarding restitution of cultural heritage to the country of origin, and despite the fact the auction would infringe upon Chinese cultural rights, hurt Chinese national feelings, and have a serious adverse effect on Christie's business in China. (b) The SACH had firmly opposed the auctioning of illicit trafficked cultural relics and Christie's would be responsible for all the adverse effects of the sale. (c) The SACH did not recognize the property rights of owners of looted cultural relics and would continue to recover looted and/or stolen cultural objects and other illegally exported relics by all necessary means in compliance with international conventions and Chinese laws. See 'The

Unexpectedly, Cai Mingchao, the winning bidder and a Chinese collector and auctioneer, advised Christie's he would not pay the purchase price and that his bid was an attempt to sabotage the sale as a protest on China's behalf.[28] Surprisingly, in 2013, French billionaire François Pinault donated the two bronzes to China in 2013.[29]

Although looting, destruction, and theft of cultural objects are not new phenomena (perhaps the first systematic plundering of fine art in Europe occurred during the Napoleonic wars, after which France was forced to return the plundered cultural trophies) and many wars, occupations, and other vicissitudes have separated peoples from their cultural heritage,[30] the problem has only become an international issue over the course of the past 50 years. Nations (especially those victimized by colonialism or imperialism) and communities of people are now demanding the restitution or return of cultural objects. Some claims have received media attention. Egypt has been seeking the repatriation of the Rosetta Stone and the Nefertiti; Nigeria has sought the return of the Benin bronzes; India has demanded the return of the 'Kohinoor Diamond' and the 'Sultanganj Buddha.' The controversy surrounding the Parthenon Marbles, also known as the Elgin Marbles, has drawn the greatest international attention, and has been a sore point in relations between the UK and Greece for many years.[31] Beginning in the 1970s, the UN General Assembly has passed a series of resolutions urging the restitution and return of cultural objects to their countries or origin.[32] Lawmakers, administrators, artists, museums, professionals, and lawyers have all played a part in informing and changing public attitudes toward such claims. Recently, international conferences have been convened to address the issue, including the Athens International

(Footnote 27 continued)
SACH Condemns the Auctions of the Bronzes', SACH, February 27, 2009, viewed July 22, 2013. http://www.sach.gov.cn/art/2009/2/27/art_722_8566.html.

[28]For more details, see T. Branigan, 'Chinese Bidder Refuses to Pay for Yves Saint Laurent-owned Artefacts', *The Guardian,* March 2, 2009, viewed June 13, 2013, http://www.theguardian.com/world/2009/mar/02/chinese-artifacts-yves-saint-laurent.

[29]Pinault's donation is seen by many as little more than a masterful stroke of corporate public relations by a firm seeking profits from newly wealthy Chinese consumers with a strong taste for luxury goods. See Hannah Xu, 'Return of Old Summer Palace Statues seen as Kering Group PR exercise', *South China Morning Post*, (29 June, 2013).

[30]Historical records show that following Napoleon's defeat at the Battle of Waterloo in 1815, the French government was forced to return approximately 5000 looted objects to their respective countries of origin. See 'Looting and Napoleon', *Looting, Hoarding, Collecting…Repatriation and Museum*, viewed March 16, 2015. http://www.niu.edu/looted/brochure/looted-tri-fold.pdf.

[31]From 1799 to 1803, while Greece was under the control of the Ottoman Empire, sculptures were removed from the Parthenon to England by a Thomas Bruce, the 7th Earl of Elgin. The sculptures are displayed in the British Museum. Since 1983, the Greek Government has officially requested the Elgin Marbles be returned to Greece but the British Museum has refused.

[32]These Resolutions include A/RES/3187(XXVIII), A/RES/3391(XXX), A/RES/32/18, A/RES/33/50, A/RES/34/64, A/RES/35/128, A/RES/36/64, A/RES/38/34, A/RES/40/19, A/RES/42/7, A/RES/44/18, A/RES/46/10, A/RES/48/15, A/RES/50/56, A/RES/52/54, A/RES/54/190, A/RES/56/97, A/RES/58/17, A/RES/61/52, A/RES/64/78, A/RES/67/80.

Conference on the return of cultural property to its country of origin, the Conferences on International Cooperation for the Protection and Repatriation of Cultural Heritage, and the International Conferences of Experts on the Return of Cultural Property. Most international conferences adopt recommendations or issue communiqués, including the Cairo Communiqué of 2010, the Seoul Recommendation of 2012, and the Dunhuang Recommendation of 2014. These recommendations and communiqués assert: cultural heritage constitutes an inalienable element of a people's cultural identity by providing a links among their past, present and future; significant cultural heritage must be returned to its country of origin; and claims for the return of cultural heritage must not be subject to time limitations.[33]

However, the cry for repatriation of cultural objects to countries of origin is not unanimous. Opposition has come from various sources. Pursuant to the Declaration on the Importance and Value of Universal Museums, 18 leading museums asserted that museums serve not just the citizens of their particular nation, but serve the people of every nation.[34] According to some scholars, claims for return and repatriation are often disingenuous because they provide little or no convincing evidence of a connection between the country of origin and the cultural heritage item.[35]

Those arguing for the repatriation of cultural objects posit that the removal of cultural objects was illegal or dishonorable and that the severance of a cultural object from its original cultural context, or the disassembly of an artistic complex, injures the object's scholarly, esthetic, and cultural integrity. In addition, they argue that because cultural heritage is an integral part of a people's cultural identity, people have an inalienable right to access the heritage created by their ancestors.[36] Opponents argue that the objects have been legally acquired by their present possessors and most countries of origin do not have adequate facilities to preserve their

---

[33]The first Conference on International Cooperation for the Protection and Repatriation of Cultural Heritage was held in Cairo, Egypt, in 2010, the second in Lima, Peru, in 2011. The first two International Conferences of Experts on the Return of Cultural Property were convened in Seoul, South Korea, in 2011 and 2012, the third was convened in Athens, Greece, in 2013, and the fourth was convened in Dunhuang, China, in 2014.

[34]The Declaration opens by stating 'the international museum community shares the conviction that illegal traffic in archeological, artistic, and ethnic objects must be firmly discouraged' before contrasting contemporarily defined and recognized illegal trafficking with historical acquisition practices such as purchase, gift, or partage. The Declaration stresses the vital role universal museums play in cultivating comprehension of different civilizations and promoting respect between civilizations, as well as the need to address claims for restitution on a case by case basis, with particular attention being paid to the historical and legal circumstances surrounding acquisition.

[35]See Cuno (2008); D. Lowenthal, 'Why Sanctions Seldom Work: Reflections on Cultural Property Internationalism', *International Journal of Cultural Property* 12 (2005), no. 3, pp. 393–424.

[36]Karen J. Warren, 'A Philosophical Perspective on the Ethics and Resolution of Cultural Properties Issues', in Phyllis Mauch Messenger (ed.), The Ethics of Collecting Cultural Property; Whose Culture? Whose Property?, New Mexico: University of New Mexico Press, 1989, at 8–10.

cultural objects. More fundamentally, opponents argue that cultural heritage belongs to a common humanity rather than to a country, and the exchange of cultural heritage promotes understanding and tolerance among nations and peoples.[37]

This book investigates the many long-lasting legal, ethical, and societal issues surrounding the allocation of cultural heritage. Whether requesting parties can recover cultural objects within existing international and national legal systems involves many preliminary inquiries. Was the original acquisition legal? What law should determine the acquisition's legality, international law or the law of a particular nation? Laws in force when the acquisition occurred or contemporary law? Which arguably nonlegal factors should affect ownership of a disputed object? What legal remedies are available for restitution of cultural objects? These issues form the basis of the first research question of this book:

> Can the original owners, or their rightful successors, of cultural objects looted, stolen, or illicitly exported before the adoption of the 1954 Hague Convention and the 1970 UNESCO Convention reclaim their cultural objects pursuant to remedies provided by international or national law?

According to some, the law is ill-suited for dealing with claims regarding the restitution of cultural objects stolen or looted in the distant past because most international conventions are not retroactive, are non-binding upon states that are not parties, and because national laws vest property rights in the possessors of the objects. Additionally, the case studies must be assumed to result in judgments against the requesting parties due to the passage of time and the consequent lapse of applicable statutes of limitation. Thus, the restitution of cultural objects most likely cannot be effected pursuant to the existing legal framework in most cases, which undermines the legitimacy of soft-law instruments such as UN Assembly resolutions promoting the restitution or return of cultural objects to countries of origin. Are such resolutions nothing more than political posturing?

What is the interconnection between cultural objects and countries? An examination of soft-law instruments and international conventions adopted since 1954 to protect cultural heritage reveals that the concept of cultural heritage being indispensable to national and cultural identity is a central tenet of such instruments and conventions. This concept is almost always prominently featured in repatriation requests. The question of why the concept of national and cultural identity matters in the disputes over cultural heritage leads to this book's second research question.

> What are the philosophical, ethical, and cultural considerations of identity underlying the international conventions protecting cultural object and claims made for repatriating cultural objects?

Following this introduction, Chap. 1 reviews several large-scale instances of the loss of cultural relics during modern Chinese history and the historical background of such losses. Generally speaking, Chinese cultural relics were 'lost' in two ways:

---

[37] *Ibid.*, at 3–8; Cuno (2008); Lowenthal *supra* note 35.

confiscation in times of armed conflicts and illegal trafficking. As to the first situation, I explore losses occurring during three wars between China and other states: the sacking of the Old Summer Palace by Anglo-French troops during the Second Opium War; the plunder of Beijing by the Eight-Nation Alliance in the Battle of Beijing; and the Japanese looting in the Second Sino-Japanese War. As to the second situation, I explore the loss of the Dunhuang manuscripts and the oracle bones.

Chapter 2 outlines the normative framework of international law, Chinese national law and international soft-lawmaking regarding cultural heritage, beginning with an overview of the laws treating cultural objects in times of war and noting that before the mid-nineteenth century cultural objects were a target of destruction and pillage in wars because of their high value and symbolic significance and, as a result, no laws prohibited looting or destroying cultural objects in times of war. Only following the mid-nineteenth century forward were laws protecting cultural property from military operations enacted. The 1954 Hague Convention and its Regulation and Protocol provides detailed protections for movable and immovable cultural property in times of war. Chapter 2 also treats two international conventions regarding illicit trafficking in cultural objects: the 1970 UNESCO Convention and the 1995 UNIDROIT Convention. Protection of cultural objects by Chinese laws during the twentieth century is also explored. The chapter with concludes by describing soft laws protecting cultural objects and the ethical aspect of combating illicit trafficking in cultural objects and their repatriation.

Chapter 3 analyzes international adjudication as it would relate to the sacking of the Old Summer Palace, the plunder of Beijing in 1900, and the Japanese pillage of China during WWII. Two issues are discussed: are states responsible for restitution of cultural objects, and are repatriation claims properly within the purview of national courts? In discussing state responsibility, I focus various international laws to determine whether confiscating cultural objects constituted a breach of a nation's international obligations. Because most the international conventions have no retroactive effect, this chapter also introduces the doctrine of inter-temporal law. Because these cases arise out of confiscations which occurred at least half a century ago, principles of post-war settlement and extinctive prescription in public international law must be examined in determining whether courts are the proper venues for adjudicating repatriation claims. The legal efficacy of resolutions regarding restitution or return of cultural objects to countries of origin is also explored.

Chapter 4 considers the Dunhuang manuscripts held by institutions in UK. English law and Chinese law are considered, especially conflict of laws. Under English law, the rights of ownership are protected under the law of torts. Because the plaintiff must demonstrate his rights to or interest in the objects in controversy in order to have standing to sue under tort law, China's ability to establish its right to the manuscripts and recognition of such title by the English courts are the initial focus of this section. Next, this section deals with the original deprivation of the manuscripts and such deprivation's effects before exploring the rules of conflict of laws in space and time, and then applying the *lex causae*. Finally the choice and application of statutes of limitations are discussed.

Chapter 5 considers cultural objects as integral to cultural identity, the human values comprising cultural identity, and cosmopolitan attitudes towards cultural heritage. Although some argue cultural identities must be respected, many criticize emphasizing cultural identity concerns of countries of origin in attempting to resolve conflicts over cultural heritage. Such criticism appears to arise out of the arguably tenuous relationship between cultural objects and their countries of origin. I broaden the inquiry by examining the connection between states and culture, concluding that repatriating cultural objects often implicates for the politics of recognition. I argue that displaying and auctioning sensitive cultural objects, as well as the prior acts of deprivation, are forms of misrecognition and non-recognition of a people's cultural identity which can deepen misunderstanding and resentment between peoples. I also argue that universal museums' possessing looted cultural objects undercuts the foundations of cosmopolitanism. Because cosmopolitanism and the recognition of cultural identity share the common root of egalitarianism, universal museums' possessing looted or other sensitive cultural objects violates cosmopolitanism's philosophical foundation.

Chapter 6 deals with Chinese attitudes towards cultural relics and the effect of their loss in modern Chinese history, as well as the implications of the repatriation of the lost cultural relics. Because Chinese cultural relics embody Chinese history and physically represent Chinese culture and because Chinese history and culture are significant in constructing and maintaining Chinese cultural identity, Chinese cultural relics are essential to Chinese cultural identity. Chinese attitudes toward the loss of cultural relics are studied by examining Chinese intellectuals' devotion to their culture and by examining the rise of Chinese nationalism. Many Chinese regard the loss of their cultural relics as a national tragedy which has left a stigma upon the nation. For many Chinese, the repatriation of lost cultural relics not only restores respect for China's cultural identity, it offers the prospect of restoring the lack of trust between China and other nations.

Chapter 7 summarizes the research, reiterates the obstacles posed by legal remedies, proposes tentative answers to the research questions and puts forth areas warranting further research.

Please note that although phrases used herein with regard to modern Chinese history, such as 'unequal treaty' and 'century of humiliation,' may carry significant political or ideological overtones for readers outside of China, such terms do not necessarily represent my opinions of the facts so described.

Chapter 1
The Loss of Cultural Relics in Modern Chinese History

1.1 Introduction

China's long history has yielded an abundance of cultural relics. Unfortunately, since the mid-nineteenth century, many Chinese cultural relics have been destroyed or removed from China by various means. The term 'lost cultural relics' refers to Chinese cultural objects looted, stolen, clandestinely excavated or illegally trafficked between 1840 and 1949.[1] Although there are no definitive totals of the lost Chinese cultural relics, the Chinese Society of Cultural Relics estimates more than ten million pieces of invaluable Chinese cultural objects have 'sunk into oblivion' in Europe, the United States, Japan, and Southeast Asian nations since the First Opium War. Approximately one million pieces are thought to be grade-one and grade-two valuable cultural relics.[2] UNESCO notes that more than two hundred museums in forty-seven countries house a total of 1.64 million Chinese relics and that ten times more Chinese antiques are held by individuals worldwide. These relics include priceless calligraphy and paintings, ancient bronze ware, pottery and

---

[1]First defined by the Chinese Social and Cultural Development Foundation, 'lost cultural relics' are differentiated from objects that were legally acquired and exported in Chinese history. According to the SACH, as a general rule, if an item was brought out of China legally, China does not seek restitution or return but instead repurchases some items selectively. China seeks repatriation of so-called 'lost cultural relics,' i.e., those looted, stolen, illegally excavated or exported from China in modern Chinese history. See Wang Zhe & Zhang Juzhong, 'Retrospect and Prospect of the Study on the Loss and Return of the Chinese Cultural Relics' (in Chinese), *Dongnan Wenhua*, (2009), no. 1, at 16.

[2]See 'How many Chinese cultural treasures "lost" overseas?' People's Daily Online, 30 January 2007, viewed July 10, 2012, http://english.peopledaily.com.cn/200701/30/eng20070130_346095.html#, Chinese cultural relics are divided into 'valuable' and 'ordinary' cultural relics. Valuable cultural relics are further broken down into grade-one, grade-two, and grade-three cultural relics. Grade-one cultural relics are 'especially important for historical, artistic, and scientific values.' Grade-two cultural relics have 'important' cultural value. Grade-three cultural relics are 'relatively important' to China's cultural heritage. Ordinary cultural relics only have 'certain historical, artistic value' (Article 3 of the Law of PRC on Protection of Cultural Relics, 2002).

Z. Liu, *The Case for Repatriating China's Cultural Objects*,
DOI 10.1007/978-981-10-0597-8_1

porcelain, sculptures, oracle bone inscriptions and classical works held primarily in Japan, Britain, France and the US. The British Museum alone holds more than 23,000 Chinese relics.[3]

This chapter discusses two different categories of lost cultural relics: cultural objects confiscated in times of war and illegally trafficked cultural objects. I begin by briefly outlining the social background of the loss of cultural relics in modern Chinese history as a result of the Opium Wars, the unequal treaty system, and the Japanese aggression. I then describe the loss of cultural relics during times of war by studying the sacking of the Old Summer Palace during the Second Opium War, the plunder of Beijing at the Battle of Beijing in 1900, and the Japanese looting during the Second Sino-Japanese War. Finally I study theft, archaeological exploration, and exportation of cultural relics in modern Chinese history by reviewing the loss of the Dunhuang manuscripts, and the loss of the oracle bones. I also discuss recovery efforts by the Chinese government, institutional organizations and individuals.

1.2 The Social Background of the Loss

For many Chinese, modern Chinese history connotes being torn asunder by imperialists and the resultant indignities such upheavals entailed.[4] To better understand Chinese sentiment regarding the loss of cultural relics in modern Chinese history, I detail three historical phenomena or events to describe the social background: the Opium Wars, the unequal treaty system, and the Japanese invasion.

1.2.1 The Opium Wars

Under the Qing government at the start of the nineteenth century, China was slipping into decline. Corruption, oppressive taxation, rural unrest, and the other ills Confucian scholars had long regarded as symptomatic of dynastic decay were everywhere. The Qing government continued the Ming dynasty's isolationist policies. Maritime trade was confined to the port of Canton and Chinese participation in such trade was monopolized by the Cohong.[5] With the onset of the Industrial Revolution, Westerners targeted China's large untapped market. By the

[3]Ibid.

[4]See Kaufman (2010), at 4–5.

[5]In Chinese feudal dynasties, ordinary Chinese did not participate in a national political life; government was conducted by the emperor and his officials with the support of local elites. See Roberts (1999), at 164; F.E. Wakeman, Jr., 'The Canton Trade and the Opium War' in: J.K. Fairbank (eds.), *The Cambridge History of China, Vol. 10: Late Ch'ing 1800–1911, Part I,* (Cambridge: Cambridge University Press 1978), at 163.

early eighteenth century, western trade with China, comprised of the exchange of Chinese tea for British woolen and metal goods, had been monopolized by the British East India Company. By the 1760s, the value of tea exports so greatly exceeded the value of British wool and metal imports that the deficit had to be made up with payments of silver.[6] Concerned about the security of its tea trade with China and the security of its commercial activity throughout Asia, Britain attempted to persuade the Chinese to increase Anglo-Chinese trade. Britain first sent an ambassador to China in 1792, to negotiate a treaty of commerce and obtain accreditation of a resident British minister. The Qing court denied Britain's request.[7] In 1816, a second British ambassador was sent in an attempt to improve Britain's Chinese trade position, but his overtures were similarly rejected.[8]

To offset their trade deficit, British merchants began smuggling opium into China. John K. Fairbank considers the opium trade 'the most long-continued and systematic international crime of modern history,' which 'provided the life-blood of the early British invasion of China'.[9] In time, the value of imported opium so increased that the balance of trade shifted against China and the deficit had to be made up with Chinese silver. By 1836, approximately 1820 tons of opium were imported into China annually and opium addiction incapacitated more Chinese each day.[10] In December 1838, the Qing government appointed Lin Zexu to proceed to Canton and suppress the opium trade. This attempted suppression, which conflicted with the interests of opium traders as well as British merchants keen to sell textiles to China, led in 1840 to the outbreak of the First Opium War. Britain defeated China and hostilities were concluded in 1842 pursuant to the Treaty of Nanjing pursuant to which the Qing government was obligated to pay 21 million silver dollars to the British government and merchants, cede Hong Kong to Britain, open five trading ports, and establish a 'fair and reasonable' tariff.[11]

To further expand their privileges, Britain demanded the Qing government renegotiate the Treaty of Nanjing to, among other things, open all of China to British merchants, legalize the opium trade, and exempt foreign imports from internal duties. When the Qing government backed away from renegotiating the treaty, Britain and France deployed a joint army of 23,000 soldiers to force the emperor's compliance. When the Chinese kidnapped a negotiating team of

[6]Wakeman, ibid., at 171–178; Roberts, ibid., at 163.

[7]See Wakeman, ibid., at 163–164.

[8]See G.T. Staunton, *Britain & the China Trade 1635–1842*: *Notes of Proceedings and Occurrences During the British Embassy to Pekin in 1816* (ed. and introd. by P.J.N. Tuck), London: Routledge 2000.

[9]J.K. Fairbank, 'The Creation of the Treaty System', in J.K. Fairbank (ed.), *The Cambridge History of China, Vol. 10: Late Ch'ing 1800–1911, Part I*, (Cambridge: Cambridge University Press 1978), at 213.

[10]Roberts (1999), at 164; Wakeman, *supra* note 5, at 178.

[11]Roberts (1999) at 166; Wakeman *supra* note 5, at 208–212.

thirty-nine diplomats and soldiers, Britain and France marched on Beijing.[12] China was defeated in what became known as the Second Opium War, and was forced to sign confiscatory peace treaties.[13]

1.2.2 The Unequal Treaty System

During the second half of the nineteenth century, following repeated battlefield defeats, the Qing government signed numerous treaties with foreign powers, pursuant to which much of China was divided into 'spheres of influence.' By the end of the nineteenth century, Germany obtained sovereignty over 'Kiautschou' for ninety-nine years; Russia obtained access to Dalian and Port Arthur as well as the right to build a railroad connecting the Chinese Eastern Railway with the Trans-Siberia Railroad; the United Kingdom leased Weihaiwei in July 1898; and France leased Canton Bay in 1899.[14] Fearing China might be completely subjugated to other powers, in 1898 the then US Secretary of State proposed the Open Door Policy to his European counterparts. Intended as a means to mediate the interests of foreign powers in China, the policy obligated foreign powers to keep China open to commercial access and to safeguard Chinese sovereignty and territorial integrity within their respective spheres of influence. By this time, the Qing government had been rendered totally powerless to resist foreign pressures,[15] and it was in the foreign powers' interest to have a weak but independent Chinese government to grant them privileges in the form of treaties.

In China, these treaties have come to be known as the 'unequal treaties'.[16] The Chinese feel these treaties were imposed upon China in so far as they were not

---

[12]G.M. Thomas, 'The looting of Yuan Mingyuan and the Translation of Chinese Art in Europe', *Nineteenth-Century Art Worldwide* 7 (2008), no. 2, at 2.

[13]China lost approximately 1,000,000 km^2 of land, ceding the district of Kowloon to Britain and land east of the Ussuri River to Russia. The burning of the Old Summer Palace was a stunning blow to the self-esteem of the once powerful Qing dynasty. See Hsu (2000), at 219.

[14]See G. Steinmetz, 'Qingdao as a colony: From Apartheid to Civilizational Exchange', Paper prepared for John Hopkins Workshops in Comparative History of Science and Technology, '*Science, Technology and Modernity: Colonial Cities in Asia*, Baltimore 16–17 January 2009; T. Daniel & L. Zhang, 'Political and Technical Factors Impinging on Port Operations: The Case of Manchuria', *Geo Journal* 30 (1993), no. 4, pp. 441–454.

[15]See Sugita, 'The Rise of an American Principle in China: A Reinterpretation of the First Open Door Notes toward China', in: R.J. Jensen, J.T. Davidann & Y. Sugita, (eds.). *Trans-Pacific relations: America, Europe, and Asia in the twentieth century*, London: Greenwood Press 2003, pp. 3–20.

[16]This term first entered the Chinese language in 1924. It is also used to conceptualize the contours of China's encounters with foreign nations throughout modern Chinese history. Before 1924, related concepts such as sovereignty, reciprocity, tariff autonomy and extraterritoriality had been gradually introduced. According to statistics from Mainland China, China was forced to sign 1182 unequal treaties with other states from and after the First Opium War. See Wang, D. (2003), at 401–407; Zhang Zhenkun, 'A Study on Unequal Treaties' (in Chinese), *Modern Chinese History*

negotiated by and between nations treating each other as equals. These treaties are regarded as little more than vehicles of imperialist invasion. The unequal treaties have caused long-standing bitterness and feelings of humiliation among the Chinese. As noted by Dong Wang, for ninety years unwavering interest in and repeated references to the unequal treaties and their humiliation of China have shaped Chinese perceptions of international law and China's relations with the world under such law.[17] Fairbank observes that Chinese resentment of the unequal treaties and the treaty system in general grew into an increasingly significant aspect of Chinese society and the Chinese state.[18]

Guo Songtao, China's first ambassador to Britain and France, wrote that 'the West should treat China as an equal', and that 'Westerners in China should fall under the jurisdiction of Chinese local authority instead of their consuls'.[19] In 1864, the American missionary, Martin, translated Henry Wheaton's *Elements of International Law* into Chinese, thus introducing the first hypothetical equivalence of 'sovereign right' to China.[20] The introduction of international law into China elicited a mixed response among Europeans. Some Western diplomats viewed Martin's work positively, while others condemned the introduction of international law into China. They feared China acquiring even an elementary understanding of international law.[21] Klecskowsky, the French chargé d'affaires, complained to Burlingame: 'Who is this man who is going to give the Chinese an insight into our European international law? Kill him–choke him off; he will make us endless trouble'.[22] As the self-appointed vanguard and promoters of Western civilization in the East, Martin's opponents assumed a patronizing attitude toward Chinese understanding of law. As beneficiaries of the unequal treaties, they feared supplying

---

(Footnote 16 continued)

Studies 1993, no. 2, pp. 4–23; Xue Hanqin, 'China's Open Policy and International law', Chinese Journal of International law *4 (2005), no. 1, pp. 133–139.*

[17]Wang, D. (2003), at 401.

[18]Fairbank, *supra* note 9, at 214.

[19]Quoted from Wang, D. (2003), at 402–403. For original reference, see Zhong Shuhe (ed.), *Guo Songtao: London and Paris Dairies*, (in Chinese), Changsha: Yuelu Shushe 1984, at 199.

[20]Marking the beginning of the systematic and formal introduction of Western international law into China, the translation of *Elements of International Law* was epoch-making in that it 'enable[d] the Chinese to have a first glimpse of what was called international law in the West'. It also led to the creation of the foreign affairs office and foreign legations in Beijing. See Li Zhaojie (2012), at 138; L.H. Liu (2004), at 109.

[21]Li Zhaojie (2012), at 139.

[22]Similarly, Samuel Wells Williams believed the introduction of knowledge of international law might enable China to find legal bases to abolish aspects of the 'unequal treaties' such as extraterritoriality. See L.H. Liu (2004), 143.

the Chinese an understanding of international law might proved the Chines with the means to roll back the West's newly acquired political and commercial privileges and frustrate future exactions of additional concessions.[23]

The unequal treaties and grievances ranging from opium traders to political invasion, economic manipulation and missionary evangelism, gave rise to a strong anti-foreign movement in China, leading to the Boxer Uprising's violent revolt against foreign interests, culminating in the Battle of Beijing in 1900 and the adoption of the Boxer Protocol.[24]

1.2.3 Japanese Aggression Against China

While the Qing dynasty was declining, Japan's rise following the Meiji Restoration enabled Japan to compete with Western powers. Fought primarily over control of Korea between August 1, 1894 and April 17, 1895, the First Sino-Japanese War ended with China's being forced to recognize the independence of Korea and cede Taiwan to Japan pursuant to the 1895 Treaty of Shimonoseki.

Mass civil disorder which flourished during the early twentieth century as a result of the Qing government's inability to effectively govern China led to its overthrow during the 1911 Xinhai Revolution and the founding of The Republic of China 1912.[25] Rather than putting an end to the chaos, the foundation of the Republic of China fractured the country into competing factions led by warlords. The North Expedition led by the Nationalist Party finally ended The Warlord Era in 1928.[26]

In 1931, the Japanese military used the Mukden Incident as the pretext for invading Northeast China. Chinese troops were over-matched and the Kuomintang government appealed to the League of Nations for help but the League of Nations was ineffectual in the face of Japanese defiance. Similarly, following the then

[23]Li Zhaojie (2012), at 140.

[24]In August 1900, forces of the Eight-Nation alliance (Austria-Hungary, France, Germany, Italy, Russia, the United Kingdom, and the United States) marched from Tientsin to Beijing and defeated the Qing Imperial Army, thereby ending the Boxer Uprising and the siege of the Legation Quarter. Pursuant to the Boxer Protocol, China's internal administration as well as its national defenses were co-opted by the Eight-Nation alliance and a huge indemnity of 450 million taels of silver placed a large burden on the Chinese people in the form of increased taxes. A final blow to what little integrity the Qing government possessed, the Boxer Protocol is regarded as one of the unequal treaties.

[25]Roberts (1999), at 206.

[26]Although the Beiyang Government was internationally recognized as the legitimate government of the Republic of China, it exercised only symbolic authority; the real power rested in the hands of warlords. See Roberts (1999), at 206.

popular trend toward appeasement rather than confrontation, Western countries took no actions against Japan.[27] Japan relentlessly seized control of great swathes of Chinese territory. After occupying Northeast China, Japan established its puppet state of Manchukuo, and made Puyi, the last emperor of the Qing dynasty, the nominal regent and emperor. Japan also invaded and demilitarized Shanghai, and attacked the Great Wall region, using collaborators to establish Japanese-friendly governments.[28]

By 1936, Japanese encroachment into north China forced the Kuomintang into a united front with the CPC. Known as the Second Sino-Japanese War, Japan's full scale invasion of China began in 1937.[29] The Japanese army captured and controlled the key cities and embarked on a campaign of murder, rape and looting. The brutality of the notorious Nanjing Massacre turned Western public opinion against Japan[30] and increased the fear of Japanese expansion, prompting the United States, the United Kingdom, and France to provide loan assistance for China's acquisition of war supplies. Japan unconditionally surrendered on August 15, 1945. The eight-year Second Sino-Japanese War directly or indirectly led to the death of between fifteen to twenty million Chinese and the devastation and destruction of an incalculable amount of property.[31]

1.3 Plunder During Times of War

Large-scale looting during wars in modern Chinese history have resulted in massive losses of Chinese cultural relics. In this section, I treat the loss of cultural relics in the Second Opium War, the Battle of Beijing, and the Second Sino-Japanese War.

---

[27]A small quantity of dynamite was detonated close to a Japanese-owned railway near Mukden (now Shenyang) on September 18, 1931. In response, the Japanese Kwantung army occupied cities and towns along the railway and ultimately extended their control to all of Manchuria. See M.B. Jansen, *The Making of Modern Japan,* Cambridge: Belknap Press 2000, at 577; L.E. Eastman, 'Nationalist China during the Sino-Japanese War 1937–1945', in: J.K. Fairbank & A. Feuerwerker (eds), *The Cambridge History of China, Vol. 13: Republican China 1912–1949, Part 2*, Cambridge: Cambridge University Press 1986, at 547–548.

[28]Roberts (1999), at 239–240; Jansen, ibid., at 577–615.

[29]Eastman, *supra* note 27, at 546, 552–553.

[30]The Nanjing Massacre's death toll is a contentious aspect of Sino-Japanese history and remains an unresolved subject of debate. Historians have proposed totals from as "few" as 40,000 to as many as 300,000. See 'Scarred by history: The Rape of Nanjing', BBC News, April 11, 2005, viewed September 14, 2013, http://news.bbc.co.uk/2/hi/asia-pacific/223038.stm; Yang Daqing, 'A Sino-Japanese Controversy: The Nanjing Atrocity As History', *Sino-Japanese Studies* 3, no. 1 (November 1990), at 22–24.

[31]For a detailed account of this war, see Eastman, *supra* note 27, at 547–608.

1.3.1 The Sacking of the Old Summer Palace

When Anglo-French forces occupied Beijing, they looted and destroyed China's most significant imperial palace, the Old Summer Palace, an amalgam of palaces, pavilions, scenic enclosures, landscapes, artificial hills, and clusters of chambers serving as courts, temples, schools, museums and libraries. Well-known for its magnificent architecture and extraordinary history, it took the Qing people from 1709 to 1772 to complete this embodiment of the apex of Qing Empire.[32] Victor Hugo described the palace and its plunder and destruction: 'There was, in a corner of the world, a wonder of the world; this wonder was called the Summer Palace. Art has two principles, the Idea, which produces European art, and the Chimera, which produces oriental art. The Summer Palace was to chimera art what the Parthenon is to ideal art…'.[33] 'This wonder has disappeared. One day two bandits entered the Old Summer Palace. One plundered, the other burned. Victory can be a thieving woman, or so it seems. The devastation of the Old Summer Palace was accomplished by the two victors acting jointly. All the treasures of all our cathedrals put together could not equal this formidable and splendid museum of the Orient. It contained not only masterpieces of art, but masses of jewellery'.[34]

The sacking of the Old Summer Palace was reported by *The Times* on December 11, 1860: 'An embassy had been taken hostage by the Chinese and held at the Old Summer Palace; the British and French had sacked the estate in retaliation and the British had razed it after learning that the prisoners had been tortured, some to death'.[35] 'The soldiers destroyed vases and mirrors, tore down paintings and scrolls, broke into the storehouse of silks and used the precious fabrics for tying up their horses; they draped themselves in the empress' robes, and stuffed their pockets full of rubies, sapphires, pearls and pieces of crystal rock'.[36] The destruction of the Old Summer Palace was a tragic loss for all of civilization.

The best visual record of the Old Summer Palace complex is embodied in a set of forty paintings in the possession of the Bibliothèque Nationale in Paris. Representing the so-called 'forty scenes' of the central garden complex, each

---

[32]Many scholars have written about the destruction and looting of Yuanningyuan and its legacy. More detailed treatments in western languages can be found in: Wong (2011); G.R. Barmé, 'The Garden of Perfect Brightness, a Life in Ruins', *East Asian History* 11 (1996), pp. 111–158; Thomas, *supra* note 12; E. Ringmar, 'Liberal Barbarism and the Oriental Sublime: the European Destruction of the Emperor's Summer Palace', *Millennium: Journal of International Studies* 34 (2006), no. 3, pp. 917–934.

[33]Victor Hugo, 'The sack of the Summer Palace', letter to Captain Butler, November 25, 1861.

[34]Ibid.

[35]Quoted from Hill (2012), at 1. Thomas is of the opinion that that in addition to being motivated by revenge, the destruction of the Old Summer Palace, coupled with a threat to burn the Forbidden City, were intended to persuade the Emperor to enter into the extremely penal forced treaty. Thus, the destruction of the Old Summer Palace was instrumental in the military conquest of China. See Thomas, *supra* note 12.

[36]See Ringmar, *supra* note 32, at 921, 922, 933.

painting depicts a unique architectural ensemble set against a semi-imaginary landscape of the sort the surrounding garden was designed to evoke.[37] There are few visual records of the 1860 looting and the extraordinary breakdown in army discipline (the war photographer Beoto made only a few plates) and the vast majority of the many hundreds of thousands of looted objects remain undocumented and dispersed. As French sources noted at the time, it was as though the Louvre and Bibliothèque Nationale had both been destroyed simultaneously.[38] The *Illustrated London News* reported that 'The loss inflicted cannot be estimated by any money valuation. Treasures of gold and silver, works of the highest Chinese art, which no sums could purchase, the accumulation of ages, the most valuable secret records of the empire, the sacred genealogical tablets of the dynasty, are all gone, and can never be replaced. The solid, indestructible stone, here and there a marble arch or gateway, and massive bronzes too ponderous to be removed, will alone remain to tell to a future generation where the beautiful palace once stood, and to bear undying record of the righteous retribution enacted by the allied armies of the foreigners'.[39] It is unknown exactly how many cultural relics were destroyed and looted from the Old Summer Palace because the documents inventorying its contents were destroyed by fire. Approximately ten thousand cultural objects have been definitively identified as the Old Summer Palace relics. The best estimate is that approximately one million relics were looted from the Old Summer Palace.[40]

In 2009, the Old Summer Palace Administration began sending delegations of Chinese experts around the world to track down the treasures looted from the Old Summer Palace. Although the Chinese officials insisted the experts were pursuing an academic investigation aimed at better identifying and cataloging the Old Summer Palace relics, many museums resisted the experts' work. Some museums presented hurriedly prepared legal documents upon the delegations' arrival. The investigation was terminated as a result of the opposition mounted by the foreign museums as well as funding difficulties.[41] On the one hundred fiftieth anniversary

---

[37]Thomas, *supra* note 12.

[38]Ringmar, *supra* note 32, at 922.

[39]Quoted from J. Greenfield, 'The Spoils of War', in: Simpson (1997), at 36. According to Hill, during the Second Opium War, British and French soldiers acquired Chinese objects in three ways: taking trophies and war prizes on the battlefield, looting government and civilian buildings, and purchasing items from merchants. See Hill (2012), at 2.

[40]An abundance of fine art items looted from the Old Summer Palace are held abroad. The most significant collections are held in Britain, France and the United States. The Empress's Chinese Museum within the Château de Fontainebleau built to Empress Eugenie's specifications in 1863, houses her collection of Far-Eastern treasures, most of which were looted during the sacking of the Old Summer Palace.

[41]The first delegation was sent to the US on November 28, 2009 and returned on December 17, 2009. During the 18-day trip, the delegation visited nine museums and collected four or five hundred old photos and pictures of the Old Summer Palace, Chengde Mountain Resort and the Summer Palace. The delegation also discovered cultural relics suspected to be from the Old Summer Palace, including the painting of Liuyin Cow Map dating from the Song Dynasty, in the Boston Museum of Fine Art. There are eighteen seals on the Liuyin Cow Map painting, a number

of the destruction of the Old Summer Palace, the Administration issued a statement urging all holders of the Old Summer Palace relics to resist the temptations of trafficking in antiquities and return the relics.[42]

1.3.2 The 1900 Plunder of Beijing

China suffered a second large-scale pillage of cultural relics as a result of the Battle of Beijing in 1900. *The Sydney Morning Herald* characterized the mad scramble a 'carnival of loot'.[43] As Hevia writes, 'a loot fever gripped the armies and Euro-American civilian population in Beijing, and a wild orgy of plunder ensued. Moreover, many accounts agree that few if any were immune from this fever.'[44]

The commander of the allied western forces documented the pillage. 'Every nation except the Germans had already received a thorough training in Plundering at Tientsin, so matters naturally took the course they did in Peking (Beijing). It is useless to discuss whether the Russians, Japanese, English, French, or Americans most distinguished themselves in these exploits. All shared in them'.[45] 'When the Forbidden City was restored to the Chinese late in 1901, most of the portion which had been under Japanese protection was in good condition, but the American section was almost completely looted'.[46] 'When the English and the Italians occupied the Summer Palace (also known as Yihe Yuan), they had all the objects of value in their respective parts of the building gathered in a great room and put under guard. But a mere glance revealed the fact that this was only part of the original contents. The Russians had already got away with the best'.[47]

Although the 1900 pillage of Beijing and the 1860 sacking of the Old Summer Palace shared a carnival-like atmosphere of unregulated plunder, there are a few significant differences. First, no one stepped forward in Beijing, as had Garner

(Footnote 41 continued)

of which were identified by experts as being from the Qing court, providing strong evidence the painting was from the Old Summer Palace. The information collected by the delegation were exhibited in January, 2010. See Le Yanna, 'Setback in the Old Summer Palace Treasure Hunt', (in Chinese), *Huanqiu Magazine*, September 15 2010, viewed September 13, 2013, http://news.sina.com.cn/c/sd/2010-09-15/145421107918.shtml.

[42]For more information on the anniversary, see 'the Old Summer Palace: 150 Years After the Fire', CCTV, online video, viewed 15 April 2014, http://cctv.cntv.cn/lm/journeysintime/special/theOldSummerPalace/.

[43]Quoted from Hevia (2007), at 94.

[44]Ibid.

[45]Waldersee (1923), at, 565.

[46]Ibid.

[47]Ibid., at 567. Chinese joined in much of the robbery and plundering. Especially in the Palaces, Chinese officials stole items but blamed the foreign troops. Although most of the loot acquired by soldiers was stolen outright, vast quantities of stolen property fell into the hands of the Chinese and were subsequently sold to soldiers. European and American curio-buyers also played a great role.

Wolseley 1860, to contain the looting by attributing it to ordinary soldiers rather than officers. Secondly, the loot from 1900 did not carry with it the aura of a being 'from the Summer Palace of the Emperor of China'.[48] One would expect to find references to objects in museum collections as being from the Forbidden City or Beijing, or as having been taken during the 1900 Boxer episode. But only a few items so labelled have surfaced in London at the time or since. Sales of Boxer Rebellion loot were not conducted in London and Paris auction houses like those that took place in the 1860s, nor were there public displays of objects looted from Qing palaces like those held in London and Paris in 1861 and 1862.[49] In addition, the area looted was much larger in 1900. In 1860, the looting was more or less confined to the Old Summer Palace, but the plunder in 1900 affected all of Beijing, including the Qing imperial palaces, residences of the Qing nobility, and private homes, as well as Tientsin and other towns and villages around Beijing.[50] The seminal work of classical Chinese figure painting attributed to Gu Kaizhi (344–406), 'Admonitions of the Instructions to the Court Ladies Scroll', is believed to have been lost during the 1900 plundering of Beijing.[51] As with the sacking of the Old Summer Palace, there is no credible figure of the number of cultural relics looted or lost during the 1900 plundering of Beijing. Chinese historians describe the 1900 plunder of Beijing in sombre tones: 'All treasures handed down from the earlier civilizations, including ancient books, paintings, curios, and national rare treasures which had been housed in Beijing, have been completely swept out of China'.[52]

1.3.3 Japanese Pillage in the Second World War

During the Second Sino-Japanese War, public museums, libraries, and private houses were all targets of pillage for Japanese troops. Innumerable cultural objects were destroyed during war operations.[53] Various statistics reflect the devastating

[48]Hevia (2007), at 93–94.

[49]Ibid., at 94.

[50]Ibid., at 93.

[51]For more information regarding the painting, see McCausland (2003).

[52]It is believed that fully one half of the collections of the Forbidden City almand almost all treasures housed in the palaces of Nanhai, Zhonghai and Beihai were been looted by the forces. See Zhang Zicheng, *A Memorandum of A Century's Loss of Cultural Relics in China* (in Chinese), Beijing: Zhongguo Lvyou Chubanshe 2001, at 46.

[53]For a general account of the Japanese plunder during the Second Sino-Japanese War, see Yan Changhong & Li Xia, 'A Review of Japan's Cultural Aggression against China during Anti-Japanese War' (in Chinese), *Journal of South-Central University for Nationalities (Humanities and Social Sciences)* 25 (2005), no. 4, pp. 12–17; Dai, X. 'A Survey on China's Loss of Cultural Relics during WWII' (in Chinese), *Republican Archives* (2003), no. 2, pp. 84–90; Peng, L. (2012), pp. 26–34.

losses to Chinese culture. Of the thirty-seven large museums in China at the outbreak of the war, only eighteen survived the war. Three quarters of the university museums and libraries were destroyed during the war. On August 17, 1937, Japanese troops marched into the Summer Palace and the Forbidden City and removed many of valuable cultural treasures. In 1944, 11,022 volumes of ancient books in the Forbidden City and 1372 pieces of treasures in the Peking History Museum were looted by the Japanese.[54] The fossils of Peking Man, discovered in 1923–1927 at the excavations at Chou K'ou-tien near Beijing, were also lost at this time.[55]

The Republic of China's Ministry of Education established its Committee on Relics Reservation in War Zones in April 1945. The committee was renamed the Committee on the Clearing up of Relics Lost in War Time in December 1945. The Committee investigated and registered relics devastated or looted during the Second Sino-Japanese War in its Catalogue on the Quantity and Evaluation of Chinese Cultural Relics Lost in War, concluding that 3,607,074 individual items, as well as 1870 cartons of Chinese cultural objects were devastated or looted during WWII. The provenance of these objects was documented by public institutes or private persons.[56] Historians now believe the totals arrived at by the Committee reflect only a fraction of the cultural objects lost for the following reasons. First, the investigation was limited to the regions under the control of Kuomintang, which accounted for no more than half of the regions occupied by Japan. Secondly, the Committee only investigated cultural relics lost after 1937 even though the systematic Japanese pillage began in 1931. As a result, relics lost between 1931 and 1937 were not included in the investigation. In addition, the complicated procedures and demanding requirements for registration discouraged individuals and institution from declaring their losses.[57] It is estimated that between 1931 and 1945, at least ten million pieces of Chinese relics were destroyed or looted during the Japanese occupation.[58]

Although Japan returned one hundred six cases of rare books to China at the beginning of the 1947 and six batches of looted relics were returned to the Nationalist government in Taiwan between 1950 and 1956, many of the cultural relics looted from China during the Second Sino-Japanese War remain in Japan.[59]

[54]Peng, L. (2012), at 27.

[55]The fossils had been placed in the safe at the Cenozoic Research Laboratory of Peking Union Medical College. In 1941 the fossils were to be transported to the USA for safekeeping until the end of the war; however, they vanished en route to the port city of Qinhuangdao in northern China. The fossils' whereabouts remain unknown. See Yan, C. & Li, X., *supra* note 53, at 10–12; Peng, L. (2012), at 28–29.

[56]Yan, C. & Li, X., *supra* note 53, at 11; Dai, X., *supra* note 53, at 84–90.

[57]Dai, X., *supra* note 53, at 84–90.

[58]Ibid.

[59]Ibid.

1.4 Foreign Expeditions, Thefts and Exportations

Throughout modern Chinese history, countless cultural relics were stolen, excavated, and/or exported from China. For example, most of the heads of the Buddha statues in the Longmen Grottoes, a UNESCO World Heritage Site, were cut off and sold to foreigners between 1907 and 1935.[60] Foreign explorers, sinologists and missionaries had come to China since the end of the nineteenth century, to collect Chinese cultural relics. One hundred fifty-one archaeological explorations were conducted by foreign expedition teams in Northwest China between 1850 and 1940.[61] I explore two important instances of illicit trafficking: the loss of the Dunhuang cultural relics and the loss of the oracle bones.

1.4.1 The Loss of Dunhuang Cultural Relics

Dunhuang, an oasis city at junction of the western end of the Hexi Corridor and the eastern end of the Takla Makan Desert now famous as a thriving tourist center for visitors to its Buddhist caves, is the home of unparalleled cultural relics scattered in various institutions throughout the world. Historically, Dunhuang marked the western limit of direct Chinese administrative control and military authority and was a major stop on the ancient Silk Road.[62] According to the renowned Chinese scholar Ji Xianlin, the four major ancient civilizations in world history, Chinese, Indian, Greek and Islamic converged on Turpan and Dunhuang.[63] Being the entry point to Central China from Central Asia, various cultures left a rich cultural heritage in Dunhuang, especially in Buddhist art. Buddhism's spread along the length of the Silk Road resulted in its art's absorbing elements from India, China, Persia, and the Ancient Greek Empire of Alexander the Great and the development

---

[60]The grottoes and niches of Longmen contain the largest and most impressive collection of Chinese art of the late Northern Wei and Tang dynasties (316–907). Devoted entirely to the Buddhist religion, these works represent the high point of Chinese stone carving.

[61]Twenty explorations were conducted by Germans, fifty-three by Russians, thirty by British, one by Hungarian, thirteen by Japanese, eight by French, three by American, twenty-two by Swedish, and one by an unknown expedition team. The most well-known organized archaeological explorations were conducted in the following sites: (a) the Mogao Grottoes at Dunhuang; (b) the ruins of Heishui Cheng; (c) the ruins of Loulan Kindom; (d) the ruins of Niya; (e) the ruins of Gaochang; (f) the Kucha Grottoes. For a general account of foreign expeditions to China, see Peng, L. (2012), at 34–55; Hsiang-yu Huang, 'Background Analysis of the Birth of Legalization of Antiques Preservation (1911–1930)' (in Chinese), *Journal of the National History Academy*, December 2012, 16–17.

[62]Hopkirk (1980), at 22; Rong, X. (2013), at 19.

[63]See Ji Xianlin 'The Status and Function of the Dunhuang and Turpan Studies in Chinese Cultural History', (in Chinese), *Hongqi*, (1986), no. 3.

of the unique form of Buddhist art known as Chinese Western art.[64] Although art and culture in the Dunhuang area achieved its greatest heights during the Tang dynasty, as the dynasty fell into decline, so did the culture along the Silk Road. Following a process of several centuries of decline, ultimately the monasteries, temples, and works of art disappeared. Two theories account for the disappearance: the gradual drying up of the glacier-fed streams which supplied water to the oasis towns; and the sudden arrival, sword in hand, of the proselytizing Islamic warriors from far-off Saudi Arabia.[65]

Evidence of Dunhuang's once-glorious era had been considered lost until the discovery of a hidden cave, known today as Cave 17 or the Library Cave, at Mogao Grottoes. No detailed account of the caves survives from the time of the discovery. The Library Cave is generally believed to have been discovered by a Chinese Taoist monk named Wang Yuanlu (hereinafter 'Taoist Wang') on May 26th during the lunar calendar of Guangxu 26th year (1900).[66] The Library Cave contained approximately 50,000 manuscripts on paper, silk, wood, and other materials. Most of the manuscripts are religious documents of Buddhism, Taoism, Manicheanism, and Nestorian Christianity in ancient Chinese, Tibetan, Uighur, Central-Asian Brahmi, Turkic, and Syriac. Other manuscripts concern history, literature, astronomy, and astrology, or contain private or official correspondence.[67] The sheer volume and excellent condition of the manuscripts made the discovery unparalleled for the study of the medieval period of China and Central Asia. Based on the manuscripts and other relevant relics, an academic discipline, named Dunhuangology or Dunhuang studies, has been developed.[68]

In 1902, Ye Changchi, the Provincial Educational Commissioner of Gansu, was provided various Library Cave items by Wang Zonghan, the Magistrate of Dunhuang. Ye Changchi recognized the value of the materials after identifying some of them as paintings dating from the beginning of the Song dynasty. Although Ye immediately urged that all the Library Cave items be sent to Lanzhou, the

[64]Because of its unique location, at least twenty-four different spellings and seventeen different languages have been found in the Turpan and Dunhuang district. In addition to the manuscripts, many grotto remains, sculptures, frescoes, silk paintings, and other cultural objects have been found. See Hopkirk (1980), at 23–24.

[65]Ibid., at 28–30.

[66]The Mogao Grottoes are also known as the Caves of Thousand Buddhas. The first caves were dug in 366 AD as places of Buddhist meditation and worship. The Mogao Grottoes became a UNESCO World Heritage Site in 1987. Taoist Wang arrived at Maogao Grottoes in the 1890s and made the Grottoes his home. In May 1900, while cleaning Cave 16, his workmen accidentally discovered a hidden door which led to a small cave filled with ancient documents and paintings dating from the fourth to eleventh centuries. See Wang Jiqing, 'Aurel Stein's Dealings with Wang Yuanlu and Chinese Officials in Dunhuang 1907', in: H. Wang (ed.), *Sir Aurel Stein: Colleagues and Collections*, London: The British Museum 2012, at 3; Rong Xingjiang (1999–2000), at 247–248; Liu Yongzeng, 'Discovery of the Library Cave in Dunhuang Mogao Caves and Running of the Historical Cultural Relics', 64 (in Chinese), *Dunhuang Research* 2000, no. 2, at 11.

[67]Rong, X. (2013), at 4–6.

[68]Ibid., at 1–2.

capital of Gansu province, due to the financial exigencies, transportation of the contents of the entire library (estimated at seven cart-loads) was delayed.[69] In May 1904, the provincial government ordered Wang Zonghan to restore all the Library Cave items to their original location in the Caves. Wang Zonghan and various provincial civil and military officials made their way to the Mogao Grottoes, looked over the manuscripts in the Library Cave and ordered Taoist Wang to take care of them in place. Taoist Wang installed a rough wooden door with a crude lock over the opening of the Cave and kept the key.[70]

In March 1907, when the local peasantry was on the verge of revolting against the sustained abuse by the Dunhuang county government, the Hungarian-born British archaeologist Aurel Stein and his Chinese interpreter Jiang Xiaowan, arrived at the Mogao Grottoes.[71] Because at that time the cave shrines were still active, important, local village holy sites, Stein broached the topic of the manuscripts cautiously. Taoist Wang was very reticent and avoided meeting Stein. With the assistance of Jiang, Stein discovered that Taoist Wang, as did Stein, greatly admired Xuanzang, a famous 7th century Chinese Buddhist monk who had traveled from Chang'an to India. The shared admiration for Xuanzang and Stein's promise to make a generous donation persuaded Taoist Wang to show Stein a handful of sample documents from the Library Cave and to allow Stein to visit the Library Cave. Ultimately, Stein prevailed upon Taoist Wang to sell over nine thousand items, including more than eight thousand manuscript scrolls and five hundred paintings, together with numerous embroideries and other artifacts. Obscured by the shadows cast by the steep river bank, the sacks full of items were furtively transferred to Stein's store-room without any one's knowledge.[72]

Stein described his acquisition of the items from the Library Cave in a letter to his friend as follows: 'For the present the new acquisition travels in huge bags, disguised as well as we could manage it… For the present we must keep this entre nous… all which the 'Thousand Buddhas' yielded has cost the Government only some £130. The single Sanskrit Ms on palm leaf with a few other 'old things' are worth this'.[73]

[69]Ye Changchi, Yuandulu Diary, 12th day of 11th month of Guangxu 29th year (1903) and 22nd day of 8th month of 30th year (1904). See Liu, Y., *supra* note 66, at 11; Wang, J., *supra* note 66, at 3; Rong, X. (1999-2000), at 249.

[70]Ibid.

[71]This was Stein's Second Expedition in Central Asia. His First Expedition was conducted between 1900 and 1901. Stein had initially considered visiting Dunhuang in 1902 when applying for permission and funding to travel into Afghanistan and Tibet, but those applications were rejected. Ultimately, Stein secured permission and funds for his Second Expedition in 1905. Funding was provided by the British Museum and the British Government of India. See Wang, J., *supra* note 66, at 1–2.

[72]See Wang, J., *supra* note 66, at 1–5; Peng, L. (2012), at 35–36; for a detailed account of Stein's acquisition of the Dunhuang manuscripts, see Stein (1928), Vol. 1, pp. 354–370.

[73]Quoted from Wang, J., *supra* note 66, at 5, original source see Stein's diary entry for June 8, 1907 (Bodleian Library, MS. 204, at 344).

Stein's collection reached England in 1909 and remained in the British Museum until the early 1920s when it was divided among various institutions in proportion to their respective percentages in funding Stein's second expedition. The manuscripts, including an exceedingly old copy of *The Diamond Sutra* considered the oldest printed book to have survived fully intact to the present day, are in the British Library. The paintings were divided between the National Museum in New Delhi and the British Museum. The British Museum retains more than three hundred paintings on silk, hemp, and paper.[74]

Ten months after Stein's departure, Taoist Wang received a second foreign visitor, Paul Pelliot, a French sinologist. Aged only twenty-seven, Pelliot had been chosen to lead a three-man expedition to Chinese Central Asia. Dazzled by Pelliot's fluent Chinese, Taoist Wang allowed Pelliot into the Library Cave on March 3, 1908. Pelliot stole a number of the finest manuscripts by hiding them in his clothes.[75] Pelliot also persuaded Taoist Wang to sell the two piles of what Pelliot considered the most valuable manuscripts for 500 taels (£90). Taoist Wang insisted that the transaction be kept a secret. Completing their exploration of Dunhuang on May 30, 1908, Pelliot and his companions sent four thousand one hundred seventy-one items to Paris, including three thousand scrolls, numerous booklets, concertinas, two hundred Buddhist pictures, and seven hundred fragments. These objects are held in the Bibliothèque Nationale.[76]

Pelliot brought a few Dunhuang manuscripts to Beijing and showed them to Chinese scholars who were shocked to learn so many rare treasures had been spirited away. The scholars immediately requested the Qing government to preserve the remaining treasures from being stolen. The Qing court ordered the governor of Shanxi and Gansu Provinces to order the magistrate of Dunhuang to arrange the transportation of the relics to Beijing. In 1911, over eight thousand scrolls and manuscript fragments reached the National Library in Beijing.[77] Unfortunately, the items deposited in the National Library were only a portion of the remaining documents. Before the items were assembled for transportation to Beijing by the government, Taoist Wang removed many manuscripts which he subsequently sold to Japanese and Russian explorers, as well as Stein during his third expedition.[78] In

---

[74]H. Wang & J. Perkins (eds.), *Hand book to the Collections of Sir Aurel Stein in the UK*, London: The British Museum 2008, at 10.

[75]'Pelliot estimated that there were between fifteen and twenty thousand manuscripts in the cave. He decided to make two piles: first the cream, which he must obtain at all cost, and then the desirable but less essential manuscripts. 'During the first ten days', Pelliot wrote in a long letter to Senart in Paris, 'I attacked nearly a thousand scrolls a day, which must be a record…' See M. Cohen, 'Dunhuang at the Bibliothèque Nationale in Paris', *IDP News* 1996, no. 4, at 1–2; Hopkirk (1980), 177–189; Peng, L. (2012), at 36; Yang Xiuqing, *Dunhuang Sees Great Changes over the Years: Mogao Grottoes Through the Hard Times*, Beijing: China Intercontinental Press 2006, at 148–151.

[76]Yang, X., ibid., at 150–151.

[77]Ibid.

[78]Ibid.

addition, Qing governmental officials were less wholehearted in packing and transporting the item, with the result that numerous items were lost or stolen while in transit to Beijing.[79] Significantly, the manuscripts from the Library Cave were just part of the lost Dunhuang relics. Some explorers detached the wall paintings from the caves. The American explorers Langdon Warner and Horace Jayne detached twenty-six of the finest frescoes dating back to the Tang Dynasty from the grottoes. The frescoes, as well as a three feet tall Tang figure of a kneeling saint, are displayed in the Fogg Museum.[80] The Russians removed items as well. A number of items collected by the Russians along the Silk Road were exhibited in Hermitage Amsterdam Museum in 2014.[81]

Thus, the manuscripts and other cultural relics from Dunhuang are held by national institutions in Britain, France, China, Germany, Japan, Russia, Korea, and the United States, among others.[82] In 1994, The International Dunhuang Project was established to catalogue and digitally document the manuscripts and other artifacts so held in their various locations.[83]

1.4.2 The Loss of Oracle Bones

Oracle bones are pieces of turtle shell or animal bone inscribed with ancient Chinese writing. Oracle bones were found in archaeological sites which have been dated to the time of the Shang dynasty. In China, the discovery of oracle bones is a thing of legend. In 1899, Wang Yirong, a director of the Qing Imperial Academy and a knowledgeable collector of Chinese bronzes, was sick with malaria. He noticed the prescription he'd been given to treat his malaria called 'dragon bones'. So-called dragon bones had long been used as medicine in China. The turtle shell fragments were prescribed for treating malaria while the other powdered animal bones were prescribed to treat knife wounds. Checking the dragon bones before they were ground into powder, Wang Yirong realized that the inscriptions on the bones were in form of the oldest Chinese writing.[84]

---

[79]Ibid.

[80]Rong Xinjiang (2013), at 107.

[81]See 'Expedition Silk Road: Treasures from the Hermitage,' Hermitage Amsterdam, 2014, viewed 14 July 2014, http://www.hermitage.nl/en/tentoonstellingen/expedition_silk_road/index.htm.

[82]For details of other collections of the Dunhuang manuscripts see Yang, X., *supra* note 75, pp. 139–188; Rong Xinjiang (2013), pp. 137–176.

[83]This project has digitized a total of 441,723 images as of July 16, 2014. For more information, see the website of IDP http://idp.bl.uk/ (revised in September 2014).

[84]See Xu Yahui, *Oracle Bone Inscriptions from the Ruins of Yin* (in Chinese), Taipei: National Palace Museum 2001, at 6; Hu Wan & Zhou Chuling, 'The Tragic Status of Oracle Bones, Chinese Cultural Treasure', (in Chinese), *Library and Information Service*, 57 (2010), no. 7, at 7.

Known commonly today as oracle bones, most of the inscribed dragon bones were found at the palace and royal ancestral shrines area on the sites of Yin-xu in Xiaotun village in Anyang within the province of Henan.[85] Over half of the inscriptions on the oracle bones record divinations or inquiries effected by means of the bones. Diviners would submit questions to the deities concerning the weather, the welfare of various members of the royal family, warfare, crops, and so forth before applying intense heat to the bones with a glowing metal rod, which would cause the bones to crack. The diviners would then determine the deities' answers by 'reading' the patterns created by the cracked bones. The questions and answers were then engraved on the bones. Although the oracle bones were carefully preserved in a cavity kiln, some were dug up from time to time by local villagers for use as medicinal 'dragon bones'.[86]

The discovery of the oracle bones is of great historical significance because they confirm the existence of the Shang dynasty. The oracle bones inscriptions constitute the earliest known significant body of ancient Chinese writing. They not only furnish evidence of the independent development of the written form of the Han language, but also set forth the rules governing of written language in ancient China which has fundamentally shaped the Chinese culture over the last three thousand years. This written language is still used by over one quarter of the human race. The oracle bones also contain important historical information such as the complete genealogy of the Shang dynasty.[87]

Once the oracle bones' significance was recognized and before the systematic excavation was organized by the Chinese academy in 1928, a large quantity of relics from the Yin-xu ruins, including many oracle bones, bronze works and jade articles, were dug up by the local peasants and sold to foreigners and antique dealers.[88] The Canadian missionary James Menzies gathered the largest private

---

[85]The Shang rulers constructed their seventh and last dynastic capital city at a bend in the Huan River approximately seven miles north of the Yellow river, calling it Yin and renaming the dynasty itself Yin, the Shang-Yin. Twelve Shang kings ruled at Yin (殷) for two hundred and seventy-three years, until 1122/1045 BC when Shang was conquered by Zhou. Zhou so completely sacked Yin that it was thereafter known as Yin-xu, the ruins of Yin. The records which survived the book-burning by China's first Emperor, Qin Shihuang, are fragmentary. Over the course of the intervening millennia, Yin was forgotten. Several centuries after the sacking of Yin, the city named Anyang was built near the site. By the beginning of the twentieth century, some historians even doubted the existence of the Shang dynasty, viewing it as, at best, a 'semi-legendary' state, like its supposed predecessor, the Xia dynasty. See Dong, L.,*Cross Culture and Faith: A New Study of James M. Menzies*, Toronto: University of Toronto Press 2005; J.M. Menzies, 'The Culture of the Shang Dynasty', *The Smithsonian Report for 1931*, Washington: Government Printing Office 1932, pp. 549–558.

[86]See Menzies, ibid., at 554–555; Hu, W. & Zhou, C., *supra* note 84, at 6.

[87]To date, approximately four thousand five hundred characters have been found on the inscriptions, some seventeen hundred of which have been identified. See Menzies, ibid., at 549–558; Hu, W. & Zhou, C. ibid., at 6.

[88]Hu, W. & Zhou, C. ibid., at 8.

collection of oracle bones, forty-seven hundred in all.[89] Theories differ as to Menzies' motivations for collecting the objects. Based on unpublished family papers and archival and museum documents, Dong argues Menzies' motivation was religious and academic rather than monetary; given his strong religious motivation, Menzies collected items in a principled and ethical manner. He bought bones from peasants and simply picked up bones from fields.[90] Today most of Menzies' collection is held by the Royal Ontario Museum. Together with collections from the White and others, the Royal Ontario Museum holds one of the largest collections of oracle bones outside China.[91] The most recent studies show approximately one hundred thirty thousand pieces of inscribed oracle bones have been unearthed in the last hundred years. Approximately one hundred ten thousand pieces are held in Mainland China and Taiwan, with more than twenty thousand scattered all over the rest of the world.[92]

Unlike the Dunhuang manuscripts and the oracle bones, most Chinese lost cultural relics, even the most sought after national treasures, have no detailed provenance. For example, there is no indisputable record of how the *Admonitions of the Instructions to the Court Ladies Scroll*, considered to have been housed in the Qing court for fifteen years (1799–1815), was removed from of China. Some art historians believe the painting was plundered from the Qing court in 1900 during the Battle of Beijing, acquired by a British Indian Army officer and then sold to the British Museum in 1903. Others believe the painting was looted during the destruction of the Old Summer Palace in 1860. Others believe the painting was stolen by court eunuchs and secretly sold. Others maintain it was granted it as a reward by the emperor to his servants who then ceded the painting to others.[93]

[89]For more details about Menzies' collection, see Dong, L., *supra* note 85.

[90]As the missionary Menzies reflected later, he believed he was guided by God: 'God seemed to guide me when he placed in my hands the discovery of the 'oracle Bones', the actual relics of the ancient religious life of the Chinese at 1400–1200 B.C.' See ibid.

[91]According to Dong, Menzies believed his collection should remain with him in China. Because he viewed his commitment to missionary work a life-long one, Menzies never contemplated sending his collection out of China. Unfortunately, Menzies left China as a result of the political turbulence during the Second Sino-Japanese War and the Civil War. Only six boxes of the Menzies collection, stored in Tianjin by his colleagues after the North Henan Mission was disbanded in 1947, remain in China. Ibid.; C. Hsü, *Oracle bones from the White and other collections*, Toronto: Royal Ontario Museum 1979.

[92]The oracles bones are housed by institutions and private collectors of Japan (approximately 7999), Canada (7407), UK (3141), US (1860), Germany (851), Russia (199), Sweden (111), Switzerland (69), France (59), Singapore (28), Netherlands (10), New Zealand (10), Belgium (7), South Korean (7). See Y. Sun, 'Statistical Material Regarding a Century of Inscribed Oracle Bone Discoveries' (in Chinese), *Palace Museum Journal* 1 (2006), pp. 25–45.

[93]See Zhang Hongxing, 'The 19th-Century Provenance of the Admonitions Scroll: A Hypothesis', in: McCausland (2003).

1.5 Recovery Activities and Chapter Conclusion

After the foundation of PRC, the Chinese government purchased and repatriated some lost cultural relics. In 1951, the central government established a task force to recover the most precious lost cultural relics. A number of Chinese cultural treasures were repatriated at this time, including the famous painting of *Penta-Bull Map* (*Wuniu Tu*) of the Tang dynasty (618–907), and two rare calligraphic works by the Wang family of the Jin dynasty: *Letter to Boyuan* (*Boyuan Tie*) by Wang Xun, and *Mid-Autumn Festival* (*Zhongqiu Tie*) by Wang Xianzhi. In addition, various regulations were promulgated during this period, including the 'Provisional Regulation on the Prohibition of Exporting Valuable Archives', 'Provisional Regulation on Excavation of Ancient Heritage Ruins and Tombs' and 'Directive on Protection of Ancient Architecture.' Unfortunately, the task force's efforts ceased upon the commencement of the destructive Cultural Revolution in 1966.[94] More recently, Chinese society has again focused on the return of cultural object and some efforts have been made to effect their recovery.

1.5.1 Recovery Efforts

Recovering its lost cultural relics has become a national project in 21st Century China. China has launched a project to catalogue Chinese lost cultural relics while the SACH funds academic research regarding China's lost cultural relics.[95] In 2002, the SACH launched a special fund to bring back Chinese lost cultural relics. Every year, fifty million *yuan* are appropriated to the fund. As of 2012, approximately ten thousand valuable cultural relics have been repatriated, including the Zilong Ding bronze and the calligraphy of *Yanshan Ming*.[96] Some municipalities and museums have also recovered lost cultural relics. Beijing established a recovery project in 2001. The Prince Gong Mansion allocates six million *yuan* annually to recovering cultural relics and established a special one hundred million *yuan* recovery fund in 2007.[97] The special fund established by the Chinese Social and Cultural Development Foundation has also drawn a great deal of public attention.

---

[94]For more details, see Peng Lei (2012), at 148–149; He, L., 'Zhou Enlai Secretly Purchased Lost Relics and Halted Raiding Ancient Tombs', (in Chinese) *Renmin Wang*, February 5, 2012, viewed July 21, 2014. http://news.xinhuanet.com/politics/2012-02/05/c_122656784.htm.

[95]See 'China Sets up Database of Lost Cultural Relics', 163.com, May 25, 2006, viewed July 22, 2014, http://news.163.com/06/0525/14/2HVPK0O00001124J.html.

[96]Ibid.

[97]For more information on regional rescue projects, see China Cultural Heritage Information and Consulting Center, March 24, 2014, viewed July 21, 2014, http://www.cchicc.org.cn/art/2011/3/24/art_412_2028.html.

Efforts to repurchase lost cultural relics have not been free of controversy. Although the Chinese are proud to be able to buy back lost cultural relics, criticism centers on two aspects of such effort. First, if the Chinese buy back objects that were looted from China, such repurchases have the unintended consequence of recognizing and validating war plunder. Second, China's frenzied repurchasing of lost cultural relics has the unfortunate side effect of pushing prices much higher than their normative value.[98]

China has been actively cooperating with UNESCO's International Criminal Policy Organization (Interpol), the World Customs Organization and other inter-governmental and non-governmental organizations, as well as entering into bilateral agreements with other countries in its efforts to recover lost cultural objects.[99] When the bronze heads from the Old Summer Palace were scheduled for auction in Hong Kong in 2000, China lodged a request with UNESCO in their Beijing office calling for a halt to the sale of objects and their restoration to China.[100] Complying with the 1970 UNESCO Convention, Denmark returned one hundred fifty-six cultural relics dating back to between the Xia dynasty and the Ming dynasty to China in April 2008.[101] In September 2014 China hosted the Fourth International Conference of Experts on the Return of Cultural Property at Dunhuang. Together with specialists from other countries, Chinese cultural and legal experts discussed the legal and logistical aspects of protecting and returning illicitly exported archaeological cultural objects. Wang Yunxia, a Chinese lawyer, argued that while the Nazi's looting of before and during World War Two has been

---

[98]Although some insist repurchase is the most effective way of repatriating lost cultural relics, most Chinese cultural relic experts, including Xie Chensheng, and Luo Zhewen, oppose repurchasing looted cultural relics, calling it as 'plunder for the second time'. In their opinion, because the bronze heads from the Old Summer Palace were looted during the Second Opium War, if Chinese buy the looted objects back, China would be plundered yet again by virtue of the economic loss inherent in such a purchase. Chinese media have widely publicized Chinese scholars' opposition to buying back looted objects. See Mo Luo, 'Opposition to Buy Back the Bronze Heads', (in Chinese), *Xin Jing Bao*, (19-2-2009);

Li Fang, 'Experts say that to Buy Back Lost Cultural Relics is Looting for a Second Time', *People's Daily,* February 26, 2010, viewed March 2, 2012, http://news.163.com/10/0226/15/60F7F23E000146BC_2.html; and others.

[99]See Gao Sheng, 'International Protection of Cultural Property: Some Preliminary Issues and the Role of International Conventions', *Singapore Year Book of International Law and Contributors,* (2008), at 77.

[100]See the Secretariat Report of the Eleventh Session of the Intergovernmental Committee for Promoting the Return of Cultural Property to its Countries of Origin or its Restitution in case of Illicit Appropriation, CLT-2001/ CONF. 202/2, (2000), 3.

[101]'Recent examples of successful operations of cultural property restitutions in the world', UNESCO, May 10, 2010, viewed July 21, 2014, http://portal.unesco.org/culture/en/ev.php-URL_ID=36505&URL_DO=DO_TOPIC&URL_SECTION=201.html.

universally condemned, Japan's systematic mistreatment and misappropriation of China's cultural heritage during the same war is seldom discussed and warrants international attention.[102]

1.5.2 Conclusion

In modern Chinese history, the sovereignty of China was often encroached upon and at other times the Chinese governments failed to protect Chinese cultural heritage from both internal and external challenges. Although to critics the reiteration of cultural loss in modern Chinese history merely satisfies the ideological needs of post-imperial Chinese governments to maintain China's independence and unity, it is incontrovertible that China suffered a huge loss of cultural objects via wartime plunder, including the sacking of the Old Summer Palace, the plunder of Beijing, and Japanese pillage during its aggression against China. Military confrontations by foreign powers repeatedly exacerbated social crises in China, leading inexorably to a nationwide loss of cultural relics. Motivated by economic interest, many Chinese willingly participated in trafficking cultural objects out of China: Taoist Wang sold the Dunhaung Library relics to foreign explorers; Chinese peasants dug up the oracle bones and sold them to missionaries. As a result of these vicissitudes, countless Chinese cultural relics have been lost to China. Now China is taking action to promote the return of its lost cultural relics.

[102]Xu Liuliu, 'Overseas Cultural Relics have a Hard Road back to China', *Global Times,* September 14, 2014, viewed September 16, 2014, http://www.globaltimes.cn/content/881381.shtml; H. Song, 'The 4th International Conference of Experts on the Return of Cultural Property Opens', *China Culture*, September 12, 2014, viewed September 16, 2014, http://www.chinaculture.org/info/2014-09/12/content_563202.htm.

Chapter 2
Law and Ethics Protecting Cultural Objects

2.1 Introduction

This chapter discusses the legal and ethical frameworks intended to protect and regulate rights in cultural objects.[1] Positing that because international threats to cultural objects originate from two different sources, James Nafziger argues there are two distinct legal frameworks intended to protect and preserve right in cultural objects.[2] The first framework deals with destruction and looting during times of war and belligerent occupation. Applicable at any time, the second framework deals with a state's ability to use international cooperation and sanctions to counter the theft and illicit trafficking of its cultural objects.[3] The first section of this chapter discusses the evolution of rules treating cultural objects in the event of armed conflict. Although historically the rules of war decreed 'to the victor go the spoils,' a countervailing argument has carried the day since the second half of nineteenth century.[4] The second section of this chapter discuses the legal framework regarding illicit trafficking of cultural objects, elaborating upon two important international conventions as well as Chinese domestic legislation from the late Qing period. This chapter concludes with an exploration of ethical guidelines regarding cultural

---

[1]Francesco Francioni and James Gordley state that 'it is safe to say that cultural heritage law is a discrete branch of international law, and at the same time it constitutes an evolving dimension of many areas of international law'. See Francioni & Gordley (2013), at 1.
[2]Nafziger (2008), at 977. As noted by Francioni, the laws protecting cultural heritage—international and domestic, private and public, peacetime and wartime—continues to increase in number, complexity, and inter-relatedness. See Francioni (2012), at 722–726.
[3]See Nafziger, *ibid.*, at 978.
[4]See W. Sandholtz, 'Plunder, Restitution, and International Law', *International Journal of Cultural Property* 17 (2010), pp. 147–176.

Z. Liu, *The Case for Repatriating China's Cultural Objects*,
DOI 10.1007/978-981-10-0597-8_2

objects promulgated by professional organizations and which have led to the successful restitution or return of some cultural objects. Although not legally binding, such ethical guidelines are valuable guides for any bodies intent upon enacting international laws regarding cultural objects.

2.2 Protection of Cultural Objects During Times of War

Cultural objects have always been looted or destroyed during armed conflict. The only practical constraint upon such destruction and looting, and a reluctance to damage buildings and works of art dedicated to religion, were out of fear the deity might seek revenge.[5] Legal constraints prohibiting destruction or looting of cultural objects during armed conflict were non-existent until the mid-nineteenth century.

2.2.1 *From Antiquity to the Eighteenth Century*

According to Henry Wheaton, the ancient law of nations provided that all property was subject to capture and confiscation in times of war, including *res sacræ* (things consecrated to gods). In ancient times, both the movable and immovable property of the vanquished passed to the conqueror.[6] This practice was codified by the Roman law of war. '[T]he Romans, with their fine legal minds, understood the ownership of the property of conquered people perfectly and absolutely.'[7] The prescribed forms for written surrender to Rome asked: 'Do you surrender the [named] people, the city, fields, water, boundaries, shrines, utensils, all things divine and human into the dominion of … the Roman people?'[8] An affirmative answer meant the Romans became 'masters of absolutely everything and those who surrender[ed] remain[ed] masters of absolutely nothing' beyond the discretion of the victor.[9] As a result, the ancient world witnessed countless instances of the destruction and plundering of property in times of conflict, such as the burning and sacking of Troy, the burning of Persepolis by Alexander the Great, and the obliteration of Corinth and Carthage.[10] The only other rules even remotely applicable to cultural objects during

---

[5]Verhoeven (2008), at 376–379; Nafziger (2008), at 978.

[6]Cicero (106–43 BCE) expressed this idea metaphorically: 'Victory made all the sacred things of the Syracusans profane.' H. Wheaton, *Elements of International Law* (2nd ed., annot. by W.B. Lawrence), London: Sampson Low 1864, at 596–597.

[7]*Ibid.,* at 597; Gillespie (2011), at 210.

[8]Gillespie (2011), at 210.

[9]*Ibid.*.

[10]Verhoeven(2008), at 378–379.

ancient times dealt with the division among the victors of the loot taken in times of conflict.[11]

Not until the Renaissance, when people began to think a work of art was unique, could not be recreated, and its loss would thus be permanent, was the plunder and destruction of art increasingly considered barbaric and as evidence of a lack of culture.[12] The Renaissance also birthed the metaphysical vision of such property as 'heritage,' a universal estate common to all peoples.[13] Although these concepts of art gained ground in the elite circles, actual sixteenth century practice usually ran contrary to such noble. The sixteenth century is replete with examples of where cultural objects were looted and destroyed in times of conflict. Despite the elevated status of art in the Renaissance, states and legal authorities did not think the destruction or looting of cultural objects was prohibited by the *jus gentium* (law of nations).[14]

Jakub Przyluski was arguably the first proponent of protecting cultural objects in times of war in the doctrine of the law of nations in 1553.[15] In his famous 'The Rights of War and Peace,' the great international lawyer Hugo Grotius asserts that 'by the Law of Nature those Things may be acquired by a just War, which are either equivalent to that, which tho' due to us, we cannot otherwise get, or which damnifies the Injurer, but within the Bounds of a just Punishment'.[16] Significantly, Grotius distinguishes between just and unjust wars.[17] According to Grotius, things taken in an unjust war must be restored, not only by those who have taken them, but by others into whose hands they may have fallen. Things taken are to be restored to their former lawful owners.[18] Grotius also considered it unnecessary to destroy an enemy's country when the victor has other sources from which to feed his troop and

---

[11]According to Gillespie, these rules were necessary for two reasons: so equity could be achieved among the victors and each would get their 'just' reward; so troops would continue to fight through a conflict rather than stop fighting to engage in private pillage, thereby affording an enemy the opportunity to regroup, as was a problem in the earliest recorded battles such as Megiddo (1479 BCE) and Kadesh. Gillespie (2011), at 211.

[12]Verhoeven (2008), at 379.

[13]R. O' Keefe, *The Protection of Cultural Property in Armed Conflict*, Cambridge: Cambridge University Press, 2006, at 5.

[14]Verhoeven (2008), at 379.

[15]Przyluski writes: 'in addition to objects of worship, outstanding works of art and literature should be exempted from the right to take spoils of war'. See Kowalski, *supra* note 18, at 87.

[16]H. Grotius, *The Rights of War and Peace,* (ed. and intr. by R. Tuck), Indianapolis: Liberty Fund 2005, at 1314.

[17]Whether a war is a 'just war' is to be determined with reference to two factors: the war's causes and its conduct. Wars may be justly undertaken in response to 'wrong not yet committed, or to wrongs already done'. The lengthy list of wrongs justifying war includes inflicting punishment, self-defense, the defense of chastity, among others. A justly undertaken war must also be fought rightly for it to be just. Grotius concludes essentially that war is justifiable when, and only when, it serves right. See *Ibid.*, at 516.

[18]*Ibid.*, at 1416, 1512.

sustain his war effort.[19] Items which by their nature could not support and prolong the war effort were to be spared even during the heat of battle.[20] As devotional works of art and related items are incapable of increasing the intensity of hostilities or retarding the conclusion of a war, it is a mark of reverence to spare them, which rule should be adhered to particularly by warring nations that worship the same God and observe the same fundamental laws, notwithstanding their having differing opinions regarding their rights.[21]

Another early jurist, Emer de Vattel, took a position similar to Grotius concerning the plundering of art during armed conflicts. Although he postis that '[I]t is lawful to take the property of an unjust enemy in order to weaken or punish him,'[22] Vattel suggests cultural objects should be protected from deliberate destruction because of their significance for humanity. 'For whatever cause a country is ravaged, we ought to spare those edifices which do honour to human society, and do not contribute to increase the enemy's strength…such as temples, tombs, public buildings, and all works of remarkable beauty'.[23] However, Vattel's prohibition of plundering cultural objects was largely ignored. Pillage was documented among British, Russian, French, and Austrian Forces as they fought their way through Prussia and elsewhere in the Seven Years War.[24]

2.2.2 The Nineteenth Century

The Napoleonic Wars saw many works of art brought to France. Originally consisting of art confiscated from clerical and aristocratic collections, under Napoleon's personal direction the Louvre's collections were enriched with art plundered from Italy, Russia, Egypt, Prussia, Italy, Spain and the Netherlands.[25] The supply wagons returning to France from conquered countries were expected to include those countries' art treasures and rare books. Napoleon supplemented these acquisitions by imposing onerous economic penalties upon his defeated enemies under treaties

---

[19] *Ibid.*, at 1464.

[20] *Ibid.*, at 1466.

[21] *Ibid.*, at 1467–1468.

[22] See E. de Vattel, *The Law of Nations, or, Principles of the Law of Nature, Applied to the Conduct and Affairs of Nations and Sovereigns, with Three Early Essays on the Origin and Nature of Natural Law and on Luxury* (ed. and introd. By B. Kapossy & R. Whitmore), Indianapolis: Liberty Fund 2008, §161–162.

[23] *Ibid.*, §166.

[24] The doctrine of 'military necessity' was developed in Prussia at this time to permit the destruction of cultural objects in extraordinary circumstances. See Gillespie (2011), at 242; Verhoeven (2008), 379.

[25] Gillespie (2011), at 247; K.F. Gibbon, 'Chronology of Cultural Property Legislation', in: K.F. Gibbon (ed.), *Who Owns the Past? Cultural Policy, Cultural Property, and the Law,* New Brunswick: Rutgers University Press 2005, at 3.

such as the Treaty of Pressburg, the Treaty between France and Prussia, and the Treaty of Vienna and then taking art in partial payment of such penalties.[26] Although some Frenchmen voiced criticism of Napoleon's massive appropriations, others supported them in light of their belief that France was by far the most enlightened and civilized nation and therefore best able to properly appreciate, and own, great art.[27]

In the second half of the nineteenth century, a consensus began to emerge regarding ethical principles governing the protection of non-combatants and non-military targets in war.[28] In his influential *Elements of International Law*, Wheaton posited that 'by the modern usage of nations, which has now acquired the force of law, temples of religion, public edifies devoted to civil purposes only, monuments of art, and repositories of science, are exempted from the general operations of war'.[29]

Promulgated in 1863, the Lieber Code marked the first time a sovereign nation established formal guidelines for the conduct of its army in the field.[30] A codification of Western military customs, the Lieber Code provides that cultural property, such as classical works of art, libraries, scientific collections, and precious instruments must be secured against all avoidable injury even when contained in besieged or bombarded fortified places (Article 35). Only public property is subject to seizure (Article 31) and cultural property is not public property (Article 34). 'In no case shall they (cultural items) be sold or given away, if captured by the armies of the United States, nor shall they ever be privately appropriated, or wantonly destroyed or injured' (para 2, Article 36).

The Lieber Code generated a great deal of interest in controlling the actions of the belligerents in European wars and a series of declarations were made and treaties were entered into, notably the 1874 Brussels Declaration and the Oxford Manual.[31] The 1874 Brussels Declaration prohibits any destruction or seizure of the enemy's property that was not imperatively demanded by the necessity of war (Article 13(9)), and provides (in Article 8) that 'The property of municipalities, that of institutions dedicated to religion, charity and education, the arts and sciences

---

[26]Gibbon, *ibid.*, 3; Gillespie (2011), at 247–248.

[27]Gibbon, *ibid.*, 3.

[28]Gibbon, *ibid.*, 3.

[29]Wheaton, *supra* note 29, at 596.

[30]For more information on the Lieber Code, see P. Maguire, *Law and War: An American Story*, New York: Columbia University Press 2001, 21; Merryman (1986), at 833–842; G.M. Hart, 'Military Commissions and the Lieber Code: Toward a New Understanding of the Jurisdictional Foundations of Military Commissions', *Military Law Review* 203 (2010), pp. 1–77.

[31]The draft of the Brussels Declaration was adopted in a conference by fifteen European states in Brussels on August 27, 1874, but remained unratified because not all the states were willing to accept it as binding. The Oxford Manual was adopted by the Institute of International law in 1880. For more information on the Brussels Declaration and the Oxford Manual, see D. Schindler & J. Toman, *The Laws of Armed Conflicts* (3rd rev. and compl. ed.), Dordrecht: Nijhoff 1988, at 22–34, 36–48.

even when state property, shall be treated as private property. All seizure or destruction of, or wilful damage to institutions of this character, historic monuments, works of art and science should be made the subject of legal proceedings by the competent authorities.' The Oxford Manual incorporates the Brussels Declaration's rules concerning the protection of cultural properties in Articles 32, 34, and 53.

The Brussels Declaration and the Oxford Manual laid the foundation for subsequent international conventions. On the initiative of the Czar Nicholas II of Russia, the First Hague Peace Conference was convened between May 18 and July 29, 1899 and attended by twenty-six delegations.[32] The Conference adopted three conventions. Rules regarding the protection of cultural objects during armed conflict are incorporated in the 1899 Hague Convention (II).[33] Article 23(g) of the 1899 Hague Convention (II) specifically forbids destroying or seizing the enemy's property unless such destruction or seizure is imperatively demanded by the necessities of war. All necessary steps should be taken to spare edifices devoted to religion, art, science, charity, and hospitals, provided they are not used also used for military purpose (Article 27). Even when taken by assault, the pillage of a town or place, is prohibited (Article 28). Prohibition of pillage of property in armed conflicts was internationally codified for the first time. Articles 47–56 of the annexed regulations provide rules regarding property in hostile territory. As a general rule, pillage was formally prohibited (Article 47). An army of occupation can only take possession of the cash, funds, and property liable to requisition belonging strictly to the state, arms depots, means of transport, stores of supplies, and generally movable property of the state which may be used for military operations (Article 53). The occupying states shall only be regarded as administrator and usufructuary of the public buildings, real property, forests, and agricultural works situated in occupied territory and belonging to the hostile state. The occupying state must protect the capital of these territories, and administer it according to the rules of usufruct (Article 55). The property of the communities and religious, charitable, and educational institutions, and those of arts and science, even State property, shall be

[32]For more information on this Conference, see B. Baker, 'Hague Peace Conference (1899 and 1907)', *Max Planck Encyclopedia of Public International Law* November 2009, opil.ouplaw.com/home/EPIL, OUP reference MPEPIL 305.

[33]The other two conventions are Convention (I) for the Pacific Settlement of International Disputes and the Convention (III) for the Adaptation to Maritime Warfare of the Principles of the Geneva Convention of August 22, 1864. Three declarations were also made: Declarations [IV,1] concerning the Prohibition of the Discharge of Projectiles and Explosives from Balloons or by Other New Analogous Methods; Declaration [IV,2] concerning the Prohibition of the Use of Projectiles with the Sole Object to Spread Asphyxiating Poisonous Gases; Declaration [IV,3] concerning the Prohibition of the Use of Bullets which can Easily Expand or Change their Form inside the Human Body such as Bullets with a Hard Covering which does not Completely Cover the Core, or containing Indentations. According to Baker, all parties in attendance signed each of the three conventions, with the exception of Convention (II), which China and Switzerland declined to sign. See *Ibid.*; Liu Pengchao, 'Diplomacy in Modern History: China's First Participation in the International Conference' (in Chinese), *Zhongguo Chengshi JingJi,* (2011), iss. 18, at 327–328.

treated as private property. All seizure of and destruction, or intentional damage done to such institutions, to historical monuments, works of art or science, is prohibited and should be made the subject of proceedings (Article 56). By the end of the second half of the nineteenth century, governments, international organizations, and lawyers had all taken a hand in increasing public awareness of the need to protect cultural properties during times of conflict.

2.2.3 The Two World Wars

The need for protecting cultural objects in times of conflict gained momentum around the turn of the twentieth century. Convened in 1907 and attended by 43 states, the Second Hague Peace Conference attempted to ameliorate the hardships incident to war and substitute non-violent dispute resolution for armed conflict as a means to settle international grievances.[34] Ten of the thirteen conventions adopted were new and the other three revised the three conventions agreed to in 1899. Most significantly for the purposes of this study, the 1899 Hague Convention (II) was the least revised, becoming known as the 1907 Hague Convention (IV).[35] The provisions respecting protection of cultural objects in the event of armed conflict in the 1907 Hague Convention (IV) are identical to those in the 1899 Hague Convention (II). Although the 1899 Hague Convention (II) and the 1907 Hague Convention (IV) were ignored by the belligerents in WWI and many cultural objects were destroyed and looted, these conventions at least provided international rules to protect cultural objects in times of war.[36]

The need for protecting cultural objects in times of war received greater attention following WWI. A report commissioned by the Peace Conference in 1919 recommended declaring confiscation, wanton devastation and destruction of cultural properties as war crimes.[37] In 1933, the Seventh International Conference of American States recommended adoption of the Roerich Pact, which was subsequently drawn up by the Governing Board of the Pan-American Union and signed on April 1935. The Roerich Pact establishes the neutrality of monuments, museums, scientific, artistic, educational, and cultural institutions, and designates a flag by which they could be identified, just as hospitals and medical personnel are identified by the red cross (Articles 1 and 3). '[T]he treasures of culture' were to be

---

[34]See Baker, *ibid.*; J.B. Scott, 'The Work of the Second Hague Peace Conference,' *The American Journal of International Law* 2 (1908), at 1.

[35]China ratified the 1907 Hague Convention (IV) on May 10, 1917. See Scott, *ibid.*, at 1–2, 12.

[36]For more information regarding such pillage and destruction, see Gillespie (2011), at 252–259.

[37]See Commission on the Responsibility of the Authors of the War and on Enforcement of Penalties, 'Report presented to the preliminary Peace Conference, March 29, 1919', *The American Journal of International Law* 14 (1920), no. 1–2, pp. 114–115.

respected and protected 'in time of war and peace' unless they had been used for 'military purposes' (Article 5).

As a result, at the opening of the Second World War, some efforts were made to protect cultural properties from damage. Hermann Goering instructed his pilots to be careful when attacking French cathedrals, which were 'under all circumstances, to be protected and not attacked, even if it were a question of troop concentration in those places.' '[I]f attacks had to be made, precision bombing Stukas were to be used primarily.'[38] Nonetheless, unprecedented loss and pillage of cultural objects occurred in WWII's Western and Eastern battlefields. The Germans destroyed four hundred twenty-seven museums, among them the wealthy museums of Leningrad, Smolensk, Stalingrad, Novgorod, and Poltava.[39] Asian countries suffered destruction by the Japanese troops. '[I]t appears that the Japanese forces acted with little restraint in the destruction of Chinese cultural heritage whereby libraries and associated cultural treasures were systematically destroyed in, inter alia, Shanghai, Nanjing, Suzhou, and Hangzhou. By the end of the war, out of 4,041 libraries in China, at least 2,500 were destroyed, along with 92 institutions of higher learning'.[40] Alexander Gillespie observes that although all the belligerents prohibited their soldiers from pillaging, soldiers stole properties in all the war's theaters. In addition, some belligerents adopted a systematic, aggressive approach to acquiring their enemies' cultural heritage, most notably the Germans and Soviets.[41] Hitler effected his collection efforts under two pretences. First, there was the art and other spoils which were to be taken in order that they could be 'safeguarded' from the vicissitudes of the war. Alternatively, items were to be acquired by sale, contract or forfeiture. After the War, the total value of the art which had been looted was estimated at between two and two and a half billion US dollars.[42] In 1943, sixteen governments and the French National Committee issued the Inter-Allied Declaration of the Allied Nations against Acts of Dispossession Committed in Territories under Enemy Occupation or Control (the Declaration of London), with the aim of combating and defeating plundering by the enemy powers. The Declaration stressed that the signatories 'reserve all their rights to declare invalid any transfers of, or dealings with, property, rights and interests of any description whatsoever which are, or have been situated in the territories which have come under the occupation or control, direct or indirect of the Governments with which they are at war, or which belong, or have belonged to persons (including juridical persons) resident in such territories'.[43]

---

[38]Gillespie (2011), at 259.

[39]The International Military Tribunal, *Tribal of the Major War Criminals before the International Military Tribunal*, Nuremberg: The International Military Tribunal 1947, *Vol.* II, at 66, 42, 54.

[40]Gillespie (2011), at 265–266.

[41]*Ibid.*

[42]*Ibid.*, at 266.

[43]Prott (2009), 4–5.

2.2.4 The Post-War Legal Regime

After WWII, war criminals were prosecuted in the Nuremberg and Tokyo Tribunals. Crimes against peace, war crimes, and crimes against humanity fell within the jurisdiction of both Tribunals.[44] The proceedings of the Nuremberg Tribunal declared 'plunder of public or private property, wanton destruction of cities, towns or villages, or devastation not justified by military necessity' war crimes (Article 6). In the Nuremberg trials, American, French and Soviet prosecutors all devoted substantial attention to prosecuting Nazi crimes against cultural property. According to the Nuremberg prosecutors, the plundering and destruction of museums, collections, libraries, and archives was part of the Nazi's plan to enhance Germany's cultural superiority by diminishing, if not annihilating, the cultural heritage of its opponents. The prosecutors also alleged such plundering and destruction violated the 1907 Hague Conventions.[45] Under the heading 'Pillage of Public and Private Property', the judgment cites the 1907 Hague Convention, quoting Article 56 in its entirety. The judgment declares that 'in addition to the seizure of raw materials and manufactured articles, a wholesale seizure was made of art treasures, furniture, textiles, and similar articles in all the invaded countries.' The verdict convicting Rosenberg states: 'Rosenberg is responsible for a system of organized plunder of both public and private property throughout the invaded countries of Europe.... He organized and directed the 'Einsatzstab Rosenberg', which plundered museums and libraries, confiscated art treasures and collections, and pillaged private houses'(Judgment, Rosenberg).[46]

Although during the formulation of the Convention on the Prevention and Punishment of the Crime of Genocide in 1948 some commentators argued the systematic destruction of cultural property should be deemed the actionable offense of 'cultural genocide,' the Convention focused its attention only on people, not objects.[47] Adopted by the UN General Assembly, The Universal Declaration of Human Rights states that 'no-one shall be arbitrarily deprived of his property (Article 17)'.[48] The first special convention for the protection of cultural property in armed conflict, the 1954 Hague Convention[49] was the result of efforts dating back

---

[44]See the Charter of the International Military Tribunal and the International Military Tribunal for the Far East Charter (IMTFE Charter).

[45]Quotd from W. Sandholtz, *Prohibiting Plunder: How Norms Change*, Oxford: Oxford University Press 2007, at 176.

[46]*Ibid.*, at, 177.

[47]This Convention was adopted by the UN Assembly on December 9, 1948 as General Assembly Resolution 260. See Vrdoljak (2006), at 164–171.

[48]Universal Declaration of Human Rights, GA Res 217 (III), UN Doc A/810, (1948) at 71.

[49]As of April 17, 2012, one hundred twenty-six countries have ratified or acceded to The Hague Convention of 1954. China acceded to the Convention on January 5, 2000.

to the Lieber Code, the Brussels Declaration, the Oxford Manual, the 1899 and 1907 Hague Conventions, and the Roerich Pact and its adoption 'satisfied a desire that many philosophers had expressed over the course of centuries'.[50]

According to its preamble, the basic principles of the 1954 Hague Convention include 'damage to the cultural property belonging to any people whatsoever means damage to the cultural heritage of all mankind, since each people makes its contribution to the culture of the world' (para 2) and 'this heritage should receive international protection' (para 3). These two principles provide the foundation for the development of all international heritage law.[51]

As summarized by O'Keefe and Prott, the obligations created by the 1954 Hague Convention and its Regulations include:[52]

A duty to safeguard cultural property (Articles 2 and 3), i.e., adequately safeguarding cultural property situated within a state's own territory against all foreseeable effects of an armed conflict;

(a) A duty to respect cultural property (Articles 2 and 4), i.e., not using either cultural property or its immediate surroundings for military purposes or for any purpose which would likely expose it to destruction or damage in the event of armed conflict;
(b) A duty to train the military in the Convention's principles (Article 7); and
(c) Special duties are imposed upon occupying powers (Convention Article 5; Regulations Articles 2 and 19; Protocol (1954) Articles 1 and 4), including assisting local authorities to safeguard and preserve cultural property and, if such authorities are unable to do so, themselves take all measures necessary to insure such property's preservation.

The two Protocols to the 1954 Hague Convention require various actions to be taken by nations desiring to be bound by their terms.[53] Drafted at the time as the 1954 Hague Convention itself,[54] the First Protocol deals with the removal of cultural property from an occupied territory. A Contracting Party must prevent the exportation of cultural property from occupied territory. If objects exported from an occupied territory are found in the territory of a Contracting Party, the Contracting

---

[50]J. Toman, 'The Road to the 1999 Second Protocol', in: A. van Woudenberg & E. Lijnzaad (eds.), *Protecting Cultural Property in Armed Conflict: An Insight into the 1999 Second Protocol to the Hague Convention of 1954 for the Protection of Cultural Property in the Event of Armed Conflict*, Leiden: Nijhoff 2010, at 2.

[51]P.J. O'Keefe & L.V. Prott (eds.), *Cultural Heritage Conventions and Other Instruments, A Compendium with Commentaries,* Crickadarn: Institute of Art and Law 2011, at 16.

[52]*Ibid.*, at 16–17.

[53]See para 6 of the First Protocol, Article 41 of the Second Protocol.

[54]The First Protocol became effective on August 7, 1956. As of October 17, 2013, one hundred three states had acceded to the First Protocol. China acceded to the First Protocol on January 5, 2000.

Party must take the objects into custody and return them to the occupied territory upon the close of hostilities.[55] Although some consider the First Protocol a 'revolutionary instrument', others consider it of little practical effect.[56] Patrick J. Bolylan states he has "not seen or received evidence of a single example of States Parties to the Protocol taking action of any kind in order to bring its provisions into practical effect in order to 'freeze' trade in, or other transfers or movements of, cultural property from areas affected by either international or internal armed conflicts".[57] Nevertheless, the recent return of four 16th Century icons from the Netherlands to Cyprus under the First Protocol is noteworthy. Belonging to the Church of Christ Antiphonitis on Cyprus, the icons were removed during the Turkish invasion in 1974 and later discovered in a private collection in the Netherlands. On September 18, 2013, the Netherlands handed the four icons over to Cyprus, the first time the Netherlands returned cultural objects under the First Protocol, and evidently the first time any cultural objects had been returned pursuant to the First Protocol.[58]

Due in large part to a succession of armed conflicts such as the First Gulf War, the conflict in the former Yugoslavia and the war in Afghanistan and their serious harm to cultural heritage, questions arose regarding the efficacy of the 1954 Hague Convention.[59] As a result, the Second Protocol to the Convention was adopted at The Hague on March 26, 1999.[60] A serious effort to update the legal protection of cultural heritage, The Second Protocol includes new provisions such as a definition of military necessity, the introduction of 'enhanced protection' and the creation of a

---

[55]According to Lijnzaad, initially there was no intention to create a separate instrument covering illegal export of cultural property from occupied territories. However, some countries opposed the inclusion of provisions on restitution of cultural property in the body of the Convention, resulting in the separation of the Convention from the First Protocol. See E. Lijnzaad, 'Sleeping Beauty, the untold story of the (first) Protocol to the 1954 Hague Convention', in: A. van Woudenberg & E. Lijnzaad (ed.), *Protecting Cultural Property in Armed Conflict: An Insight into the 1999 Second Protocol to the Hague Convention of 1954 for the Protection of Cultural Property in the Event of Armed Conflict*, Leiden: Nijhoff 2010, at 148–149.

[56]*Ibid.*, at 149.

[57]P. J. Boylan, *Review of the Convention for the Protection of Cultural Property in the Event of Armed Conflict* (The Hague Convention of 1954), UNESCO Doc CLT-93/WS/12, (1993), at 101.

[58]For more information of the case, see 'Mutual Presentation of Cyprus and the Netherlands on the Return of 4 Icons from the Netherlands to Cyprus under the Protocol of the Hague Convention of 1954', *10 Meeting of the High Contracting Parties to the Hague Convention, UNESCO, Monday 16 December 2013*, viewed March 16, 2015, http://www.unesco.org/culture/laws/1954/NL-Cyprus-4icons_en.

[59]A. Bos, 'Words of Welcome', in: A. Van Woudenberg & E. Lijnzaad (eds.), *Protecting Cultural Property in Armed Conflict: An Insight into the 1999 Second Protocol to the Hague Convention of 1954 for the Protection of Cultural Property in the Event of Armed Conflict*, Leiden: Nijhoff 2010, at xvi.

[60]The Second Protocol entered into force on March 9, 2004. As of February 11, 2015, 68 states have ratified or acceded to the Second Protocol. China has not been a party member to this protocol.

new monitoring body for the implementation of the Protocol, the intergovernmental Committee for the Protection of Cultural Property in the Event of Armed Conflict.[61] The Second Protocol also provides additional penalties, jurisdiction based on the territorial and active personality theories for all 'serious violations', and universal jurisdiction for violations listed in Article 15 sub-paras (a) to (c). The Second Protocol also establishes individual criminal responsibility for violators.[62] Although the Second Protocol makes great strides in strengthening the rules regarding protection of cultural property during wartime, as Van Woudenberg says, we can only hope that the provisions of criminal liability and jurisdiction do not need to be applied too often.[63] The 1954 Hague Convention and its two Protocols greatly enhanced the rules governing protection of cultural property in the event of armed conflict and their basic principles concerning respect for cultural property have become part of customary international law.[64]

Cultural property also benefits from a certain amount of protection under international criminal law. Crimes against cultural property were treated as crimes against public and private property in the Nuremberg Tribunal and in the Tokyo Tribunal. The ICTY Statute makes a step forward by naming 'seizure of, destruction or wilful damage done to institutions dedicated to religion, charity and education, the arts and sciences, historic monuments and works of art and science' violations of the laws or customs of war (Article 3(d)).[65] The ICTY convicted a number of individuals of crimes against cultural property arising out of the 1991 attacks on educational, cultural, and religious sites in the former Yugoslavia.[66] Considering intentional direct attacks on cultural property as separate indictable offenses follows from the Rome Statute of ICC (Article 8, para 2(b) (ix)).[67]

---

[61]Bos, *supra* note 59, at xvi.

[62]For more information about the 'penal elements', see Nafziger (2008), at 987–988.

[63]A. van Woudenberg, 'Elaboration and legal implementation of the 1999 Second Protocol: The Dutch finger on the pulse', in: A. van Woudenberg & E. Lijnzaad (eds), *Protecting Cultural Property in Armed Conflict: An Insight into the 1999 Second Protocol to the Hague Convention of 1954 for the Protection of Cultural Property in the Event of Armed Conflict*, Leiden: Nijhoff 2010, at 115.

[64]Nafziger (2008), at 1001.

[65]U.N. Doc.S./25704 at 36, annex (1993) and S/25704/Add.1(1993), adopted by Security Council on 25 May 1993, U.N. Doc.S/RES/827(1993).

[66]In 2000, the ICTY convicted General Tihomir Blaskic on charges related to looting and pillage of Bosnian sites. In 2004, Vice Admiral Miodrag Jokic was convicted of targeting Dubrovnik. In 2005, Pavel Strugar, the commander of the Yugoslav People's Army Forces, received an eight-year sentence for ordering attacks on targets in the Dubrovnik region without prohibiting attacks on Dubrovnik's Old Town. See Nafziger (2008), at 990.

[67]The Rome Statute of the International Criminal Court circulated as document A/CONF. 183/9 of 17 July 1998 and corrected by process-verbaux of November 10, 1998, July 12, 1999, November 30, 1999, May 8, 2000, January 17, 2001 and January 16, 2002. The Statute became effective July 1, 2002.

The Nuremberg Tribunal and Tokyo Tribunal and the ICTY Statute and Rome Statute of the ICC have established that wilful destruction and pillage of cultural property are war crimes under the general category of crimes against public and private property or in their own right. Despite international efforts, cultural property remains the target of pillage and destruction. One million books, ten million documents and fourteen thousand archaeological artifacts have been lost in the US-led invasion and subsequent occupation of Iraq.[68] According to Eric A. Posner, treaties have failed because of the lack of sufficient preciseness in existing conventions, insufficient numbers of parties agreeing to the conventions, insufficient enforcement mechanisms, governmental unwillingness and lack of interest in protecting cultural heritage. [69] According to Mattew Bogdanos's investigation into the looting of Iraq's National Museum, people in Iraq believe the US cares for no culture other than its own. The history of looting, as well as the US's failure to protect cultural heritage, reinforces their belief. Because the protection of cultural heritage does not command the same degree of attention or resources as do terrorism or other violent crimes in wartime, relatively few resources were made available for tracking down stolen artifacts.[70] In brief, although protection of cultural objects during wartime is well regulated pursuant to international conventions, in practice, such conventions are largely unenforced.

2.3 Protection of Cultural Objects Against Illicit Trafficking

The legal regime purporting to protect cultural property other than in times of war includes: (1) the UNESCO Convention and other agreements generally applicable to cultural heritage; (2) regional and bilateral laws and agreements, including European law and bilateral provisions regarding extradition of criminals; and (3) domestic customs control and prosecutions based in part upon foreign and international laws.[71] This section treats international conventions protecting cultural objects from illegal movement or illicit trafficking and Chinese law regarding protection of cultural relics.

[68]See H. Marquez, 'The Plunder of Iraq's Treasures', *Asia Times,* (17-2-2005).

[69]E.A. Posner, 'The International Protection of Cultural Property: Some Skeptical Observations', *Chicago Journal of International Law* 8 (2007), no. 1, at 218–221.

[70]See M. Bogdanos, 'Thieves of Baghdad: Combatting Global Traffic in Stolen Iraqi Antiquities', *Fordham International Law Journal*, 31 (2007), no. 3, pp. 725–740.

[71]Nafziger (2008), at 992.

2.3.1 International Conventions

The 1970 UNESCO Convention and the 1995 UNIDROIT Convention are the most significant international conventions regarding illegal movement of cultural objects.[72]

2.3.1.1 The 1970 UNESCO Convention

According to Askerud and Clement, the 1970 UNESCO Convention was drafted in response to increasing theft and unauthorized export and import of cultural objects in the 1960s.[73] Designed to reinforce the solidarity among its signatories in order to stem the illicit import, export and transfer of ownership (defined as illicit traffic in cultural property), the Convention established a system of import and export control.

The 1970 UNESCO Convention requires party states to adopt certification procedures to control exportation of cultural property (Article 6). Party states must also prevent museums and similar institutions from acquiring illegally exported property from other party states (Article 7(a)); prohibit the importation of stolen cultural property and return such items to their state of origin upon request (Article 7(b)). Unlike theft, which has been prohibited by all legal systems (with the exception of taking booty in times of war), cultural object import and export control is a recent development. Such efforts have been debated and criticized from their inception.[74] Acording to Forrest, the difficulty arises from the need to require sovereign states to enforce exportation laws of other sovereign states. The equality of states and respect for their sovereignty is a fundamental principle of international

[72]The 1970 UNESCO Convention was adopted at the 16th UNESCO General Conference of November 1970 and entered into force on April 24, 1972. The 1995 UNIDROIT Convention was adopted in 1995 and became effective on July 1, 1998. As of August 27, thirty-four states have ratified or acceded to the Convention; China ratified the Convention on May 7, 1997.

[73]In its early years, regarded 'fatally flawed,' the Convention won little support, but with its accession by market countries such as the US, Canada, Australia, France, Japan, the United Kingdom, Switzerland, Germany, Belgium and the Netherlands, the Convention has become the most important multilateral international treaty in this regard. As of April 18, 2014, one hundred twenty-seven states have acceded to or ratified the Convention. China acceded to the Convention on November 28, 1989. See P. Askerud & E. Clement, *Preventing the Illicit Traffic in Cultural Property: a Resource Handbook for the Implementation of the 1970 UNESCO Convention*, Paris: UNESCO 1997, at 16; P.J. O'Keefe, *Commentary on the UNESCO 1970 Convention on Illicit Traffic,* Leicester: Institute of Art and Law, 2000, at 8.

[74]*Ibid.*; also see C. Forrest, 'Strengthening the International Regime for the Prevention of the Illicit Trade in Cultural Heritage', *Melbourne Journal of International Law* 4 (2003), no. 2, at 594; S. Gruber, 'Protecting China's Cultural Heritage Sites in Times of Rapid Change: Current Developments, Practice and Law',*Asia Pacific Journal of Environmental Law* 10 (2007), at 267; K. Siehr, *International Art Trade and the Law* (Recueil des Cours 243), Leiden: Nijhoff Online 1993, DOI: 10.1163/ej.9780792332831.009-41810.1163/ej.9780792332831.009-292, at 162.

law. As a result, states are reluctant to require other states to enforce their public laws, including penal laws, revenue laws and exportation laws.[75]

Pursuant to Article 9, state parties must join in a concerted international effort to identify and implement concrete measures to control the import of cultural property. State parties have interpreted their obligation to counter the import of cultural property both broadly and narrowly. The broad interpretation involves ensuring all cultural property is protected. If cultural property is illegally exported, the state into which it is imported must regard the importation as illegal and ensure the cultural property is returned to its state of origin. This broad interpretation applies to all states whose cultural heritage is illegally exported.[76] The narrow interpretation provides that party states need merely prevent museums and similar institutions over which they have direct control from acquiring cultural property illegally exported from other party states. For example, the US does not consider it illegal for a private individual or an institution it does not directly control to import cultural property illegally exported from a foreign state if it was not stolen from a museum or religious institution of the foreign state.[77]

The import and export controls in the 1970 UNESCO Convention have been criticized by some as jeopardizing legal international trade in cultural property. Some consider it nonsensical to attempt to control export of privately held cultural property because export does not, in and of itself, damage the contextual value of

[75]Forrest, *ibid.*, at 597. Although some countries are reluctant to enforce the export controls of other states, most states attempt to protect their cultural property through export regulations. Attempts to control the movement of cultural objects have been made throughout history. The first modern export ban dates from the chirography of Cardinal Giuseppe Doria Pamphili of October 2, 1802 and the confirming edict Pacca of April 7, 1820. In the late nineteenth and early twentieth centuries, similar efforts were made legislatively in Greece (1834), Italy (1872) and France (1887). According to Siehr, different states have adopted different cultural property export policies: (a) a few states such as the US and the Swiss cantons, have no cultural property export control and make no attempt to protect their cultural property from sale to other countries; (b) several countries such as Italy and some Ibero-American countries prohibit the export of all cultural property without distinguishing between classified/registered items and unclassified/unregistered or between national treasures and pieces of art inadvertently located within their boundaries; (c) many countries take a middle position by restricting export control to classified items or pieces of great importance—for example, most European museums are state owned and their treasures can only be sold by Government permission. See Siehr, *ibid.*, at 162–165, 249.

[76]Forrest, *ibid.*, at 601–602.

[77]*Ibid.* The US legislation implementing the 1970 UNESCO Convention, the Convention on Cultural Property Implementation Act, allows the US to enter into bilateral agreements (Memoranda of Understanding) with a requesting state party. While the bilateral agreement is being negotiated, the U.S. may impose import restrictions if the criteria for an 'emergency' situation are satisfied. Four criteria must be met to impose import restrictions: (a) the cultural property must be in danger; (b) the other state must have taken sufficient actions to protect the cultural property; (c) the import restriction must be beneficial and not overly restrictive; and (d) there is international interest in restricting the importation of the cultural property involved (19 U.S.C. § 2602(a) (1)). Some authors consider the Act little more than an 'agreement to agree'.

the objects or the objects themselves and does not deprive living cultures of objects of ritual or ceremonial importance. [78] Others argue that because the 1970 UNESCO Convention contains such a broad, normative definition of cultural property,[79] it is only useful if state parties specify by law what national cultural property should be protected. The Convention requires signatory states to establish and up-date a list of protected property whose export would constitute an appreciable impoverishment of their national cultural heritage (Article 5).[80] The Convention's allowing signatory states unilaterally to declare their cultural property 'inalienable' and its export therefore 'illicit' has been called the 'blank check' provision by the American lawyer John Henry Merryman.[81]

Like other conventions, the 1970 UNESCO Convention is not retroactive. During negotiations, China had proposed the inclusion of the following article directly relating to restitution and return of cultural objects: 'Any state party which, when the Convention comes into force, is in possession of important cultural property, illicitly acquired, inalienable to, and inseparable from, the history and civilization of another state, shall, in the interest of international good will, endeavor to restore such property to that state.'[82] Some states feared any degree of retroactivity would cast doubt upon ownership of cultural objects within their borders in contravention of the rules of their domestic legal systems, and they made it clear that they would not participate in any Convention which included such a

---

[78]See Merryman, (2001), at 53–67; R.D. Abramson & S.B. Huttler, 'The Legal Response to the Illicit Movement of Cultural Property', *Law and Policy in International Business* 5 (1973), 972; P. Askerud & E. Clement, *Preventing the Illicit Traffic in Cultural Property: a Resource Handbook for the Implementation of the 1970 UNESCO Convention*, Paris: UNESCO 1997, at 7.

[79]The two major international regimes underlying the free movement of goods, the Treaty of European Communities and the World Trade Organization, both prohibit export controls on 'goods'. The European Court of Justice defines 'goods' as 'products which can be valued in money and which are capable of forming the subject of commercial transaction.' Although both regimes make an exception for restrictions 'imposed for the protection of national treasures possessing artistic, historic, or archaeological importance', neither includes a detailed definition of 'national treasures'. Judge Pierre Pescatore has held that 'exceptions from the rules barring export controls are to be strictly construed.' The term 'treasures' cannot apply to the generality of cultural objects, but only to those having unusual value because of their uniqueness and their importance to a people. See Commission v. Italy (Re Arts Treasures), Case 7 /68[1968] ECR 42; [1969] CMLR1.

[80]According to the Council Regulation (EEC) No 3911/92 of 9 December 1992 on the export of cultural goods, member states of the European Communities retain the right to define their national treasures and to take the necessary measures to protect them within the European Community.

[81]Merryman (1986), at 844–845.

[82]UNESCO Doc. SHC/MD/ 5 Annex II, 10; see L.V. Prott,'Editor's Preliminary Note', in L.V. Prott (ed.), *Witnesess to History: A Compendium of Documents and Writings on the Return of Cultural Objects*, Paris: UNESCO 2009, at 13.

provision. Eventually, the retroactivity provision was rejected on the grounds the Convention was not intended to be retroactive, to the frustration of various states. [83]

2.3.1.2 The 1995 UNITROIT Convention

Because the 1970 UNESCO Convention failed to address the differences among private law systems, one their most glaring weaknesses, in 1984 UNESCO commissioned the UNIDROIT to develop as set of private law rules covering illicit trafficking in cultural objects to complement the 1970 UNESCO Convention. The final text of the 1995 UNIDROIT Convention was adopted after years of study and negotiation.[84] Although the categories of cultural objects covered by the 1970 UNESCO Convention and the 1995 UNIDROIT Convention are identical, the 1995 UNIDROIT Convention does not require cultural objects to be 'designated' as such by a state. As a result private cultural objects are protected by the 1995 UNIDROIT Convention regardless of whether they are designated as such by a state.[85]

The 1995 UNIDROIT Convention provides two distinct regimes for illicitly trafficked cultural objects.[86] The first regime treats stolen cultural objects, establishing the principle that stolen cultural objects must be returned.[87] This regime does not distinguish between public or private property or good or bad faith purchasers, the latter being determinative only in relation to the purchaser's right to compensation (Article 4). Excavated cultural objects are regarded as stolen 'when consistent with the law of the state where the excavation took place' (Article 3(2)).

[83]Dissatisfaction was expressed at the Conference of Heads of State or Government of Non-aligned Countries at its Fourth Conference in Algiers in 1973. States found propsective controls of little utility because significant culturally significant objects were already in other countries. *Ibid.* at 12–13.

[84]L.V. Prott, 'UNESCO and Unidroit A Partnership against Trafficking in Cultural Objects', *Uniform Law Review* 1 (1996), at 59–61.

[85]*Ibid.*, at 61–62.

[86]See UNITROIT Secretariat, 'UNIDROIT Convention on Stolen or Illegally Exported Cultural Objects: Explanatory Report', *Uniform Law Review* 2001, no. 3, at 502.

[87]The Convention counterbalances the principle of restitution of stolen cultural objects by the bona fide possessor's right to compensation for her loss of her cultural object. Compensation is subject to two prerequisites: the possessor 'neither knew nor ought reasonably to have known that the object was stolen' and the possessor 'can prove that it exercised due diligence when acquiring the object'. The notion of 'good faith' is interpreted variously in different legal systems. The Convention requires the court or competent authority to take into consideration 'all the circumstance of the acquisition' (Article 4(7)), paying particular attention to certain criteria defined largely by reference to Article 7(2)(3) of the draft Uniform Law on the Acquisition in Good Faith of Corporeal Movables. Although compensation is to be 'fair and reasonable,' the Convention goes no further in establishing the amount of compensation, relying instead on the discretion of the courts. See *Ibid.* at 514–520.

Claims may be brought by private parties or states dispossessed of cultural objects as a consequence of theft. Thus, while the 1970 UNESCO Convention only provides that the return should be made 'through diplomatic offices,' under the 1995 UNIDROIT Convention a private owner may avail himself of the normal legal channels available in the country where the object is located in order to obtain a court order requiring the return of a stolen object. States may act in the place of a private person who cannot or does not wish to bring a claim.[88] Claims for restitution must be brought within three years from the time the claimant knew the location of the cultural object and the identity of its possessor, but special treatment is given to certain 'identified' objects.[89] The absolute statute of limitations is fifty years from the time of the theft, and states party to the Convention may declare that claims are subject to an absolute time bar of seventy-five years or such longer period as they may provide by law.[90]

The second regime treats illegally exported cultural objects.[91] Illegally exported cultural objects include not only items exported without a permit according to the law of the requesting state, but also include cultural objects temporarily exported under permit but not returned in accordance with the terms of the permit (Article 5 (3)). Although a private owner can initiate proceedings to reclaim stolen cultural objects, only states party to the Convention are entitled to order the return of an illegally exported cultural object. Because such claims are brought on the basis of a breach of public law protecting cultural heritage ((Article 5(1)), it is the state that has an interest in initiating proceedings. The state may act on its own initiative or at the request of a private owner. If the object was first stolen and then unlawfully removed to another state, a claim for restitution may be brought by the dispossessed owner.[92] Significantly, only when the illegal export of a cultural object impairs the interests protected by the Convention, or when a cultural object is determined to be of great cultural importance to the requesting state, may the court or other

[88] *Ibid.*, at 506.

[89] 'Identified' cultural objects are items forming an integral part of a particular monument or archaeological site, or items belonging to a public collection. A 'public collection' consists of a group of inventoried or otherwise identified cultural objects owned by: (a) a state party to the Convention, (b) a regional or local authority of a state party to the Convention, (c) a religious institution in a state party to the Convention, or (d) an institution that is established for an essentially cultural, educational or scientific purpose in a state party to the Convention and is recognized in that state as serving the public interest (Article 3 (4), (7)).

[90] Nine states party to the Convention had made such a declaration and introduced a longer limitation by December 1, 2011. China declares the absolute period of seventy-five years.

[91] In the absence of specific international commitments, the removal of a cultural object from a state in breach of the state's rules is not regarded by many states as an unlawful act and does not, in itself, constitute a legal obstacle to the object's acquisition. This attitude was condemned by the International Law Institute in Wiesbaden in 1975 and the 1989 Swiss Law on Private International Law was instrumental in 'softening' the inapplicability of the foreign public law. See UNITROIT Secretariat, *supra* note 86, at 524.

[92] *Ibid.*, at 526.

competent authority order its return.[93] The limitation period for the return of illegally exported objects is the same with that for restitution of stolen cultural objects, except there is no exceptional limitation system for certain 'identified' objects.

Like the 1970 UNESCO Convention, the 1995 UNITROIT Convention is not retroactive. When signing the Convention in 1996, 'China reserve[d] the right to recover the cultural relics illegally confiscated in the history'.[94] Although the 1995 UNITROIT Convention is considered the most recent and sophisticated multinational treaty on restitution because it achieves a delicate compromise between importing and exporting countries and between civil and common law jurisdictions, the Convention's sophistication does not guarantee its popularity among states. It's ratification by so few states and its rare application signal the Convention's practical failure.[95]

2.3.2 *Chinese Legislation Protecting Cultural Relics*

As of the end of 2013, pursuant to the 1970 UNESCO Convention, China has entered into Memorandum of Understanding (MOU) with nineteen states prohibiting the illicit transfer, import, and export of cultural property.[96] The SACH lists over five hundred legal and administrative instruments intended to protect cultural objects in China.[97] Significantly, legislative efforts to protect cultural relics in China date from well before the PRC's foundation.

---

[93]Interests include: (a) the physical preservation of the object or of its context; (b) the integrity of a complex object; (c) the preservation of information of, for example, a scientific or historical character; (d) the traditional or ritual use of the object by a tribal or indigenous community (Article 5(3)).

[94]See Peng, L. (2012), at 73.

[95]According to Forrest, the unsatisfactory degree of ratification can be attributed to the constituent and political composition of many states. While states whose constituents seek to acquire cultural heritage are obligated to promote free trade in cultural heritage, source states seek protection of national cultural heritage by preventing any such trade whatsoever. See Forrest, *supra* note 74, at 601.

[96]Peru, India, Italy, the Philippines, Greece, Chile· Cyprus, Venezuela, the US, Australia, Turkey, Ethiopia, Egypt, Mongolia, Mexico, Colombia, Nigeria, and Switzerland. Concluded in 2009 and garnering the majority of public interest, the MOU with the US imposes import restrictions on categories of archaeological material from the Palaeolithic Period through the Tang dynasty, and monumental sculpture and wall art at least two hundred fifty years old.

[97]Adopted in 1982 and amended in 2002, the Law of PRC on Protection of Cultural Relics is the most important. The instruments include one law, five administrative regulations by the State Council, eight department regulations, six national standardizations, thirty-three industry standardizations, one hundred fifty regulatory documents, eighty provincial regulations, twenty regional regulations, one hundred sixty regional normative documents, one military regulation, accession to four international conventions, fifteen bilateral agreements. For more details, see 'There are over five hundred existing legal instruments to protect cultural relics in China', China

Faced with a series of challenges at the end of the nineteenth century, the late Qing government attempted to modernize China. Modernizing the legal system included providing legal protection for cultural heritage. In charge of the protection of historical sites and antiquities at that time, the Ministry of Interior issued the Promotional Measures on Conservation of Antiquities in 1906, requiring the regional governments to investigate all heritage sites within their administrative areas and report their findings to the Ministry.[98] The Statute on Regional Autonomy of Cities, Town and Villages promulgated in 1908 designated protection of heritage sites one of the 'autonomous affairs' (Article 5).[99] Drafted in 1909 by the Ministry of Interior and submitted to the to the Qing Court for approval, the Promotional Statute on Conservation of Antiquities defined antiquities as, among other things, stiles, stone pillars with Buddhist inscription, stone resonators, stone statues and inscriptions, ancient paintings, inscriptions on cliffs, paintings and works of calligraphy, from the Zhou and Qin dynasties to 1909 and required the provincial governments to prepare and submit to the Ministry a list of antiquities. The statute prohibited and harshly punished traffic in antiquities. Each province was required to establish museums to collect and protect cultural relics. Unfortunately the statute was never effectively implemented due to the political upheavals of the late Qing dynasty.[100]

Following the demise of the Qing dynasty, the Beiyang Government continued governmental attempts to regulate the preservation of antiquities by issuing the Grand President's Decree Restricting the Export of Antiquities in June 1914, requiring all exports of antiquities to be examined and approved by the Ministry of Interior and the Tax Bureau. Although the decree required the Tax Bureau to formulate guidelines regarding the export of antiquities to be implemented by all customs services in China, such guidelines were never formulated; instead, heavy export duties were simply imposed.[101] Promulgated in 1916, the five articles of the Provisional Regulation on the Conservation of Antiquities delineate five categories of antiquities: tombs of royals and their predecessors, places of interest, works of art, precious plants and other kinds of relics which were to be inventoried and conserved. Movable antiquities owned or discovered by individuals were to be

(Footnote 97 continued)

News, December 11, 2012, viewed April 2, 2013, http://www.chinanews.com/cul/2012/12-11/4400271.shtml.

[98]See Peng, L. (2012), at 77; Guan Xiaohong, 'The Ministry of Education in the Late Qing Dynasty and Modern Cultural Institutions' (in Chinese), *Journal of Sun Yatsen University (Social Science Edition)* 40 (2000), no. 2, at 81.

[99]Zhang Song, 'Legal History of Protecting Cultural Heritage in China' (in Chinese), *China Ancient City* (2009), no. 3, at 27.

[100]See Peng, L. (2012), at 77–78.

[101]Ma Shuhua, *Protection of Cultural Relics during the Period of Republic of China*, (in Chinese) [Dissertation], Jinan: Shangdong Normal University 2000, at 7–8.

purchased and conserved by public institutions in case the objects could be purchased by foreigners and exported abroad (Articles 3 and 5).[102]

On September 13, 1928, the Chinese Ministry of Interior promulgated Regulations Governing the Preservation of Scenic Resorts, Ancient Remains and Relics. Established in the same year, the Central Commission for the Preservation of Antiquities played an important role in the preservation of antiquities at that time.[103] The Commission sent telegrams to cities all over China requiring municipal authorities to stop all excavations by foreign explorers.[104] On June 2, 1930, the Nationalist Government promulgated the Law on the Preservation of Antiquities governing the preservation, ownership, excavation, circulation and export of antiquities.[105] Regulations implementing the law were promulgated throughout the 1930s.[106]

2.3.2.1 Rules for Archaeological Excavation

The 1930 Law on the Preservation of Antiquities led to more effective control of excavations. The law declared national ownership of all antiquities buried underground or exposed on the ground and required persons discovering any antiquities

---

[102]The President of the Republic of China issued a presidential decree on the restriction of export control of antiquities in 1914. See Ma, S., *ibid.* at 7–8; Peng, L.(2012), at 78.

[103]Established in April 1928 as the successor to the Chinese Association of Academic Organizations, the Association was intended to stop explorations by Swedish explorer, Sven Hedin. Following extensive negotiations, the Association and the exploration team signed a detailed cooperation agreement defending China's interest. See Luo Guihuan, 'As regards the Founding and Significance of the Central Committee for the Preservation of Antiquities in the Early 20th Century', (in Chinese), *The Chinese Journal for the History of Science and Technology* 27 (2006), no. 2, at 137–139.

[104]Chinese authorities intercepted eighty-seven cartons of antiquities collected by the American expedition team led by Roy Chapman Andres from the Gobi Desert and Mongolia. The items included many fossilized dinosaur eggs and ancient animal specimens. On October 20, 1928, representatives from China and the US reached an agreement pursuant to which all historical cultural relics were to remain in China; fossils of vertebrate animals were to be sent to the Museum of Natural History in New York for research, two complete sets of which were to be returned to China following the research; fossils of invertebrate animals were to be researched in China, and one specimen would be sent to New York; and the other items were divided equally between the two parties. See Luo, G., *ibid.*, at 139–140; Ma, S., *supra* note 101, at 27–28.

[105]The categories of antiquities provided include those related to archaeology, science or history, paleontology and other cultures (Article 1). See Hsiang-yu Huang, 'Background Analysis of the Birth of Legalization of Antiques Preservation (1911–1930)' (in Chinese), Journal of the National History Academy, December 2012,; Ma, S., *ibid.* at 22–26.

[106]The regulations include: Implementation of the Antiquities Preservation Law, Rules on Excavation of Antiquities, Rules on Export Permit for Antiquities, Rules on Excavation of Antiquities by Foreign Academic Institutes and Individuals, Provisional Scope and Species of Antiquities, Rules on Encouragement and Reward Respecting Antiquities and Measures of Conservation of Antiquities in Unusual Times. See Ma, S., *ibid.*, at 22–26.

to report the discovery to the government in return for a reward. Failure to report a discovery resulted in the discoverer being punished as a thief (Article 7). Excavations of antiquities required permits from both the Ministries of Education and Interior and excavations done without permits were deemed theft (Article 8). In addition, excavations were to be supervised by supervisors appointed by the Central Commission for the Preservation of Antiquities (Article 11).[107]

When Stein entered China for his fourth expedition in 1930, on behalf of the Central Commission for the Preservation of Antiquities, nineteen Chinese professors, heads of colleges and directors of research institutes asked Stein's sponsors at Harvard University, the Archaeological Survey of India, and the British Museum to consider 'whether in the interest of science and international good feeling they should continue their support promised to Sir Aurel Stein'.[108] The experts claimed: Stein intended to take archaeological objects from Xinjiang and had obtained his permit under false pretenses; the wholesale smuggling of the Dunhuang manuscripts was effectively 'commercial vandalism'; and other countries had enacted laws prohibiting the unauthorized excavation and the export of archaeological treasures. They said the Chinese government had promulgated just such a law in 1930, and they believed they had the 'sympathy of all true students of scientific archaeology all over the world' in opposing any attempt by Stein or other foreigners to excavate under false pretenses and smuggle historical objects out of China.[109] Unlike his previous expeditions, Stein's activities during the fourth expedition were kept under strict surveillance by the Chinese government. The Chinese Ministry of Interior sent an extra urgent telegram to Jin Shuren, the provincial director of Xinjiang, on September 21, 1930, prohibiting Stein from conducting archaeological excavations in Xinjiang and ordered Jin Shuren to observe Stein's activities closely.[110] Jin Shuren sent decrees to municipalities in Xinjiang to implement the order from the central government.[111] When Stein and his followers engaged in archaeological excavations, the Chinese Ministry of Interior ordered the Ministry of

[107]The Law of PRC on Protection of Cultural Relics declares that all cultural relics remaining underground, in China's waters, or in collections of state-owned intuitions are owned by the state, as are all sites of ancient ruins, ancient tombs, temples, other monuments, ancient architecture and stone carvings designated for protection by the state (Article 5). State-owned cultural relics may not be donated, rented or sold to other organizations or individuals (Article 44). In order to protect cultural relics within China, the law imposes harsh criminal sanctions (including the death penalty until 2011) upon the theft, robbery or smuggling of cultural relics. For more regarding the PRC's law on cultural relics in English, see S. Gruber, 'Protecting China's Cultural Heritage Sites in Times of Rapid Change: Current Developments, Practice and Law', *Asia Pacific Journal of Environmental Law* 10 (2007), no. 3–4, pp. 272–276; J.D. Murphy, 'An Annotated Chronological Index of People's Republic of China Statutory and Other Materials Relating to Cultural Property', *International Journal of Cultural Property* 3 (1994), no. 1, pp. 159–167.

[108]Quoted from A. Walker, *Aurel Stein: Pioneer of the Silk Road,* London: Murray 1995, at 287.

[109]*Ibid.*

[110]Xu Xinjiang, Tong Lu, and others (ed.), *Modern Historical Materials about Foreign Explorers in Xinjiang*, (in Chinese), Urumqi: Xinjiang Meishu Sheying Chubanshe 2001, at 134–135.

[111]*Ibid.*, at 134–153.

Foreign Affairs to revoke Stein's visa and deport Stein.[112] Stein was deported on May 18, 1931. On his departure, all the antiquities found upon a search of his luggage were detained by the Chinese authorities.[113]

The Rules on Excavation of Antiquities and the Rules on Excavation of Antiquities by Foreign Academic Institutes and Individuals provided more detailed procedures and conditions for excavations in China. Pursuant to the rules, only academic institutes under the direct control of the central or provincial governments were allowed to conduct excavations. If an excavation required facilities or support from foreign academic institutes or individuals, the Chinese academic institute was required to report such requirement to the Central Commission for the Preservation of Antiquities. Without the approval of the Central Commission, foreign academic institutes or individuals were prohibited from participating in the excavation. Marking the beginning of the standardization of archaeological excavations in China, the first excavation permit was issued for the archaeological excavation at the ruins of Yin-xu by the Ministries of Education and Interior in 1935.[114] These efforts halted the previously rampant excavations in China by foreign explorers. There was one excavation in northwest China by foreign explorers in the 1920s, and no such excavations in the 1930s.[115]

2.3.2.2 Antiquities Export Control

Following the Beiyang Government's attempt to reduce the export of antiquities pursuant to the Presidential Decree in 1914, more regulations regarding export of antiquities were promulgated, including the 1916 Provisional Regulation on the Conservation of Antiquities, the 1924 Act on Protecting Ancient Books, Antiquities, and Historical Sites, the 1930 Law on the Preservation of Antiquities and the 1935 Rules on Export Permits for Antiquities.[116] Not everyone welcomed antiquities export control. Various individuals even requested the Tax Bureau to issue them tax exemptions for the export of antiquities, but the Tax Bureau refused on the ground that such tax exemptions violated the 1916 Promotional Regulation on Conversation of Antiquities.[117] The Tax Bureau did request the Ministry of Interior to specify the

---

[112] *Ibid.*, at 143.

[113] According to archival documents, all of Stein's acquisitions were temporarily kept in the British Consulate in Kashi before being handed over to the Chinese authorities after negotiations. Stein took photographs of the objects, which photographs are now in the British Library. *Ibid.*, at 27.

[114] See Li Ji, 'The First License of Archeological Excavation issued by Republic of China' (in Chinese), in: National Museum of History (ed.), *Bao Zunpeng Xiansheng Jinian Wenji,* Taipei: National Museum of History 1971, at 69–70.

[115] From 1850 to 1920, each decade respectively recoded five, twelve, twenty-eight, twenty-two, twenty-two, forty-five and sixteen excavations in northwest China. For more information, see Huang, H., *supra* note 105, at 9–18.

[116] Quoted from Ma, S., supra note 101, at 8.

[117] *Ibid.*

exportable and non-exportable antiquities. In response, the Ministry of Interior stressed that because antiquities embodied China's culture there was no reason to promote the export of antiquities, concluding that in principle, all export of antiquities should be prohibited. As to the categorization of antiquities, the Ministry of Interior distinguished antiquities from general goods rather than distinguishing exportable antiquities from the non-exportable antiquities.[118] In 1927, the Beiyang Government issued another Decree of the Grand President on the prohibition of the export of antiquities.[119] When the 1930 Law on the Preservation of Antiquities was promulgated, it was established that 'the circulation of antiquities shall be limited within China.' Antiquities could only be exported for research purposes, which were to be jointly approved by the Ministries of Education and Interior. Exported antiquities were to be returned to China within two years (Article 13). The 1935 Rules on Export Permits for Antiquities provided the detailed procedures for obtaining export permits.

Under the existing law of the PRC, all cultural relics extant as of or prior to 1911 are not subject to exportation, except for exhibition or upon approval by the State Council.[120]

2.4 Soft Laws Protecting Cultural Objects

In addition to the two legal frameworks discussed above, in recent decades some ethical strictures concerning the circulation, restitution and return of cultural objects have been developed. The development of such ethical strictures is often described as "soft law-making."[121] According to Lorenzo Casini, because 'traditional international law instruments do not seem to ensure an adequate level of protection for cultural heritage,' 'securing such protection requires procedures, norms, and

---

[118] *Ibid.*

[119] See *ibid.*, at 8–13.

[120] For more details, see Examining Standards for Export of Cultural Relics issued in 2007. This documents also lists sixteen categories of cultural objects which are prohibited from being exported: fossilized objects, materials related to architecture; works of paintings and calligraphy before 1911 and some items between 1911 and 1949, rubbings before 1949, statues, and others.

[121] Although the concept of soft law has existed for years, scholars have not reached a consensus on why states use soft law or whether 'soft law' is a coherent analytic category. See A.T. Guzman & T.L. Meyer, 'International Soft Law', *Journal of Legal Analysis* 2 (2010), no. 1, at 171; Lorenzo Casini, "Italian Hours': The Globalization of Cultural Property Law', *International Journal of Constitutional Law* 9 (2011), no. 2, at 369; M. Barelli, 'The Role of Soft Law in the International Legal System: the Case of the United Nations Declaration on the Rights of Indigenous People', *International and Comparative Law Quarterly* 8 (2009), no. 4, at 960; K. Siehr, *International Art Trade and the Law* (Recueil des Cours 243), Leiden: Nijhoff Online 1993), DOI: 10.1163/ej.9780792332831.009-41810.1163/ej.9780792332831.009-292, at 251.

standards [to be] produced by international organizations' such as UNESCO and ICOM.[122] For Casini, a comprehensive global regulatory regime to complement the law of cultural property has yet to be achieved.[123] Alessandro Chechi agrees, stating: 'Cultural heritage has a variety of emotional and symbolic meanings that can be described, but not fully captured, in legal terms.... Indeed, the various interests associated with cultural assets could be better accommodated through a shift from adversarial processes and the strict application of positive law towards a model that puts greater emphasis on information exchange, consultation, consensus-building, and sharing.'[124] Because I agree that a positive legal regime protecting cultural heritage has yet to be achieved and that soft law-making likely reflects the trends in law-making regarding cultural objects, I next treat two aspects of soft law-making respecting cultural objects: ethical guidelines combating illicit trafficking in cultural objects and the ethics of repatriating cultural objects.

2.4.1 Ethical Guidelines Regarding Illicit Trafficking in Cultural Objects

Following the adoption of the 1970 UNESCO Convention, museums, art dealers and art historians embraced ethical guidelines regarding their acquisition, trading and publication practices. Despite their not being legally binding, some such ethical codes have been quite effective.[125] In the archaeological community, institutions like the World Archaeological Congress and Archaeological Institute of America have adopted ethical guidelines aimed at fighting against the illicit trafficking in cultural objects.[126] Museum associations have made similar attempts to combat illicit trafficking in cultural objects. The most well-known ethical guidelines are found in the ICOM Code of Ethics for Museums. The code bars member museums from acquiring cultural objects without full provenance even if positive law does

---

[122]Casini, *ibid.*, at 369.

[123]*Ibid.*

[124]A. Chechi, *The Settlement of International Cultural Heritage Disputes*, Oxford: Oxford University Press 2014, at 4.

[125]Because they are not legally binding, although they may influence the elaboration of a legal rule or even articulate a principle identical to the content of a specific legal instrument, ethical guidelines do not generally create legal sanctions per se, unless a legal instrument expressly stipulates consequences.

[126]Adopted in 1990, The World Archaeological Congress's First Code of Ethics sets forth the obligation of archeology and heritage management professionals to recognize of the importance of indigenous cultural heritage (sites, places, objects, artifacts, human remains, etc.) to indigenous peoples and that such cultural heritage rightfully belongs to the indigenous people. Also approved in 1990, The Archaeological Institute of America's Code of Ethics requires its members to refuse to trade in undocumented antiquities and refrain from activities that enhance the commercial values of objects. Members are also required to inform the appropriate authorities of threats to or plunder of archaeological sites and the illegal import or export of archaeological material.

not forbid their acquisition.[127] Similar ethical guidelines are found in other museum associations such as the Department for Culture, Media and Sport's Illicit Trade Advisory Panel in the UK, and the Association of Art Museum Directors in the US, Canada and Mexico.[128] Ethical guidelines for art dealers also prohibit their members from trading in objects of dubious provenance. For instance, the Code of Practice for the Control of International Trading in Works of Art prohibits members from to importing, exporting or transfering ownership of stolen or illegally exported objects or objects acquired dishonestly or illegally from excavation sites or monuments.[129] Similarly, the International Code of Ethics for Dealers provides: 'Professional traders in cultural property will not import, export, or transfer the ownership of this property when they have reasonable cause to believe it has been stolen, illegally alienated, clandestinely excavated or illegally exported'.[130]

The Principle of Due Diligence

Used throughout the ethical codes discussed above, in cases involving recovery of stolen or looted cultural property, "due diligence" is required in two situations: (1) a buyer's investigation of suspicious circumstances; and (2) a victim's search for his stolen property.[131]

In the first situation, due diligence relates to a buyer's obligation to verify the provenance of an object, that is, a buyer must make a legitimate effort to ascertain

---

[127]Created in 1946 by and for museum professionals, ICOM is a network of almost thirty thousand members of the global museum community. Adopted in 1984 and revised in 2004, the ICOM Code of Ethics seeks to provide a 'global minimum standard' upon which more specific or rigorous requirements may be built.

[128]In 2004 The Department for Culture, Media and Sport's Illicit Trade Advisory Panel issued ethical guidelines to assist museums, libraries and archives when considering the acquisition of cultural property originating outside the UK. Pursuant to the guidelines, museums should acquire and borrow an item only if its provenance is legally and ethically sound. Museums, libraries and archives should reject an item if, after undertaking due diligence, there is any suspicion about the item or its surrounding circumstances. In 2004 the Association of Art Museum Directors promulgated guidelines advising members not to acquire objects without clear proof the object was outside the US prior to 1970 or that it was legally exported from another country after 1970. See Department for Culture, Media and Sport (DCMS), *Combating Illicit Trade: Due Diligence Guidelines for Museums, Libraries and Archives on Collecting and Borrowing Cultural Material,* London: DCMS 2005.

[129]The terms of this Code were translated into French and adopted by the Confédération Internationale des Négociants en Oeuvres d'Art (CINOA) at Florence on September 25, 1987, and amended in Stockholm in 1998 and in New York in 2005. Established in 1935 for dealers, CINOA represents five thousand dealers from thirty-two leading national and international member associations in twenty-two countries.

[130]The International Code of Ethics for Dealers in Cultural Property was prepared by the Intergovernmental Committee for Promoting the Return of Cultural Property to its Countries of Origin or its Restitution in Case of Illicit Appropriation and endorsed by the UNESCO General Conference in 1999.

[131]See L.F. Pinkerton, 'Due Diligence in Fine Art Transactions', *Case Western Reserve Journal of International Law* 22 (1990), no. 1, at 1.

the veracity and accuracy of all information supplied, and uncover additional data about the history of the object, to fully explain the object's history of ownership. The goal of performing an investigation with due diligence is to fill in any gaps in the object's published provenance and to ascertain whether the object's current owner holds the proper title.[132] A guideline issued in the UK provides that due diligence involves: (1) examining the item; (2) considering the type of item and likely place of origin; (3) taking expert advice regarding the item and its provenance; (4) determining whether the item was lawfully exported to the UK; and (5) evaluating the account of the item's ownership given by its vendor or donor.[133] Although exercising and demonstrating due diligence in investigating the provenance of cultural objects has become a necessary element of acquiring a valid title to cultural objects, not all cultural objects are registered or otherwise subject to a public recording system. Not all cultural objects have complete, unbroken records of ownership, and most cultural objects have gaps in their provenance. Some commentators have criticized the due diligence requirements of ethical guidelines, arguing that museums should be able to acquire unprovenanced objects unless there is clear and convincing evidence such objects were looted or are of questionable status as to legal title.[134] Cuno argues that a museum should be able to acquire an antiquity without having all the ownership and provenance history as long as certain procedures are followed.[135]

In the second situation, due diligence involves a victim's obligation to search for stolen objects and an owner's obligation to verify the provenance of owned cultural objects (owners are not necessarily individual collectors, they include individuals who have inherited perhaps only one particularly significant cultural item, a gallery, a corporation, a church, a museum, a historic house, or even a cemetery).[136] First of all, a victim must report a theft to law-enforcement and other agencies. Such reporting is essential to facilitating buyers' exercising their due diligence by their researching a proposed acquisition in available databases and registries of stolen and missing items.[137] Victims are also obligated to make a diligent search for its stolen objects although even a diligent search may not save a victim's claim from the effects of the passage of time.[138]

---

[132] *Ibid.*; M.J. Masurovsky, 'Why is Contextual Analysis needed In The Resolution of Cultural Heritage Litigation Cases?', *CLE Program, The Center for Jewish History*, October 11, 2013.

[133] DCMS, *supra* note 128, at 8–10.

[134] L.M. Kaye, 'Provenance Research: Litigation and the Responsibility of Museums', in J.A.R. Nafziger & A.M. Nicgorski (eds), *Cultural Heritage Issues: The Legacy of Conquest, Colonization, and Commerce,* Leiden: Nijhoff 2009, at 405.

[135] J.B. Cuno, 'Ownership and Protection of Heritage: Cultural Property Rights for the 21st Century: U.S. Art Museums and Cultural Property', *Connecticut Journal of International Law* 16 (2001), no. 2, at 189–196.

[136] A. Kisluk, 'Forum: Stolen Art and 'Due Diligence'', *Curator: The Museum Journal* 41 (1998), no. 3, at 162.

[137] *Ibid.*, at 164.

[138] Pinkerton, *supra* note 131, at 10.

2.4.2 *Ethics of Restitution of Cultural Objects*

The last few decades have witnessed increasing scholarly debate and public concern regarding claims for restitution and return of cultural objects, most notably restitution of Nazi looted art and claims by formerly colonized or occupied countries. Proving the legitimacy of the desire for restitution and return of cultural objects, a number of resolutions and principles have been adopted to address these concerns.

2.4.2.1 Restitution of Nazi Looted Art

The campaign to return Nazi looted art began in the early 1990s with the publication of an abundance of scholarly and journalistic research, resulting in increasing popular awareness of both the extent and the brutality of the Nazis' art spoliation.[139] On December 3, 1998, the international community convened the Washington Conference on Holocaust-Era Assets where the participating nations developed non-binding principles to assist in resolving issues relating to Nazi looted art. Now known as the Washington Principles, they provide minimum conditions and starting points for a restitution policy to achieve 'a just and fair solution.' Unfortunately, the Washington Principles fail to specify what solutions qualify as 'just and fair.'[140]

On November 4, 1999, The Parliamentary Assembly of the Council of Europe adopted Resolution 1205 on Looted Jewish Cultural Property, asserting that restoring such cultural property to its original institutions, communities, nations or individual owners or their heirs is a significant aspect of returning Jewish culture to its rightful place in Europe. The Resolution called for 'the organization of a European conference, further to that held in Washington on the Holocaust-era assets, with special reference to the return of cultural property and the relevant legislative reform'.[141] In response to the Resolution, in October 2000, Lithuania hosted a conference. Adopted at the conclusion of the conference's plenary session, the Vilnius Forum was a significant first step in calling on all participating States 'to take all reasonable measures' to implement Resolution 1205.[142] Three major

[139]Tensions during the Cold War years left little room for introspection into, or discussion about, Germany's wartime past. The collapse of communism and the disintegration of the Eastern Bloc played an important part in opening up the historical information on trophy art, providing key evidence for a great deal of the current title disputes. B. Demarsin, 'Let's Not Talk About Terezin: Restitution of Nazi Era Looted Art and the Tenuousness of Public International Law', *Brooklyn Journal International Law* 37 (2011), no. 1, at 122–123.

[140]*Ibid.* at 138; T.I. Oost, *In an Effort to do Justice? Restitution Policies and the Washington Principles,* Amsterdam: University of Amsterdam 2012, at 3, 17.

[141]See P.J. O'Keefe, 'A Comparison of the Washington and Vilnius Principles and Resolution 1205', in: L.V. Prott (ed.), *Witnesses to History: A Compendium of Documents and Writings on the Return of Cultural Objects*, Paris: UNESCO 2009, at 158–159.

[142]*Ibid.*, at 158.

themes ran through the forum: access to information; modalities of restitution, particularly regarding property with no heirs; and restitution implementation procedures.[143] To the extent valuable information was exchanged and advances were made in providing information services, the Vilnius Forum was a success.[144]

In June 2009, the Czech Republic hosted the Prague Conference on Holocaust Era Assets. Focusing on immovables, Nazi-looted art, Holocaust education and remembrance, archival access, and the recovery of Judaica, the Prague Conference closed with the Terezin Declaration's endorsement by the forty-six participating governments.[145] The Terezin Declaration reaffirms the Washington Principles and urges all stakeholders to ensure that their legal systems or alternative processes facilitate just and fair solutions. At the national level, some countries like Austria, the Czech Republic, France, The Netherlands, Russia and the U.K. have adopted explicit policies on restitution of Nazi-looted cultural assets. Most countries have demonstrated a willingness to make a legitimate effort at restitution.[146]

Efforts toward the restitution of Nazi-looted art are significant in two ways; they recognize the need to provide "transitional justice" to the victims of WWII[147] and, as stated in Resolution 1205, they enable the restoration of Jewish culture to its proper place in Europe and its culture.

2.4.2.2 General Assembly and UNESCO Resolutions

During the second half of the twentieth century, various UN organizations have focused their attention on cultural heritage issues.[148] The UN General Assembly

---

[143] *Ibid.*, at 159.

[144] *Ibid.*, at 158–162.

[145] For the declaration, see *Holocaust Era Assets conference,* June 30, 2009, viewed October 25, 2012, http://www.holocausteraassets.eu/program/conference-proceedings/declarations/.

[146] For more information regarding the national practices on the restitution of Nazi looted art, see Oost *supra* note 140.

[147] The UN defines 'transitional justice' as 'the full range of processes and mechanisms associated with a society's attempt to come to terms with a legacy of large-scale past abuses, in order to ensure accountability, serve justice and achieve reconciliation'. See UN Security Council, *The Rule of Law and Transitional Justice in Conflict and Post-Conflict Societies*, S/2004/616, para 8.

[148] The Preamble to its charter states that one of the UN's objects is to 'establish conditions under which justice and respect for the obligations arising from treaties and other sources of international law can be maintained.' Encouraging and fostering the development of international law to regulate international relations has been a major objective of the United Nations since its inception. According to Rosalyn Higgins, the process by which the content of norms is clarified or developed within UN organs include: (a) decisions which UN organs take concerning their own jurisdiction and competence, (b) resolutions declaratory of existing law, (c) resolutions confirmatory of existing law, (d) claims within an area of law generally agreed upon, (e) resolutions recommending the adoption of new rules of law, (f) decisions applying specific rules to particular situations, and (g) rules internal to the organizations. See R. Higgins, 'The Development of International Law by the Political Organs of the United Nations', *Proceedings of the American Society of International Law at Its Annual Meeting (1921–1969)* 59 (1965), at 117–123.

and UNESCO have become the primary forums for countries of origin to demand the return of their cultural objects.[149] During the 1960s, states recently released from colonial rule lodged increasingly strong demands at the UN for the recovery of their cultural objects. From and after the 1970s, the UN General Assembly has adopted a series of resolutions addressing restitution or return of cultural property. Sponsored in 1973 by twelve African states (A/RES/3187(XXVIII)), 'Restitution of works of art to countries victims of expropriation' deplores 'the wholesale removal, virtually without payment, of objets d' art from one country to another, frequently as a result of colonial or foreign occupation', and affirms that the prompt restitution to a country of its cultural property without charge is calculated to strengthen international cooperation inasmuch it constitutes 'just reparation for damage done.'

As a specialized agency of the UN, UNESCO leads international efforts to safeguard tangible and intangible cultural heritage. UNESCO has contributed to the development and clarification of norms regarding cultural heritage law by drafting and promoting international multilateral conventions.[150] In 1978, the UNESCO Director-General made a Plea for the Return of an Irreplaceable Cultural Heritage to Those Who Created It, stating that cultural heritage is one of the most noble incarnations of a people's genius, bearing witness to the history of a culture and nation whose spirit they perpetuate and renew. According to the Plea, restitution of the cultural heritage will help people to greater self-knowledge as well as enable others to understand them better. The Plea calls for the return of cultural heritage to people who have created it.[151] The Plea is regarded as providing ethical basis for the return of cultural objects to their countries or origin. Also in 1978, UNESCO established the Intergovernmental Committee for Promoting the Return of Cultural

---

[149]Although its efforts have not always been clearly recognized or universally embraced, since the late 1940 s the UN General Assembly has attempted to modernize international law. The General Assembly's obligation to treat legal matters and participate in the formulation of international law can be found in Articles 10, 11, and 13 of its Charter. In addition to appointing ad hoc special committees, the General Assembly has utilized the Six (Legal) Committees of the General Assembly and the International Law Commission to encourage the betterment of international law. See C.C. Joyner, 'U.N. General Assembly Resolutions and International Law: Rethinking the Contemporary Dynamics of Norm-Creation', *California Western International Law Journa*l 11, (1981), no. 3, 448–450.

[150]UNESCO has drafted and promoted the 1954 Hague Convention, the 1970 UNESCO Convention, the 1972 Convention Concerning the Protection of the World Cultural and Natural Heritage, the 2001 Convention for the Protection of the Underwater Cultural Heritage, the 2003 Convention for the Safeguarding of Intangible Cultural Heritage, and the 2005 Convention on the Protection and Promotion of the Diversity of Cultural Expressions.

[151]The Plea also acknowledges that people seeking return of cultural heritage "know, of course, that art is for the world and are aware of the fact that this art, which tells the story of their past and shows what they really are, does not speak to them alone. They are happy that men and women elsewhere can study and admire the work of their ancestors. They also realize that certain works of art have for too long played too intimate a part in the history of the country to which they were taken for the symbols linking them with that country to be denied, and for the roots they have put down to be severed.' See A.M. M'Bow, 'A Plea for the Return of an Irreplaceable Cultural Heritage to Those Who Created it,' *UNESCO* 7 June 1978.

Property to its Countries of Origin or its Restitution in Case of Illicit Appropriation (ICPRCP) to facilitate the resolution of restitution claims for objects removed prior to the implementation of the 1970 UNESCO Convention.[152] UNESCO's most important arm in the area of return and restitution of property to its country of origin, in its advisory role the ICPRCP provides a framework for discussion and negotiation although its recommendations concerning inter-State disputes are not legally binding. The ICPRCP's enabling statute provides that a return request can 'be made for any cultural property which has a fundamental significance from the point of view of the spiritual values and cultural heritage of the people' (Article 3 (2)). As does the 1970 UNESCO Convention, the ICPRCP privileges the state. Only states that are UNESCO members or associate members may assert a claim or sit on the ICPRCP.[153] The ICPRCP has helped settle a number of claims. The dispute over the Parthenon Marbles between Greece and UK is pending before the ICPRCP. The parties have been unable to agree whether the marbles were illicitly exported by Lord Elgin.[154] According to Prott, the establishment of the ICPRCP and the Director-General's appeal are important 'because both, on the surface, apply equally to cultural heritage items taken during hostilities and those taken during colonial times. Whatever the legality of the original taking, the emphasis here rests on allowing each country an appropriate representation of its own national cultural heritage—a desire with which, it must be said, many museum curators have sympathy'.[155]

2.5 Chapter Conclusion

The broad acceptance of the 1954 Hague Convention and the 1970 UNESCO Convention signals the global community's awareness of the need for protection of cultural heritage. Although the notion that 'to the victors go the spoils' was previously recognized throughout human history, it has been universally established that destruction and confiscation of cultural objects are illegal in the event of armed

[152]The twenty-two Committee members are elected from among the UNESCO Member States at elections held every two years during the General Conference.

[153]Vrdoljak (2006), at 214.

[154]The Committee successfully concluded the six following cases through mediation or bilateral agreement where international conventions were deemed inapplicable: Germany and Turkey regarding the Bogazkoy Sphinx; Barbier-Mueller Museum and the United Republic of Tanzania regarding a Makonde Mask, the U.S. and Thailand regarding Phra Narai; the German Democratic Republic and Turkey regarding seven thousand Bogazkoy cuneiform tablets; the Cincinnati Art Museum and Jordan regarding parts of the sandstone panel of Tyche; and Italy and Ecuador regarding twelve thousand pre-Columbian objects. The dispute between the U.K. and Greece regarding the Parthenon Marbles, and the dispute between Iran and Belgium regarding archaeological objects from the Necropolis of Khurvin are pending before the Committee. Most of the successful resolutions followed the 1970 UNESCO Convention.

[155]Prott, *supra* note 82, at 15.

conflict, and looted cultural objects should be returned to their rightful owners. Although combating illicit traffic in cultural objects has been identified by the international community as a worthy objective, due to differences between domestic legal regimes, especially as they relate to illegally exported cultural objects, disagreement remains regarding the definition of 'illicit traffic.' In addition to international conventions, even though they are of no legally binding effect, soft-law instruments are playing a vital role in the protection of cultural objects. The ethical guidelines adopted by professional associations to deal with cultural objects, the practices surrounding restitution of Nazi-looted art, and the resolutions adopted by UN organs are of normative value in practice insofar as they reflect developing trends in international law.

Chapter 3
Restitution Through International Adjudication: Looted Cultural Objects Case Studies

3.1 Introduction

This chapter assesses the viability of seeking restitution of cultural objects in international legal tribunals.[1] Although in theory because it is the only global and permanent court of general subject matter jurisdiction the ICJ should be the leading international legal forum,[2] in practice the ICJ has rarely had an opportunity to address questions of cultural property. In its May 26, 1961 judgment in the case of the Temple of Preah Vihear, the ICJ found that Thailand was obligated to restore to Cambodia sculptures, stelae, fragments of monuments, a sandstone model and ancient pottery which were most likely removed from the Temple or its environs by Thai authorities during their 1954 occupation of the Temple. But the case was essentially a territorial dispute rather than one involving the restitution of cultural objects. In 2001, Liechtenstein brought a case to the ICJ against Germany seeking the return of certain works of art confiscated after WWII and held in a third country, but the case never moved beyond the preliminary objection phrase at which point the ICJ declined to assert jurisdiction.[3] Because the ICJ can only hear cases between states upon their consenting to jurisdiction, nor can the ICJ entertain complaints

[1]Notably, international cultural heritage law provides no mechanism of norm enforcement and dispute resolution. See Francioni (2012), at 726.
[2]Chechi (2014), 208.
[3]See Francioni (2012), 726–728; ICJ June 15, 1962, Case concerning the Temple of Preah Vihear (Cambodia v. Thailand), Judgment, Rep 6; ICJ February 19, 2005, Certain Property (Liechtenstein v. Germany), Judgement, Rep 6.

Z. Liu, *The Case for Repatriating China's Cultural Objects*,
DOI 10.1007/978-981-10-0597-8_3

made by non-state actors.[4] Hence, jurisdiction would most likely be the first obstacle to international adjudication of disputes involving cultural property in the ICJ particularly and in any other contemporary international legal forum.

Even assuming the ICJ could obtain jurisdiction over such parties and cases, it is unclear whether the restitution of cultural objects stolen or looted years, decades or centuries in the past is permissible under international law. The following cases concerning confiscation of cultural objects in the wars fought by China illustrate this problem: the sacking of the Old Summer Palace during the Second Opium War; the plunder of Beijing during the Battle of Beijing; and the Japanese pillage during the Second Sino-Japanese War (see Chap. 1).[5] First, I discuss whether there is a duty of restitution. This involves the determination and application of the rules of international law, such as treaties, custom, general principles of law. I also discuss the intertemporal law principle in public international law. Next I analyze the admissibility of restitution claims, paying particular attention to post-war settlement and the principle of extinctive prescription in public international law. I also discuss the legal effect of resolutions by international organizations concerning restitution of cultural objects.

3.2 Are States Responsible for Restitution?

According to international jurists, responsibility lies at the heart of domestic and international law.[6] According to the law of state responsibility, a party seeking reparation must prove a breach of an obligation which can be attributed to a

---

[4]See Article 36(2) of the Statute of the ICJ. When the claim is presented before an international tribunal, objections to jurisdiction may be raised. Objections to jurisdiction relate to conditions affecting the parties' consent to have the tribunal decide the case. If successful, jurisdictional objections terminate all proceedings in the case because they deprive the tribunal of the authority to make rulings as to the admissibility of the claim, never mind its substance. See J.R. Crawford (ed.), *Brownlie's Principles of Public International Law* (8th ed.), Oxford: Oxford University Press 2012, at 693.

[5]Since the 1900s, China has been governed by the Qing dynasty, the ROC and the PRC. In discussing the issues raised by such a succession of states or governments, the 1983 Vienna Convention on Succession of States in respect of State Property, Archives and Debts, comes to mind but it has not yet entered into force. Due to its One-China policy providing that the successions in China were governmental rather than state successions, China has refused to ratify the Vienna Convention. Because the PRC has been recognized as the only legitimate government of China by the international community since the 1970s, this chapter does not discuss the issues of succession. See 'Status of the Vienna Convention on Succession of States in respect of State Property, Archives and Debts', *Unitedd Nations Treaty Colletion*, viewed October 16, 2014, https://treaties.un.org/Pages/ViewDetails.aspx?src=UNTSONLINE&tabid=2&mtdsg_no=III-12&chapter=3&lang=en.

[6]See I. Brownlie, *System of the Law of Nations: State Responsibility, Part I*, Oxford: Clarendon 1983, at 1; J.R. Crawford, *State Responsibility: The General Part*, Cambridge: Cambridge University Press 2013, at 3; K.M. Maranga, 'The Changing Role of State Responsibility: Comparative Approach', *Journal of Global Affairs and Public Policy* 1 (2011), no. 1, at 2.

state.[7] According to Ian Brownliee, one of the world's leading international lawyers, 'In international relations, as in other social relations, the invasion of the legal interest of one subject of the law by another legal person creates responsibility in various forms'.[8] Following the adoption of the *Draft Articles on Responsibility of States for Internationally Wrongful Acts*, it is generally acknowledged that state responsibility may arise from acts or omissions by any of its powers or organs, irrespective of their hierarchy (Article 2). State responsibility arises upon the occurrence of the international wrong imputable to the state. State responsibility obligates State to make full reparation for the injury caused by the internationally wrongful act (Article 31).

Because 'the question of restitution does not arise if art plunder is permissible,'[9] (i.e., if confiscating cultural objects during wartime is legal no responsibility of restitution arises) a party seeking restitution of disputed cultural objects must demonstrate the breach of an obligation arising under international law.[10] Thus if China were to seek the restitution of cultural objects confiscated as a result of armed conflicts which occurred during modern Chinese history, Chine would have to prove the confiscation constituted a breach of an international obligation, and the breach of obligation was attributable to the states involved. Because the three armed conflicts discussed here were clearly contested by China and other states, the attributability of such a breach of an obligation to a state should not be controversial.

Although the law of state responsibility provides a general framework for establishing the consequences of a breach of an obligation, the law relating to the content and the duration of substantive state obligations arises from 'primary rules'[11] contained in a various treaties, customary law, *jus cogens*[12] and general

---

[7]In Crawford's view, responsibility was not identified as a legal category by Vitoria, Suarez, Bodin and other early writers. Even though Grotius may have promulgated the general principles of responsibility in his work on the civil law, such principles are not found in his work on the law of nations. Not until the 1850s did a writer use recognizably modern language of responsibility in a systematic way. Since the beginning of the twentieth century, the codification of State responsibility has been regarded as a major area of interest in the development of international law. It was selected for codification by the League of Nations and was one of the principal subjects of the unsuccessful conference in The Hague in 1930. Upon the establishment of the ILC in 1948, state responsibility was among the first fourteen topics to be dealt with. See *ibid*, pp. 3–42.

[8]According to Brownlie, responsibility has its basis both in religious thought and in the secular morality. 'It is the idea of being liable, answerable, accountable, for wrong doing'. See Brownlie, *supra* note 6, at 1.

[9]Sandholtz (2010), at 148.

[10]M. Roscini, 'Establishing State Responsibility for Historical Injustices: The Armenian Case', *International Criminal Law Review* 14 (2014), no. 2, at 2.

[11]According to Hart, primary rules govern actions by spelling out particular obligations (or their absence); secondary rules, in contrast, govern the procedural methods by which primary rules are enforced, prosecuted and so forth. See H.L.A. Hart, *The Concept of Law* (3rd ed.), Oxford: Oxford University Press 2012, at 94.

[12]The notion of *jus cogens* (peremptory norms) dates primarily from the development of natural law doctrine. According to Grotius, principles of natural law were so immutable that not even God could change them. As with natural law theories, although most of these peremptory norms

principles of law.[13] In terms of confiscation of cultural objects in the event of armed conflict, following the broad acceptance of the 1954 Hague Convention, it is universally accepted that pillage of cultural objects during armed conflict is illegal, and looted cultural objects must be restored to their rightful owners. The cases discussed here concern cultural objects confiscated during wars fought at least more than half a century ago. In establishing whether there is state responsibility for restitution of such cultural objects, the application of legal rules plays an important role. As discussed in Chap. 2, the legal rules concerning cultural objects during wartime have changed with the passage of time. Throughout human history, people looted cultural objects as well as other property during wartime. Because legal prohibitions of looting cultural object during times of war have only come into favor since the mid-nineteenth century, whether a court would choose to apply the old rules or the new rules in deciding these cases would, to a large extent, determine the outcome. If the old rules allowing confiscation of cultural objects during wartime apply, no responsibility for restitution arises; if the existing rules prohibiting confiscation of cultural objects during wartime apply, state responsibility for restitution of cultural objects arises. The doctrine of intertemporal law has been developed in public international law to govern the application of law which have changed over time.

3.2.1 The Doctrine of Intertemporal Law

Because legal rules have changed over time, the question of whether to apply the international law that was contemporaneous with the acts in question, or whether to apply the international law that is contemporaneous with the adjudication, arises. Anthony D'Amato maintains 'it is a well-settled principle of international law that

(Footnote 12 continued)

originate from ethical or sociological considerations, their character arises from within international law and the will of the state. Because of significant differences in philosophical premises and methodologies, scholars disagree as to what constitutes a peremptory norm and how a given norm rises to that level. Consensus was finally reached during the Vienna Conference held in 1969 and codified in Article 53 of the Vienna Convention on the Law of Treaties 1969. It is generally recognized that *jus cogens* includes prohibitions of aggression, genocide, crimes against humanity, war crimes, piracy, slavery and slave-related practices, and torture and that sufficient legal basis exists to support the conclusion that all such crimes are prohibited by *jus cogens*. See R. Nieto-Navia, 'International Peremptory Norms (*Jus Cogens*) and International Humanitarian Law', in: L.C. Vohrah et al. (eds), *Man's Inhumanity to Man: Essays on International Law in Honour of Antonio Cassese,* The Hague: Kluwer Law International 2003, at 599; M.C. Bassiouni, 'International Crimes *Jus Cogens* and *Obligatio Erga Omnes'*, *Law and Contemporary Problems* 59 (1996), no. 4, at 68.

[13]See J.R. Crawford, 'Articles on Responsibility of States for Internationally Wrongful Acts', *United Nations Audiovisual Library of International Law* 2012, legal.un.org/avl/ha/rsiwa/rsiwa.html. Also see also Article 38 of the Statute of the ICJ.

the rules of law contemporaneous with the acts in the distant past, and not present rules of law, control their legal significance'.[14] In the case of *Island of Palmas*, Judge Max Huber stated that 'a juridical fact must be appreciated in the light of the law contemporary with it, and not of the law in force at the time when a dispute in regard to it arises or falls to be settled.'[15] The ICJ has recently reasserted this principle. Following its earlier case law, the facts and situations it must take into consideration are those "with regard to which the dispute has arisen or, in other words, only those which are its 'real cause' rather than those which are the source of the claimed rights."[16]

This principle is embocied in the Vienna Convention on the Law of Treaties 1969. According to the Convention, a treaty does not have retroactive effect so as to bind a party with respect to any act or fact which took place, or any situation which ceased to exist, before its entry into force for that party, unless explicitly provided in the treaty (Article 28).[17] According to James Crawford, a leading scholar on the law of state responsibility, when a new peremptory norm of general international law comes into existence, as contemplated by Article 64 of the Vienna Convention, it does not create a retrospective assumption of responsibility.[18] Article 71(2) of the Convention provides that a new peremptory norm 'does not affect any right, obligation or legal situation of the parties created through the execution of the treaty prior to its termination, provided that those rights, obligations or situations may thereafter be maintained only to the extent that their maintenance is not in itself in conflict with the new peremptory norm.'

The non-retroactivity of legal rules, called variously the doctrine, theory or principle of intertemporal law appears in ICJ case law. However denominated, the principle of intertemporal law is one of the most important principles in public international law.[19] The principle is essential to some human rights instruments such as the International Covenant on Civil and Political Rights, which provides 'No one shall be held guilty of any criminal offense on account of any act or omission which did not constitute a criminal offense, under national or international

[14]According to D'Amato, parties involved in international disputes occasionally disagree about the legal significance of acts or situations occurring, or treaties entered into, in the distant past. See Anthony A. D'Amato, 'International Law, Intertemporal Problems', *Encyclopedia of Public International Law,* 1992, at 1234–1235.

[15]Permanent Court of Arbitration 14 April 1925, Island of Palmas (Netherlands *v.* United States), 2R. International Arbitration Awards, 831, 845.

[16]ICJ February 3, 2012, Jurisdictional Immunities of the State (Germany v. Italy; Greece intervening).

[17]Adopted on May 22, 1969 and opened for signature on May 23, 1969 by the United Nations Conference on the Law of Treaties, the Convention entered into force on January 27, 1980 and one hundred and thirteen states are now party to it.

[18]See J.R. Crawford, *The International Law Commission's Articles on State: Introduction, Text and Commentaries*, Cambridge; Cambridge University Press 2002, at 132.

[19]D' Amato, *supra* note 14, at 1235; also see T.O. Elias, 'The Doctrine of Intertemporal Law,' *American Journal of International Law* 74 (1980) no. 2, at 285.

law, at the time when it was committed….' (Article 15).[20] When formulating its Draft Articles, the ILC considered whether there were exceptions to the principle of intertemporal law. The commission examined 'hypothetical cases [such as genocide and freeing of slaves] which do not happen to have arisen in the past and are likely to arise only very rarely in the future, but which nevertheless cannot be ruled out.'[21] However, the commission avoided providing exceptions to the general rule in its Draft Articles on the ground that doing so might weaken the general rule.[22] Crawford states it is appropriate to apply the principle of intertemporal law to all international obligations, but such application should not prejudice the possibility that states may agree to provide compensation for damages caused as a result of a conduct which was regarded as legal under prior rules.[23]

As a result, although contemporary international law criminalizes the plunder of public and private cultural property in times of either international armed conflict (during hostilities or belligerent occupation) or non-international armed conflict, contemporary law cannot be applied to the three historical cases under discussion.[24] Pursuant to the principle of intertemporal law, the legality of the confiscation of cultural property must be governed by the legal rules in effect at the time of the confiscation. Again, state obligations can be contained in *jus cogens,* conventional law, customary law and general principles of law. In light of *jus cogens,* in 1977 the ICOM carried out its study of the 'Principles, Conditions and Means for Restitution or Return of Cultural Property in View of Reconstituting Dispersed Heritage' which observes, 'It would certainly be unrealistic to go back indefinitely into the past, and thus be confronted with hazards of national history and the succession of States. But it is equally true that the community of nations now considers as an element of *jus cogens* the right of all peoples to recover cultural property which forms an integral part of their cultural identity.'[25] Nonetheless, other than declarations in soft-law instruments, there is no support for the notion that the right of all people to recover cultural heritage is an element of *jus cogens*. On the contrary, serious reservations have been expressed regarding extending such an obligation to include returning acquisitions or appropriations that were legal and legitimate at the time they were made and possessors are entitled to invoke the principle of non-retroactivity.[26]

[20]The Covenant on Civil and Political Rights was adopted and opened for signature by UN General Assembly resolution 2200 (XXI) of December 16, 1966 and it entered into force on March 23, 1976.

[21]Such norms can have such effect because they are *jus cogens*. See S. Rosenne (ed.), *The International Law Commission's Draft Articles on State Responsibility, Part 1, Articles 1–35,* Dordrecht; Nijhoff 1991, Vol. 1, at 173.

[22]*Ibid.* at 174.

[23]Crawford (2002), at 132.

[24]Sandholtz (2010), at 148; also see R. O'Keefe, 'Protection of Cultural Property under International Criminal Law', *Melbourne Journal of International Law* 11 (2010), pp. 256–357.

[25]ICOM, 'Study on the Principles, Conditions and Means for the Restitution or Return of Cultural Property in View of Reconstituting Dispersed Heritages,' *Museum International* 31 (1979), no. 1, at 63.

[26]See B.O. Okere (1987/88), at 146.

Notwithstanding the ICOM report's assertion, I think, it is premature to conclude the right to recover significant cultural heritage is an element of *jus cogens*. "In order to be a 'Peremptory Norm of general international law'" a norm must be "accepted and recognized by the international community as a whole."[27] Due to the substantial disagreement regarding repatriation of cultural objects, I hesitate to regard the right to cover cultural heritage an element of *jus cogens*. Even if the right to recover cultural heritage were currently accepted as an element of *jus cogens*, under the principle of intertemporal law, I think it is extremely problematic to apply such a recently developed peremptory norm to acts which took place in the distant past. According to some, international law frowns against retroactivity of legal rules in general, only admitting retroactivity in the case of treaties which explicitly impose an obligation to make restitution. The UNESCO recommendations are not legally binding. Such recommendations cannot vest the principles of restitution of cultural property with retrospective force; they can only exhort member states to do so.[28] In light of the controversy surrounding considering the right to recover cultural heritage an element of *jus cogens*, I only analyze whether the confiscation of cultural objects constituted a breach of international obligation contained in international law's sources: treaties, customs, and general principles of law, as enumerated in Article 38 of the Statute of the ICJ.[29] Although the Statute of the ICJ was adopted after the occurrence of the events in the cases studied in this chapter, the sources of the public international laws regulated in Article 38 of the Statute of the ICJ have long been recognized as sources of public international law and have been codified since the beginning of the twentieth century. For example, Article 7 of the unratified Twelfth Hague Convention Relative to the Creating of an International Prize Court of 1907 provides: 'If an question of law to be decided was covered by a convention in force between the belligerent captor and the Power which was itself, or whose subject was, a party to the proceedings, the Court has to apply the provisions of that Convention. In the absence of such provisions, the Court shall apply the rules of international law. If there are no rules generally

---

[27]F.A. Mann, *Furthur Studies in International Law*, Oxford; Clarendon Press 1990, at 86.

[28]See Okere, *supra* note 26, at 146.

[29]As stipulated in Article 38, in the settlement of disputes submitted to the ICJ, the Court shall apply international conventions, international custom and general principles of law, to which are added, as 'subsidiary means', judicial decisions and teachings of the most highly qualified publicists. Sources enumerated in Article 38 are called 'formal sources' by some international lawyers. Notably, classic doctrine made a distinction between 'formal sources' of international law, sources enumerated in Article 38 of the Statute of the ICJ, and 'material sources'—the substratum—wherefrom the former are originated. Schwarzenberger insists that Article 38 of the Statute of the ICJ establishes a hierarchy of sources of international law: 'treaties take precedence over international customary law, and international customary law comes before the general principles of law recognized by civilized nations.' Others maintain Article 38 does not establish a hierarchy. See G. Schwarzenberger, 'The Inductive Approach to International Law', *Harvard Law Review* 60 (1947), no. 4, at 551; J.H.W. Verzijl, *International Law in Historical Perspective*, Vol. 1, Leiden: Sijthoff 1968, at 1–3; A.A.C. Trindade, *International Law for Humankind: Towards a New "Jus Gentium"*, Leiden: Nijhoff 2010, at 113–114.

recognized, the Court will decide according to the general principles of justice and equity.'[30] The Statute of the Permanent Court of International Justice of 1920 contains a similar provision in Article 38.

3.2.2 International Conventions

Promulgated in 1863, the Lieber Code is the first legal document providing protection of cultural property in the event of armed conflict. Subsequent international legal instruments have incorporated rules exempting cultural objects from war operations. The 1899 Hague Convention (II) is the first international convention protecting cultural property in armed conflicts.

The 1899 Hague Convention (II) is clearly inapplicable to the 1860 sacking of the Old Sumer Palace. Can the 1899 Hague Convention (II) be applied to the 1900 plunder of Beijing? The plunder of Beijing took place in August 1900 during the Battle of Peking between China and the Eight-Nation Alliance (Russia, United Kingdom, France, Germany, Italy, United Stated of America, Japan and Austria-Hungry). During the battle, Beijing was occupied until the Dowager Cixi returned to Beijing from her 'tour of inspection' on January 7, 1902, thereby restoring the rule of the Qing dynasty over China (see Chap. 1).

Significantly, because Article 3 of the 1899 Hague Convention (II) states 'the present Convention shall be ratified as speedily as possible,' the Convention was not subject to 'definitive signature[31];' instead, it was subject to ratification. As a result, mere signature did not create legal obligations binding upon the signatory states. Even though they had all signed the Convention on July 29, 1899, not all eight members of the Alliance had ratified the 1899 Hague Convention (II) before the plunder of Beijing took place.[32] Moreover, the Qing government did not sign the Convention until June 12, 1907.[33] Historical documents indicate the foreign

[30]Quoted from V.D. Degan, Sources of International Law, The Hague: Kluwer Law International 1997, at 3.

[31]According to the definition in the UN Treaty Collection, when a treaty is not subject to ratification, acceptance or approval, 'definitive signature' establishes the consent of the state to be bound by the treaty. Most bilateral treaties dealing with more routine and less politicized matters come into force upon definitive signature, without recourse to ratification· See *United Nations Treaty Collection*, viewed March 24, 2105 https://treaties.un.org/pages/Overview.aspx?path=overview/glossary/page1_en.xml.

[32]The Convention was ratified on September 4, 1900 by Austria-Hungary, France, Germany, the Netherlands, the UK, and Italy. Japan ratified the Convention on October 6, 1900, and the US on April 9, 1902. See the information on the website of the ICRC.

[33]The Qing dynasty delegates signed the other two Conventions on July 29, 1899, but did not sign the Convention on the Laws and Customs of War on Land and its annex.

affairs department of the Qing Court feared that accession to the Convention would be disadvantageous to Qing government in subsequent wars with foreign states.[34] Pursuant to Article 2 of the Convention, its regulations are only binding on contracting powers and they cease to be binding on a contracting power when it enters into conflict with a non-contracting power. As a result, even though the Convention provides cultural property shall be immune from confiscation during armed conflicts, because China was a non-contracting power when the war was fought in 1900, the Convention is inapplicable to the plunder of Beijing.[35]

In addition, western legal positions legitimized the alliance's military intervention. According to Wolfgang Heinze and Friedrich Klein, western legal authority, the resistance of the legation quarter constituted an act of legitimate self-defense and the intervention of the alliance was justified on the grounds the Chinese government was either unwilling or unable to fulfil its duty to protect foreigners. A few Chinese officials came to a similar conclusion.[36] However, the alliance's actions during the intervention contravened the 1899 Hague Convention (II), to which all the states of the alliance were party. One of the few critics of the alliance's disregard of the Convention, the historian Thoralf Lynch, observed: 'Legal discourse thus created a double ambivalence on the Allied side: at a theoretical level, the intervention was designed to enforce international law in a country that refused to acknowledge it. At a practical level, the method of enforcing international law consisted in its constant violation.'[37]

The provisions of the other relevant international convention, the 1907 Hague Convention (IV), are identical to those regarding protection of cultural heritage set forth in the 1899 Hague Convention (II). Japan signed the 1907 Hague Convention (IV) at the conference, and ratified it on November 13, 1911. The Convention became bindging upon Japan on February 11, 1912.[38] The Qing dynasty did not sign this Convention during the Conference but did sign the other eight

[34]See Liu Pengchao, 'Diplomacy in Modern History: China's First Participation in the International Conference' (in Chinese), Zhongguo Chengshi JingJi, (2011), iss. 18, at 328; Tang, C., 'A Study on China's Participation of the Hague Peace Conferences, 1899–1917' (in Chinese), *Guoli Zhengzhi Daxue Lishi Xuebao* 23 (2005), at 47–55.

[35]The public international law maxim, known as *pacta tertiis nec nocent nec prosunt,* provides that a treaty applies only to the parties, which is a corollary of the principle of consent and of the sovereignty and independence of states. See A. Kaczorowska, *Public International Law* (4th ed.), New York: Routledge 2010, at 118.

[36]Quoted from T. Klein, 'The Boxer War-The Boxer Uprising', *Online Encyclopedia of Mass Violence*, July 23, 2008, viewed August 4, 2014, massviolence.org/The-Boxer-War-The-Boxer-Uprising, at 9–10.

[37]*Ibid.*, at 10.

[38]Japan made a reservation to Article 44 of the Regulation annexed to the Convention. Article 44 reads: 'A belligerent is forbidden to force the inhabitants of territory occupied by it to furnish information about the army of the other belligerent, or about its means of defence.'

conventions.[39] Following the Xinhai Revolution, the government of the Republic of China signed the 1907 Hague Convention (IV) on 27 December 1915, and ratified it on December 11, 1916.[40] Thus, both Japan and China were party to the 1899 Hague Convention (II) and the 1907 Hague Convention (IV) prior to the outbreak of Second Sino-Japanese War.[41]

Established by both the practice of civilized nations and Conventions and Assurances, including the 1907 Hague Convention (IV), the laws and customs of war were cited as authority by the Tokyo Tribunal. 'Destruction of enemy property, without military justification or necessity, and pillage,' and 'failure to respect … private property and religious convictions and worship in occupied territories,' listed among the alleged acts in breach of the laws and customs of war in Sects. 11 and 12 of Appendix D of the Indictment also contravenes the 1907 Hague Convention (IV).[42] Insisting it was merely an 'incident,' successive Japanese governments refused to acknowledge that the hostilities in China were a war to which the laws and customs of war applied.[43] The Tribunal found the war had been envisaged by Japan's military leaders as punitive war to punish the people of China for their refusal to acknowledge the superiority and leadership of the Japanese race and cooperate with Japan. The military leaders sought to make the war so brutal and savage in all its consequences as to break the will of the Chinese people to resist.[44] Because both China and Japan had signed and ratified the 1907 Hague Convention (IV), the Tribunal referred to the Convention to determine whether the Japanese military leaders' acts constituted a breach of international obligations arising under the Convention.[45]

Because the 1907 Hague Convention (IV) is referred to in the Judgment of the Tokyo Trial, and because both China and Japan had signed and ratified the Convention in the first decade of the twentieth century, the Convention clearly applies to the Japanese destruction and pillage of property (including cultural property) during the Second Sino-Japanese War.[46] In addition, the 1907 Hague Convention (IV) remained in force throughout and following World War II. As a

---

[39]The Qing dynasty acknowledged eight of the fourteen conventions (Conventions 1, 2, 3, 5, 9, 10, 13, and 14). See Tang, C., *supra* note 34, at 55–65.

[40]*Ibid.*, at 84–86.

[41]The 1907 Hague Convention (IV) stipulates in Article 2: 'The provisions contained in the Regulations referred to in Article 1, as well as in the Present Convention, do not apply except between Contracting powers, and then only if all the belligerents are parties to the Convention'.

[42]See N. Boister & R. Cryer (eds), *Documents on the Tokyo International Military Tribunal: Charter, Indictment, and Judgments,* Oxford: Oxford University Press 2008, *Vol.* 1, at 62.

[43]J. Pritchard & S.M. Zaide (eds), *The Tokyo War Crimes Trial*, *Vol.* 22, Tokyo: Court House of the Tribunal War Ministry Building 1981, *Vol.* 22, at 490.

[44]*Ibid.*, at 490.

[45]*Ibid.*, at 60.

[46]The Chinese lawyer Wang Yunxia contends the 1899 Hague Convention (II) and the 1907 Hague Convention (IV) do not apply to pillage in WWII because not all the belligerent states were party to the Conventions. I disagree with her contention. See Wang Yunxia (2007), at 142.

result, because both the 1907 Convention (IV) and the 1899 Convention (II), which both prohibit confiscation and destruction of cultural objects, were binding upon China and Japan during WWII, the Japanese destruction and pillage of cultural objects during WWII constituted a breach of international obligations arising under international conventions.

3.2.3 International Customary Law

A second source of international law is international customary law, also known as custom-evidence of a general practice accepted as law. Some conventions have become sources of customary international law. For example, it is now widely accepted that the 1907 Hague Conventions are part of customary law binding on all states regardless of whether they are parties to these conventions. In its 2004 Legal Advisory Opinion on Legal Consequence of the Construction of a Wall in the Occupied Palestinian Territory, the ICJ confirmed the provisions of the Hague Regulations have become part of international customary law: "The Court observes that, in the words of the Convention, those Regulations were prepared to 'revise the general laws and customs of wars' at that time. Since then, however, the International Military Tribunal of Nuremberg has found that the 'rules laid down in the Convention were recognized by all civilized nations, and were regarded as being declaratory of the laws and customs of war.'" The ICJ reached the same conclusion when examining the rights and duties of belligerents in their conduct of military operations.[47] The provisions on the protection of cultural property in Article 23(g), 47 and 56 of the 1907 Hague Convention (IV) were deemed applicable to all states in an international armed conflict.[48] Had the 1907 Hague Convention (IV) been recognized as customary international law during and immediately following WWII, the conventions could have allowed China to claim that the Japanese random destruction and pillage of cultural objects constituted a breach of international obligations under international customary law.

But the determination of international customary law has been called 'more an art than a science,'[49] and it is considered as 'one of the most cumbersome' sources of international law.[50] As Hersch Lauterpacht, one of the leading international

[47]ICJ July 9, 2004, Legal Consequence of the Construction of a Wall in the Occupied Palestinian Territory.

[48]See W. Fiedler, 'Safeguarding of Cultural Property during Occupation: Modifications of the Hague Convention of 1907 by World War II?', in: M. Briat & J.A. Freedberg (eds.), *Legal Aspects of International Trade in Art,* The Hague: Kluwer Law International 1996, at 175–183.

[49]M.W. Janis, *An Introduction to International Law* (2nd ed.), Boston: Little Brown & Co 1993, at 44.

[50]G.J.H. van Hoof, *Rethinking the Sources of International Law*, Deventer: Kluwer Academic 1983, at 85.

lawyers in the 20th century, explains 'There is no rule of thumb which renders it possible to predict with any degree of assurance what amount of precedent will cause an international tribunal to assume in any given case the degree of accumulation of precedent qualifies as custom.'[51] Custom is generally considered to have two constituent elements: the objective element, represented by the international practice itself, and the subjective element, *opinio juris sive necessitatis* (the belief that such practice is in accordance with law and accepted as such).[52] Some have criticized making *opinio juris* a constituent element in determining custom, arguing that the objective element alone is sufficient to render custom a legitimate source of law because the more subjective *opinio juris* is difficult to determine. Others insist upon the necessity and relevance of *opinio juris* in the formation of custom.[53] In its opinions regarding North Sea Continental Shelf cases, the ICJ looked for both elements: 'Not only must the acts concerned amount to a settled practice, but they must also be such, or be carried out in such a way, as to be evidence of a belief that this practice is rendered obligatory by the existence of a rule of law requiring it.'[54] The importance of *opinion juris* has been increasing.[55] The ICJ's decision reveals that the Court rarely relies solely on actual practice to determine the content of customary rules; rather it frequently bases its conclusions on non-binding resolutions of international bodies and its own decisions. Hence, to determine the international customary law regarding cultural objects in the situation of armed conflicts, attention must be paid to both the subjective element and the objective element.[56]

---

[51]Hersch Lauterpacht, *International Law: Collected Papers* (ed. by E. Lauterpacht), Cambridge: Cambridge University Press 1970, at 61.

[52]In the past, international law was characterized as 'the generalization of the practice of state', while nowadays, international practice has a much wider scope, comprising not only that of state, but that of international organizations and of other subjects of international law. The two elements of customary law was considered by the PCIJ as early as in 1927, in the Lotus cases. See Permanent Court of International Justice September 7, 1927, The Case of the S.S. Lotus (France/Turkey); Trindade, *supra* note 29, at 116–118; A.E. Roberts, 'Traditional and Modern Approaches to Customary International Law: A Reconciliation', in: C. Ku & P.F. Diehl, *International Law: Classic and Contemporary Readings* (2nd ed.), London: Lynne Rienner 2003, at 81; A.C. Arend, 'A Methodology for Determining and International Legal Rule', in: C. Ku & P. F. Diehl, *International Law: Classic and Contemporary Readings,* (2nd ed.), London: Lynne Rienner 2003, at 27.

[53]Trindade, *supra* note 29, at 116–117.

[54]ICJ February 20, 1969, North Sea Continental Shelf Cases (Federal Republic of Germany/Denmark; Federal Republic of Germany/Netherlands), at 45.

[55]Trindade, *supra* note 29, at 119; also see P. Weil, 'Towards Relative Normativity in International Law', *The American Journal of International Law* 77 (1983), at 417.

[56]In the Asylum case (Colombia v. Peru, 1950), the ICJ ruled that the proof of custom was to abide by the principle of division or distribution of the burden of proof between the contending parties in international litigation. See Trindade, *supra* note 29, at 117.

Determining the customary international law regarding pillage of cultural objects in time of war is not easy given the countless instances of wartime pillage throughout history and the established notion "to the victor go the spoils" (see Chap. 2). For most of human history war has gone hand in hand with the destruction and pillage of property. Moreover, early international lawyers such as Grotius and Vattel considered it legal to take an enemy's property in a just war even though booty taken in an unjust war should be restored (see Chap. 2). Not until the Napoleonic Wars did anyone begin examining the legitimacy of pillaging art. Articulating the Allied position, the Duke of Wellington observed that Napoleon's systematically looting cultural property from the rest of Europe was 'contrary to the principles of justice and the rules of modern war.'[57] Unlike Grotius and Vattel, Wheaton and Atlay distinguished 'public property' and 'private property' in discussing confiscating property during wartime in the nineteen century. Wheaton argued that since the time of William's conquest of Normandy, among Christian civilizations, although property belonging to the government of the vanquished nation passes to the victorious state, which also takes the place of the former sovereign with respect to the right of eminent domain, private rights are unaffected by conquest.[58] Wheaton reiterated that 'The modern practice of nations has firmly established the general rule of exempting private property on land from confiscation,' and 'by the modern usage of nations, which has now acquired the force of law, temples of religion, public edifices devoted to civil purposes only, monuments of art, and repositories of science, are exempted from the general operations of war. Private property on land is also exempt from confiscation, with the exception of such as may become booty in special cases.'[59] Although Vattel did not specify whether such cultural objects should be treated as 'private property,' his followers analyzed the sacking of the Old Summer Palace in 1860 and the plundering of Beijing in 1900 in the fourth edition of Elements of International Law published in 1904, concluding that: 'The plunder of the Emperor of China's summer palace by the troops of France and England, in the 1860 war against China, and still more, the organized looting that was permitted to some of the European contingents after the relief of the Peking Legations in 1900, show that the most civilized nations do not, even now invariably restrain their troops from pillaging private property.'[60] Also the accumulation of legislation since the 1860s, such as the Lieber Code, the Brussels Declaration, the Oxford Manual, the 1899 Hague Convention (II) and the 1907 Hague Convention (IV) provides evidence supporting the existence of international customary law prohibiting destruction and pillage of cultural objects in the event of armed conflicts, even though it is still difficult to determine exactly when such customary law came into existence.

---

[57]Gillespie (2011), at 249.

[58]H. Wheaton & J. Beresford Atlay, *Elements of International Law* (4th ed.), London: Steven and Sons 1904, at 481.

[59]*Ibid.*

[60]*Ibid.* at 482.

3.2.4 General Principles of Law

General principles of law recognized by civilized nations are also important sources of public international law. According to Verdross, a founder of international constitutionalism, 'The general principles of law are at the basis of custom and of conventional law. The latter are usually no more than the crystallization of those principles. The concrete rules cannot be construed to conflict with the principles of which they constitute the application.'[61] Likewise, according to ICJ judge Fernandes: 'The priority given by Article 38 of the Statute of the Court to conventions and to custom in relation to the general principles of law in no way excludes a simultaneous application of those principles and of the first two sources of law. It frequently happens that a decision given on the basis of a particular or general convention or of a custom requires recourse to the general principles of law…. A court will have recourse to those principles to fill gaps in the conventional rules, or to interpret them.'[62] 'International practice shows that a court or an arbitrator cannot ascertain the true meaning of the provisions of a treaty without considering these within the framework of certain general principles which dominate them.'[63]

However, the determination and application of general principles of law in inter-state disputes warrant careful examination. As ICJ Judge Tranidade suggests, doubts and uncertainties persist as to the meaning of "general principles of law." For some, the term pertains to the principles of international law properly, while for others, it refers to the principles of comparative domestic law of the various states.[64] In Judge Tranidade's view, the term "general principles of law" link domestic law and international law because beginning in the 1950s repeated references have been made to general principles of law such as good faith, *res judicata*, and prohibition of rights abuses.[65] As to general principles of law regarding to taking spoils during times of armed conflict, although all national legal systems criminalize theft and robbery, because no cases adjudicated by the ICJ attest to such a principle it is doubtful whether 'pillage is illegal' can be argued to have risen to the level of a general principle of law.

Even if the existence of such a principle could be successfully argued, it is doubtful it could be applied to the cases under discussion here. During their early days, international courts and tribunals often turned to general principles of law to

[61]Quoted from E. Hambro, *The Case Law of the International Court, Vol. IV, 1959–1963*, Leiden: Sijthoff 1966, at 97. For original source, see Verdross, Derecho International Publico, (1963), 205–206.

[62]ICJ April 12, 1960, Right of Passage over Indian Territory (Portugal/India), dissenting opinion of Judge Fernanedes, p. 139–140.

[63]*Ibid.*, at 139–140.

[64]Trindade, *supra* note 29, at 122.

[65]*Ibid.*

fill legal "gaps," interpret legal rules, and reinforce legal reasoning.[66] Although international courts and tribunals still may occasionally turn to general principles of law when dealing with less-developed branches of international law, this practice has not resulted in a fully-fledged set of legal rules sufficient to regulate all the legal issues that may arise in judicial practice.[67]

There are significant legal obstacles to the direct application of general principles of law in international law. 'Chiefly, [opponents] have invoked the prevalence of the principle of state sovereignty in international relations and the special character of international law.'[68] According to Raimondo, because of the absence of a centralized legislative body, a specific general principle of law may be unsuitable for regulating inter-state legal disputes. The analogy pursuant to which the applicability of a specific general principle of law would be based may be inappropriate or, there may not even be an analogy which sustains the applicability of the general principle of law.[69] Raimondo's critique is the most likely reason the PCIJ and the ICJ have failed to apply general principles of law directly in adjudicating inter-state cases.[70]

Interim conclusion

Japanese pillage in China during WWII violated international obligations arising under the 1899 Hague Convention (II) and the 1907 Hague Convention (IV), which were most likely inapplicable to the plunder of Beijing in 1900 because China was not then a party to the Conventions even though the Conventions, and other laws outlaw looting cultural objects in armed conflicts, are now considered international customary law. No international convention existed at the time of the sacking of the Old Summer Palace in 1860 and no specific time can be identified as when the destruction and confiscation of cultural objects during time of war came to be deemed illegal under international customary law. Although all legal systems prohibit theft and robbery, it is disputable whether the prohibition of theft and robbery in national, domestic legal systems can be applied as a general principle of law directly to an inter-state dispute. Although international norms concerning war pillage have changed, the evolution of legal rules takes time. The belief that pillage of cultural object in times of war has been outlawed rests on the proliferation of legal prohibitions and increased awareness from and after the second half of the nineteenth century. As Weil states, '[I]t is not always easy to draw the frontier between the prelegal and the legal. This is a problem that recurs every time law

[66]For instance, the Iran-United States Claims Tribunal applies general principles of law pertaining to private law. F.O. Raimondo, *General Principles of Law in the Decisions of International Criminal Courts* (dissertation), Amsterdam: University of Amsterdam 2007, 11–12; C.I. Jonathan, *Is International Law Threatened by Multiple International Tribunals?* (Recueil des Cours 271), Leiden: Nijhoff Online 1998, DOI: 10.1163/ej.9789041112101.101-382, at 196–197.

[67]See Jonathan, *ibid.*, at 226–228; Raimondo, *ibid.* at 12.

[68]Raimondo, *ibid.*, at 6.

[69]Raimondo, *ibid.*, at 74.

[70]Raimondo, *ibid.*, at 4, 74.

resorts to the technique of the threshold: between the reasonable and nonreasonable, the equitable and the nonequitable, the essential and the nonessential, the appurtenant and the nonappurtenant.'[71]

3.3 Admissibility of the Restitution Claims

Even if a requesting state proves a confiscation of cultural objects during an armed conflict violated an international obligation and gave rise to state responsibility, the requesting state must still establish the admissibility of its restitution claim. Although a lack of admissibility does not, in principle, exclude a tribunal's authority to hear the case, it affects the possibility or propriety of the tribunal's deciding the particular case at the particular time. A respondent state may raise objections to the admissibility of a claim and invite the tribunal to dismiss (or perhaps postpone) the claim. Objections to admissibility may be based on undue delay in presenting the claim, failure to exhaust local remedies, mootness, or failure to join a necessary third party.[72] This section treats two issues affecting admissibility of restitution claims: post-war peace treaties and the principle of extinctive prescription in international law.

3.3.1 Settlement by Post-war Peace Treaties

The Second Opium War concluded with the Treaties of Tientsin and the Conventions of Peking. The war in 1900 concluded with the Boxer Protocol (known as The Peace Agreement between the Great Powers and China in the west). Because these treaties were signed by the Qing government under the threat of "gunboat diplomacy," the question arises as to whether they can be seen as being dispositive of the question of possession of looted cultural objects? These treaties recall Napoleon including his acquisition of art from his defeated enemies in a series of peace treaties. What effect should express surrenders of works of art in peace treaties with defeated Italian states have in determining whether France was

[71]Weil, *supra* note 55, at 417· Lefkowitz describes the chronological paradox in customary international law formation as resting on two misconceptions; the first regarding the process whereby customary rules comes to exist, and the second regarding the process whereby customary rules becomes law. For instance, at some initial point in time a few members of a group may believe falsely in the existence of a certain customary rule. However, if that group persists in their belief other members of their group may come to share their belief with the result that at some later point in time the customary norm truly does exist and applies to the members of the group. See D. Lefkowitz, 'The Sources of International Law: Some Philosophical Reflections,' in S. Besson (ed.), *The Philosophy of International Law,* Oxford: Oxford University Press 2010, at 202.

[72]See Crawford (2012), at 693.

ethically or legally entitled to remove those works to Paris.[73] In 1943, China signed treaties with the U.S. and the U.K. providing for the abrogation of extraterritoriality in China. Both the Chinese Nationalist Party and the Communist Party pronounced the treaties unequal.[74]

Most Western states viewed the notion of unequal (i.e., illegal or invalid) treaties as vague, easily manipulated, and likely to jeopardize the stability of treaty relations.[75] The equality of states is juridical; as a practical matter, states vary enormously in size, resources, population, military capacity, and economic strength.[76] The 'unequal treaty' concept has been espoused by states victimized by imperialism and colonization, focusing especially on colonial-era treaties granting states extensive trade, mineral or other rights in their former colonies as a condition of independence, and on neo-colonial treaties viewed as perpetuating colonialism through economic domination.[77]

International law theorists have long referenced equal and unequal treaties. Grotius considered unequal treaties with an inferior party 'commands,'[78] but wrote: 'Unequal Leagues are made, not only between the Conquerors and Conquered … but also between People of unequal Power, even such as never were at War with one another.'[79] But for Vattel, 'to authorize [a rule invalidating imposed treaties] would amount to an attack upon the common safety and welfare of Nations, the principle would be condemned as abhorrent by the same reasons which made the faithful observance of treaties a universally sacred duty.'[80] According to Hans Kelsen, although the conclusion of a contract must be voluntary on both sides in national law of civilized nations, this principle is not generally recognized as a rule of positive international law applicable to treaties. In his words, 'peace treaties are, as a rule, imposed by threat or use of force excised by a victorious state against a vanquished state. But peace treaties are not considered to be null or annullable for

[73]Merryman & Elsen et al. (1998), at 8.

[74]Wang argues that the pronouncements by the Nationalist Party and the Communist Party illuminated the rivalry between the two parties over 'who gets the credit' for the redemption of 'a century of national ignominy.' Wang, D. (2003), 399.

[75]See J.L. Dunoff, S.R. Ratner & D. Wippman, *International Law: Norms, Actors, Process*, New York: Aspen 2006, at 50–51; S.S. Malawer, "Unequal Treaties are not Necessarily Illegal", *The New York Times*, September 12, 1983, viewed December 12, 2013, http://www.nytimes.com/1983/09/12/opinion/l-unequal-treaties-are-not-necessarily-illegal-156706.html?smid=pl-share; L.F. Chen, *State Succession Relating to Unequal Treaties*, Hamden: Archon Books 1974, at 232.

[76]*Ibid.*

[77]See Dunoff, Ratner & Wipmann, *ibid.*, at 50–51.

[78]H. Grotius, The Rights of War and Peace, (ed. and intr. by R. Tuck), Indianapolis: Liberty Fund 2005, at 826.

[79]*Ibid.*, at 827.

[80]Wang, D. (2003), 51.

this reason.'[81] The applicable principle of public international law is *pacta sunt servanda* (promises must be kept).[82]

However, because Chapter VII of the United Nations Charter declares it illegal to use armed force in circumstances other than self-defense or with the permission of Security Council, a treaty imposed by the use or threat of armed force might arguably be considered illegal by organs of the UN. Although aggressive military force has long been universally acknowledged as illegal, and the Vienna Convention on the Law of Treaties provides that a treaty is void if its conclusion has been procured by the threat or use of force in violation of the principles of international law embodied in the UN Charter (Article 52), it is unclear whether a state is entitled to retroactively invalidate historical 'unequal treaties.' China was the first nation to challenge the legal validity of its treaties with foreign countries, a remedy not mentioned by either Grotius or Vattel. Originally considered invalid, China's presentation of the unequal treaties case led to international law accepting that a treaty imposed upon a defeated and weak state under duress is not viable.[83] In the 1964 UN debates on Cyprus, the Greek Cypriots suggested because they had no choice but to accept the treaties they were 'unequal, inequitable and unjust.'[84] The Turkish representative successfully defended the adoption of the treaties.[85] In the territorial dispute *Libyan Arab Jamahiriya v. Chad*, Libya argued the ICJ should make allowance for Libya's relative lack of diplomatic experience placing it at a disadvantage when negotiating the contested Treaty with France, but the ICJ evidently took no notice of the Libyans' submission.[86]

Thus, although it is arguable a historical unequal treaty can be retroactively invalidated in international law, for the Chinese, the unequal treaties theory has yet to provide assistance in obtaining the restoration of looted cultural objects.

Waiver of Claims?

Japan signed the Treaty of Peace (also known as the San Francisco Peace Treaty) with the Allied Powers at the San Francisco Peace Conference on September 8, 1951. Article 14 (b) of the Treaty waives the allied powers' rights to claim war

---

[81]H. Kelsen, *Principles of International Law* (2nd ed., rev. and ed. by R.W. Tucker), New York: Holt, Rinehart & Winston 1966, at 464.

[82]According to Greenberg, the reasons for validating all treaties were twofold. First, the essential consideration was the need for a state to be able to ensure its survival by consenting to an agreement to prevent that state and its people from further destruction. Second, there was the need to ensure the observation of treaties by all states in the international community. See K.A. Greenberg, 'Hong Kong's Future: Can the People's Republic of China Invalidate the Treaty of Nanking as an Unequal Treaty?' *Fordham International Law Journal* 7 (1983), no. 1, at 537–538.

[83]Wang, D. (2003), at 399–401.

[84]See Dunoff, Ratner & Wipmann, *supra* note 75, at 47–48.

[85]*Ibid.*, at 47–49.

[86]See G.J. Naldi, 'Case Concerning the Territorial Dispute (Libyan Arab Jamahiriya/Chad)', *International and Comparative Law Quarterly* 44 (1995), no. 3, at 689–690.

reparations from Japan.[87] Arguably, fearing Soviet and Chinese communist expansion in Asia and wanting to rid Japan of the burdens of responsibility for its war-time aggression and make Japan its closest ally in the Pacific, the U.S. pressured victimized countries not to demand large reparations from Japan and persuaded most of the Allied Powers to accept the terms of the Treaty,[88] although another reason may have been not to repeat the failure of the Versailles Treaty. Many analysts have blamed the harsh indemnity imposed upon Germany after WWI as the primary cause of the German economic and financial crisis of 1929–33 which contributed to the outbreak of WWII.[89]

Significantly, neither the Republic of China nor the People's Republic of China was invited to attend the Conference. The ROC government entered into a separate peace treaty with Japan on April 28, 1952, commonly known as Treaty of Taipei, which recognized the San Francisco Peace Treaty.[90] Although the PRC published a statement by Zhou Enlai declaring the Treaty a violation of the Cairo Declaration, the Yalta Agreements, the Potsdam Declaration and Agreement, and the Basic Post-Surrender Policy of the Far Eastern Commission,[91] in normalizing diplomatic relations with Japan China entered into the Joint Communique of the Government of Japan and the Government of the People's Republic of China on September 29, 1972, Paragraph 5 of which provides: 'The Government of the People's Republic of China declares that in the interest of the friendship between the Chinese and the Japanese peoples, it renounces its demand for war reparation from Japan.'[92] Significantly, it is controversial for a government to waive its citizens' private rights. According to Steven C. Clemons, one day before the San Francisco Peace Treaty was to be signed, the Dutch government threatened to walk out of the conference because of their fear they lacked the constitutional authority to waive

[87]Article 14 (b) reads: 'Except as otherwise provided in the present Treaty, the Allied Powers waived all reparations claims of the Allied Powers, other claims of the Allied Powers and their nationals arising out of any actions taken by Japan and its nations in the course of the prosecution of the war, and claims of the Allied Powers for direct military costs of occupation'.

[88]See R. Stich, *Japanese and U.S. World War II Plunder and Intrigue*, Walnut Creek: Silverpeak 2010, at 19; O. Yasuaki, 'Japanese War Guilt and Postwar Responsibilities of Japan', *Berkeley Journal of International Law* 20 (2003), no. 3, at 614.

[89]See J.M. Keynes, *The Economic Consequences of the Peace*, New York: Harcourt, Brace & Howe 1920; M.F. Boemeke, G.D. Feldman & E. Gläser (eds), *The Treaty of Versailles: A Reassessment after 75 Years,* Cambridge: Cambridge University Press 1994, at 2.

[90]See See the 'Treaty of Peace between the Republic of China and Japan', *United Nations Treaty Series* (138–4) 1952, no. 1858.

[91]See Price (2001).

[92]Okazaki states that "It was Zhou Enlai who said emphatically that China and Japan should cooperate to make Asia a better place and to bring strength to Asia. To that end, he said that (China) was going to forget its grudge against Japan. This would be great if it could be accomplished. From that standpoint, our cooperation with China's 'four modernizations' and our attitude toward the entire Korean Peninsula should be changed considerably, in our conception and ways, in my view". See K. Byosei, 'The Shifting Nature of Japan-China Relations after the Cold War', in: P.E. Lam (ed.), *Japan's Relations with China: Facing a Rising Power,* New York: Routledge 2006, at 29.

such private rights.[93] As a result, the Japanese Prime Minister pledged: 'The Government of Japan does not consider that the Government of the Netherlands by signing the Treaty has itself expropriated the private claims of its nationals so that, as a consequence thereof, after the Treaty comes into force these claims would be non-existent.'[94] Following the declassification of more historical documents, it has become apparent the U.S. and Japan sought to use the San Francisco Peace Treaty to eliminate any possibility of war reparations being imposed upon Japan. But according to Clemons, the Treaty also 'fostered a deliberate forgetfulness whose consequences haunt us today.'[95] The Japanese lawyer Yasuaki has suggested the generous and lenient attitudes of the Chinese government must have been beyond the comprehension of the Chinese war victims, but their opposition and dissatisfaction were suppressed.[96]

Beginning in 1995, Chinese war victims have filed a number of lawsuits in Japanese courts seeking compensation from the Japanese government and Japanese corporations. All the cases have been dismissed variously on the grounds of 'limitation of actions,' 'state immunity,' and 'abandonment of the right to claim.'[97] Although the Chinese government has repeatedly officially stated that the right of Chinese citizens to assert private claims for war reparation was not waived in the Joint Communique, the Chinese stance has been rejected by the Japanese government and its judicial organs. In the Nishimatsu Construction Case and the second Chinese Comfort Women Case, the Japanese Supreme Court overturned a number of legal decisions made by lower courts, holding claims of individual Chinese nationals had been waived pursuant to the Joint Communique.[98] Even though the Chinese government considers Japan's unilateral interpretation of the Joint Communique illegal and invalid, Japan will probably continue to rely on the waiver of claims by the Chinese government to dismiss any and all future claims seeking war reparations.[99]

---

[93]S. C. Clemons, 'Recovering Japan's Wartime Past—and Ours,' *The New York Times*, September 4, 2001, viewed March 26, 2015, http://www.nytimes.com/2001/09/04/opinion/recovering-japans-wartime-past-and-ours.html.

[94]Quoted from *ibid.* In the article, Clemons reports that in 1956 the Dutch successfully pursued a claim against Japan on behalf of private citizens pursuant to which Japan paid ten million dollars as a way of 'expressing sympathy and regret'.

[95]*Ibid.*

[96]Yasuaki, *supra* ntoe 88, at 605, 609.

[97]'The lawsuits involve cases of massacre, indiscriminate bombing, abandoned chemical weapons and shells, Unit 731's experiments using live human subjects and its deployment of germ bombs, sexual exploitation of 'comfort women' and cases of forced labor.' See W. Underwood & J. Kang, 'Japan's Top Court Poised to Kill Lawsuits by Chinese War Victims,' *The Asia- Pacific Journal: Japan Focus* March 2, 2007.

[98]M. Asada & T. Ryan, 'Post-war Reparations between Japan and China and Individual Claims: The Supreme Court Judgments in the Nishimatsu Construction Case and the Second Chinese "Comfort Women" Case,' *Journal of Japanese Law* 14 (2009), no. 27, at 258–284.

[99]*Ibid.*, at 283; Yasuaki *supra* note 88, at 600–620.

The fact the 1972 Joint Communique does not define 'war reparations' raises the question of whether requests for the return of cultural objects retained by Japan fall in the category of 'war reparations.' Although the First Protocol to the 1954 Hague Convention specifies cultural property shall not be retained as war reparations (Section I, paragraph 3),[100] when it signed this Protocol Japan inserted a reservation to this provision declaring that: 'In applying the provisions of paragraph 3 of I of the Protocol, Japan will fulfill the obligation under those provisions in a manner consistent with its domestic laws including the civil code. Japan will be, therefore, bound by the provisions of Section I of the Protocol to the extent that their fulfilment is compatible with the above-mentioned domestic laws.'[101] The International Committee of the Red Cross's study of customary rules of international humanitarian law [102] lists as its Rule 41: 'The occupying power must prevent the illicit export of cultural property from occupied territory and must return illicitly exported to the competent authorities of the occupied territory.' The study considers Rule 41 a 'norm of customary international law applicable in international armed conflicts.'[103] Rule 41's source is paragraph 3 of the First Protocol of the 1954 Hague Convention. There is official opposition to Rule 41. The 1997 Russian Federal Law on Cultural Values Removed to the USSR as a Result of the Second World War and Located on the Territory of the Russian Federation declares Russia's right to such cultural objects as an exercise of its right to 'compensatory restitution.' The law was upheld by the Russian Federation's Constitutional Court in 1999.[104] Even though it is now generally established as an international customary rule that cultural objects shall not be retained as war reparation, the waiver of claims provision in the Joint Communique increases the uncertainty of the admissibility of China's claims for the return of looted cultural objects.

---

[100]Para 3 of Section I of the Protocol reads: 'Each High Contracting Party undertakes to return, at the close of hostilities, to the competent authorities of the territory previously occupied, cultural property which is in its territory, if such property has been exported in contravention of the principle laid down in the first paragraph. Such property shall never be retained as war reparations.'

[101]Protocol to the Convention for the Protection of Cultural Property in the Event of Armed conflict 1954 (14 May 1954), see unesco.org.

[102]For an overview of the study, see J.M. Henckaerts, 'New Rules for the Protection of Cultural Property in Armed Conflict: The Significance of the Second Protocol to the 1954 Hague Convention for the Protection of Cultural Property in the Event of Armed Conflict,' in: A. van Woudenberg & E. Lijnzaad (eds), *Protecting Cultural Property in Armed Conflict: An Insight into the 1999 Second Protocol to the Hague Convention of 1954 for the Protection of Cultural Property in the Event of Armed Conflict*, Leiden: Nijhoff 2010, pp. 175–212.

[103]ICRC, Customary IHL, viewed March 27, 2015, https://www.icrc.org/customary-ihl/eng/docs/v1_rul_rule41.

[104]For a general view of this Russian law, see 'Spoils of War', *International Newsletter*, no. 4, (1997).

3.3.2 The Principle of Extinctive Prescription

In discussing the Articles on Responsibility of States for Internationally Wrongful Acts, the ILC's report lists 'delay' as justification for losing the right to invoke responsibility.[105] Although extinctive prescription appears to be generally recognized as grounds for denying the admissibility of a claim of responsibility,[106] no generally accepted time limit, expressed in years, has been laid down and no attempts to establish a precise or finite time for international claims in general have succeeded.[107] Cases will be held inadmissible on grounds of delay if the respondent State has been clearly disadvantaged, and international courts have carefully weighed the relevant aspects in each case, including, for example, the conduct of the respondent state and the importance of the rights involved,[108] but the adopted Draft Articles do not provide for the loss of the right to invoke responsibility.

Nonetheless, international law appears to recognize the principle of prescription. Decisions rendered by international judges indicate international tribunals are willing to apply the doctrine of laches against state claims tainted by undue delay.[109] The earliest instances of states successfully asserting laches as a defense in international law are the 1858 Macedonian Case decided by a Belgian arbitrator,[110] and the 1863 Case of Louis Brand.[111] The seminal authority affirming the efficacy of laches doctrine in international law is the 1890 Williams Case, announced by Commissioner Little. In 1868, the US sued the Venezuelan government on behalf of a New York merchant who alleged Venezuela had breached its contractual obligation in 1841.[112] Commissioner Little opined that even if it was well established in international law that there was no time limit on a valid claim between sovereign states, a claim riddled with undue delay cannot be 'valid.'[113] Following the Williams Case, the efficacy of laches was affirmed by a series of international

[105]J.R. Crawford (Special Rapporteur), *Third Report on State Responsibility*, UN-doc A/CN.4/507, 15 March—4 August 2000, para 257–259.

[106]*Ibid.*, para 257.

[107]*Ibid.*, para 258.

[108]*Ibid.*, para 259.

[109]A.R. Ibrahim, 'The Doctrine of Laches in International Law', *Virginia Law Review* 83 (1997), no. 3, at 655.

[110]In the Macedonian Case, the US sued Chile for the seizure of a US Ship in violation of international maritime law. Although the seizure occurred in 1819, the US did not assert its claim until 1841. Chile argued the claim was barred by 'prescription.' Arbitration by King Leopold of Belgium May 15, 1863, Case of the Brig Macedonian (United States/Chile). See J.B. Moore, *History and Digest of International Arbitrations to Which the United States Has Been a Party,* Washington: Government Print Office 1898, at 3138–89.

[111]In the Case of Louise Brand, the US sued Peru on behalf of an American citizen alleging tortious injuries by Peruvian soldiers incurred twenty-six years prior to the filing of the suit. See *ibid.* at 1615, 1625.

[112]Ibrahim, *supra* note 109, at 658–660.

[113]*Ibid.*, at 659.

arbitrations conducted in The Hague in 1903 by various Venezuelan tribunals and in the late 1920s by various international tribunals.[114] In 1925, the Institute of International Law announced that the limitation of actions in public international law was a general rule that 'should influence international arbitrators and judges in rendering their awards.'[115]

The ICJ endorsed the principle of extinctive prescription in deciding the 1992 case of Certain Phosphate Lands in Nauru. 'The Court recognizes that, even in the absence of any applicable treaty provision, delay on the part of a claimant state may render an application inadmissible. It notes, however, that international law does not lay down any specific time-limit in that regard. It is therefore for the Court to determine in the light of the circumstance of each whether the passage of time renders an application inadmissible.'[116] According to Hober, in international law extinctive prescription is a procedural tool with substantive law consequences because it both precludes the claim from being tried and extinguishes the claim so it cannot be used for set-off. A finding of extinctive prescription appears to require delay in presenting a claim which results in a disadvantage to the respondent.[117]

The events giving rise to China's claims for the return of looted cultural objects all occurred between seventy and a hundred and fifty-five years ago. Chief among the causes was China's political bipolarity following the establishment of the PRC, which was aggravated by the fact that until the 1970s the PRC held itself aloof from the international community, rendering western countries skeptical and suspicious of the PRC. But during the 1970s, the PRC finally gained enough support for the UN General Assembly to declare the PRC, and not the Republic of China (ROC), China's rightful representative in international affairs.[118] Notwithstanding the reasons for the delay, given the length of the delay, any state responding to a claim for the return of looted Chinese cultural objects would most likely successfully invoke the principle of extinctive prescription as a defense, thereby rendering China's application inadmissible.

3.3.3 Legal Effects of the Resolutions

The doctrine of intertemporal law, the post-war settlement and the principle of extinctive prescription in public international law, militate against restitution claims pursued through international adjudication. To overcome these legal obstacles,

---

[114]*Ibid.*, at 661–665.

[115]J.B. Scott, 'Institute of International Law', *American Journal of International Law* 19 (1925), no. 4, at 759–760.

[116]ICJ June 26, 1992, Certain Phosphate Lands in Nauru (Nauru/Australia), 253–254, para 32.

[117]K. Hober, *Extinctive Prescription and Applicable Law in Interstate Arbitration*, Uppsala: Iustus 2001, at 280–304.

[118]UNESCO, CLT-99/CONF.203/2. Tenth Session, (Paris, January 25–28, 1999).

scholars and international organizations have argued that claims for the repatriation of cultural objects merit special consideration. Concerning cultural objects looted during WWII, the UNESCO Intergovernmental Committee for Promoting the Return of Cultural Property to its Countries of Origin or its Restitution in case of Illicit Appropriation states: 'Where there have been successive displacements, the objects will be returned to the territory where they were located at the outbreak of hostilities in 1939,' and 'no time limits can be set.'[119] Since the 1970s, the UN General Assembly has adopted a series of resolutions on restitution and return of cultural objects to the countries of origin (see Chap. 2).

A critical aspect of UN resolutions concerns their binding effect.[120] Most international lawyers insist that only formal sources of intentional law are legally binding and not being formal sources, UN resolutions have no binding effect[121] while others argue the connection between law and morality is fundamental and the resolutions' ethical content provide a legitimate basis for a binding international obligation.[122] A third group takes a middle position by arguing UN resolutions are legally binding due to their 'quasi-legislative force' or their 'political effect.'[123]

The ICJ has considered the legal effects of UN resolutions. In the 1955 Voting Procedure case, Judge Lauterpacht stated that although General Assembly resolutions are legally binding in some matters upon the Secretary-General and UN Members, in general they are 'in the nature of recommendations.'[124] Judge Klaestad concurred, stating that 'such a decision (recommendation) adopted by the General Assembly without the concurrent vote of the Union Government does not

---

[119]*Ibid.*, Annex I.

[120]Because the binding effect of a resolution involves its ability to create obligations on its addressee(s), some argue resolutions' ability to bind is closely linked to the concept of state consent. See Trindade, *supra* note 29, at 113; R. Higgins, *Problems and Process: International Law and How We Use it*, Oxford: Oxford University Press 1995, at 24–25; M.D. Oberg, 'The Legal Effects of Resolutions of the UN Security Council and General Assembly in the Jurisprudence of the ICJ', *European Journal of International law* 16 (2006), no. 5, at 880.

[121]Some are of the opinion that although the General Assembly serves a valuable function as a forum for the expression of momentary indignation and deeply held sentiments, its strength as an international political body are also its weakness as a legislative body. See Verzijl, *supra* note 29, at 1–3; G.J. Kerwin, 'The Role of United Nations General Assembly Resolutions in Determining Principles of International Law in United Courts,' *Duke Law Journal* 1983, at 892–899.

[122]Trindade, *supra* note 29, at 140; J.L. Brierly, *The Basis of Obligation in International Law*, Oxford: Clarendon Press 1958, at 65.

[123]'Political effect' of a General Assembly resolution refers, particularly when the resolution is addressed to a certain Member or Members of the United Nations, to those Members running the risk of losing the political friendship and understanding of their fellow Members who voted for the Resolution if they fail to follow the course 'recommended' in the Resolution. See D.H.N. Johnson, 'The Effect of Resolutions of the General Assembly of the United Nations', *British Year Book of International Law* 32 (1955–1956), at 121; R.A. Falk, 'On the Quasi-Legislative Competence of the General Assembly', *American Journal of International Law* 60 (1966), no. 4, pp. 782–791.

[124]ICJ June 7, 1955, Voting Procedure on Questions relating to Reports and Petitions concerning the Territory of South West Africa, at 118.

create a binding legal obligation for that Government'[125] and the legal effects of such resolutions are 'not of legal nature in the usual sense, but rather of moral or political character.'[126] Notwithstanding their positions on the non-legal binding effect of UN resolutions, Judges Lauterpacht and Klaestad both argued that Member States have a duty to consider in good faith a recommendation adopted by the General Assembly.[127]

In the case of South West Africa, the court confirmed that the 'General Assembly is in principle vested with recommendatory powers,' and 'it is debarred from adopting, in specific cases within the framework of its competence, resolutions which make determinations or have operative design.'[128] The court went on to discuss the legal effects of resolutions adopted by the UN Security Council, holding that the legal basis of the resolution (Security Council Resolution 269) was Article 24 of the UN Charter which 'vests in the Security Council the necessary authority to take action such as that taken in the present case.'[129] Thus, if a declaration has been made by the Security Council under Article 24 of the UN Charter on behalf of all member states, the members would not be free to act in disregard of this declaration.[130] We can deduce from this advisory opinion by the ICJ that a UN Security Council resolution adopted under the UN Charter is legally effective. Hence, UN 'resolutions' can be categorized into recommendations and decisions. Recommendations are not legally binding while decisions are legally binding. Significantly, even though the ICJ does not consider them legally binding, the ICJ continues to reiterate that some General Assembly resolutions are of normative value and can, in certain circumstances, provide important evidence for establishing the existence of a customary rule, including the emergence of an *opinio juris*.[131]

In the *Texaco Case*, the arbitrator found General Assembly Resolution 1803 represented current international law because it had been passed with the support of importing and exporting states.[132] Thus, it may be inferred that if a General Assembly resolution receives unanimous support it may be viewed as confirmation of international law. As to the resolutions by General Assembly and UNESCO concerning restitution or return of cultural objects to their countries of origin, such

[125] *Ibid.*, at 88.

[126] *Ibid.*, at 88.

[127] *Ibid*, at 88, 119.

[128] ICJ June 21, 1971, Legal Consequences for States of the Continued Presence of South Africa in Namibia (South West Africa) notwithstanding Security Council Resolution 276 (1970), para 105.

[129] *Ibid.,* para 110.

[130] *Ibid.*, para 112.

[131] See Oberg, *supra* note 120, at 880; Higgins, *supra* note 120, at 24–25; Advisory Opinion on the Western Sahara, (1975); ICJ June 27, 1986, Military and Paramilitary Activities in and against Nicaragua (Nicaragua/United States); ICJ July 8, 1996, Legality of the Threat or Use of Nuclear Weapons, at 254–255.

[132] Quoted from Higgins *supra* note 120, at 27–28. For original source, see January 19, 1977, Texaco Overseas Petroleum Co. v. Libyan Arab Republic, 53 ILR 389.

resolutions have been initiated and supported by claiming states but the targeted countries targeted have refused to be bound by such resolutions.[133]

3.4 Conclusion

The foregoing analysis focuses on the legal obstacles to recovering cultural objects through international adjudication: no compulsory jurisdiction, no retroactivity of existing conventions, the post-war settlement, and the principle of extinctive prescription. Due to the non-retroactivity of existing conventions, the qualification of the acts of confiscating cultural objects during wartime will be determined by the intertemporal law, but the determination of intertemporal law regarding pillage of cultural objects during wartime is challenging, especially in cases where no international conventions apply. No international convention prohibiting pillage of property in the event of armed conflict existed at the time of the sacking of the Old Summer Palace in 1860. The persistent state practice of pillage at wartime conflicted with *opinio juris* prohibiting pillage of cultural objects, which makes the determination of custom difficult. Although all legal systems make robbery or theft illegal, the abstraction of these rules as general principles of law is problematic; general principles of law are seldom directly applied to inter-state disputes by international courts and tribunals. In addition, there is no defining moment since which taking spoils from war has been universally outlawed. Post-war settlements by peace treaties also cast doubt upon the admissibility of repatriation claims. As noted discussing the situation between Japan and China during their normalizing their diplomatic relationship, the Chinese government's waiver of claims in the Joint Communique places requesting parties in a disadvantageous position. Although contemporary international law recognizes that cultural objects may not be retained as war reparations, the lack of binding precedent and the doctrine of intertemporal law, makes it questionable whether this rule would be applicable to the cases under discussion. In addition, Japan's reservation in the First Protocol to the 1954 Hague Convention would make Japan a consistent objector to the now customary rule. Thus, even if China succeeds in proving Japanese looting during WWII constituted a breach of an international obligation, it is extremely likely Japan would invoke the waiver of rights as a defense. Also, due to the principle of

[133]A Resolution is voted on by all UN members States in the General Assembly, which usually requires a simple majority (50 percent of all votes plus one) to pass. If the issue is an 'important question,' a two-thirds majority is required. Since 1999, resolutions in this respect have been adopted without vote. Resolution (A/RES/52/24) adopted in 1997 was passed with support of eighty-seven states, with twenty-three abstentions and seventy-five non-voting in the one hundred eighty-five total voting membership. See C.C. Joyner, 'U.N. General Assembly Resolutions and International Law: Rethinking the Contemporary Dynamics of Norm-Creation', California Western International Law Journal 11, (1981), no. 3, at 445, 470. See United Nations Dag Hammarskjold Library, http://www.un.org/Depts/dhl/.

extinctive prescription in public international law, the lapse of time would most likely make a repatriation claim inadmissible. In an attempt to overcome all these legal obstacles, UNESCO and other international organizations have adopted numerous resolutions on restitution or return of cultural objects to their countries of origin, and although these resolutions have normative value, it is unlikely a court would apply such resolutions to cases lacking the respondent state's consent. The legal obstacles discussed in this chapter demonstrate that seeking restitution of looted cultural objects through international adjudication within the present international legal framework is virtually impossible.

Chapter 4
Restitution Through Civil Litigation: A Case Study of the Dunhuang Manuscripts

4.1 Introduction

Although all legal systems recognize the wrongfulness of theft, in practice, claims upon stolen property may be defeated by countervailing policies protecting bona fide purchasers or by rules applying a concept of 'theft' which is less inclusive than that of the victimized state.[1] Jurisdictions differ in allocating rights and obligations between bona fide purchasers and victims of theft. In general, civil law systems favor good-faith possessors insofar as a bona fide purchaser may obtain valid title even from a thief and exercising due diligence provides strong evidence of an acquisition in good faith. And even though common law systems afford greater protection to victimized owners, the good faith of the purchaser is similarly important. For example, under English common law, a bona fide purchaser is protected by statutes of limitation and in the US a buyer in good faith can obtain valid title from a seller who has nothing more than voidable title.[2]

This chapter discusses the possibility of recovering the Dunhuang manuscripts through transnational civil litigation. French and English institutions hold most of the Dunhuang manuscripts. While French civil law favors the possessor of property, English common law gives priority to its original owner. Because the claimant (most likely the PRC or the municipality of Dunhuang) would most likely obtain a better result by maintaining an action in an English rather than a French court, this chapter discusses China bringing an action against the British holders of Dunhuang manuscripts—the British Museum and the British Library—in an English court.

Because such a case involves both English and Chinese law, conflict of laws issues would also arise. The English court would have to examine various matters

---

[1]Prott and O'Keefe (1989), at 612.

[2]English limitation law, see Section 4 of the Limitation Act 1980; also see L.F. Pinkerton, 'Due Diligence in Fine Art Transactions', Case Western Reserve Journal of International Law 22 (1990), no. 1, at 17; D. Fincham, 'How Adopting the Lex Originis Rule Can Impede the Flow of Illicit Cultural Property', *Columbia Journal of Law & the Arts* 32 (2008), no. 1, at 111.

Z. Liu, *The Case for Repatriating China's Cultural Objects*,
DOI 10.1007/978-981-10-0597-8_4

in sequence: jurisdiction, the characterization of the cause of action, and the choice of law. English courts generally have jurisdiction to entertain *in personam* claims so long as the defendant is either served with process in England or is domiciled in England.[3] In this case, because both the British Museum and the British Library are domiciled in England, English courts would have jurisdiction.

In characterizing a cause of action involving ownership and involuntary transfer of personalty, two aspects must be considered: first, the act of deprivation and any consequence thereof, and second, whether the person ultimately in possession of the item has acquired ownership.[4] In practice, a claimant must also prove he has title to or possessory rights in the objects in dispute. This chapter discusses three questions: (1) whether the claimant has title to or possessory rights to the Dunhuang manuscripts; (2) the legal effect of the deprivation of the manuscripts in 1907; and (3) whether the present possessors have acquired ownership of the manuscripts.

4.2 Characterization of the Cause of Action and Proof of Title

Following jurisdiction, "classification" is the second procedural step in resolving a lawsuit involving foreign law elements filed in an English court. Classification involves allocating the question presented to its correct legal category in order to reveal the relevant rule for determining the correct choice of law.[5] Although according to English lawyers English case law does not detail how classification should be conducted,[6] in the view of Fawcette, Cheshire and North, 'there can be little doubt that classification of the cause of action is in practice effected on the basis of the law of the forum.'[7] Thus an English court would undoubtedly classify an action seeking the return of the Dunhuang manuscripts pursuant to English law.

Excluding an owner from his property constitutes an infringement upon his property rights. When a person seeks to recover an asset held by another, the matter is prima facie within either the law of torts or the law of property. In classical Roman law, a claimant could go into court and simply assert his ownership of the goods in question: 'That cow, Buttercup, is mine!' Such an assertion was called *vindicatio*, a pure proprietary claim.[8] There is no equivalent of *vindicatio* in English common law.

---

[3]Under English law, a claim *in personam* may be negatively described as any claim which is not an Admiralty claim *in rem*, a probate claim, or an administrative claim. See Dicey (2012), at 371, 645.

[4]Prott & O'Keefe (1989), at 367.

[5]Court of Appeal for British Columbia January 14, 1992, Tezcan v. Tezcan, 87 DLR (4TH), 509–511; A. Mayss, *Principle of Conflict of Laws* (3rd ed.), London-Sydney: Cavendish 1999, 6.

[6]Mayss, ibid., at 6–7.

[7]P.M. North, J.J. Fawcett & G.C. Cheshire, *Private International Law* (12th ed.), London: Butterworths 1992, at 45.

[8]See S. Frisby & M. Jones, 'National Report on the Transfer of Movables in England and Wales', in: W. Faber & B. Lurger (eds.), *National Reports on the Transfer of Movables in Europe, Vol. 2*, Munich: Sellier 2011, at 12.

English law protects property rights pursuant to the law of torts rather than property law.[9] Under English common law, the claimant asserts the defendant has committed a tort and must return the property or pay damages.[10] According to Norman Palmer, four principal torts can be committed against the chattels of another: conversion, trespass, negligence, and damage to a reversionary interest.[11] Among the four, the torts specific to chattels, and the most important concerning misappropriation, are conversion and trespass to chattels by asportation (removal).[12]

4.2.1 Trespass to Chattels and Conversion

The tort of trespass to chattels arises out of an immediate and direct interference with a possessory interest without the authority of the person entitled to possession. If trespass is to act as a form of de facto *vindicatio*, the right to possess must provide a claimant with sufficient standing to sue.[13] In addition to showing a direct and voluntary act of trespass, a claimant must prove a mental element in order to succeed.[14] 'It is strongly arguable that the claimant must show negligence (and perhaps also actual loss) in order to establish liability'.[15] Palmer also believes that a person who acts neither deliberately nor negligently in interfering with an other's ownership rights in a chattel cannot be sued for trespass to the chattel.[16]

The distinction between trespass and conversion is well settled: trespass is founded on possession, while conversion is founded upon property.[17] Conversion

[9]Common law is used here in its most narrow sense, that is, as opposed to equity where an action akin to *vindicatio* does exist. Although English law also recognized vindication of property rights with which the defendant has interfered, there is most likely only one principle on which the law of restitution is dependent, namely the principle of unjust enrichment. As Virgo claims, the body of law which exists to secure the reversal of unjust enrichment is the law of restitution. See G. J. Virgo, *The Principles of the Law of Restitution* (2nd ed.), Oxford: Oxford University Press 2006.

[10]Dicey (2012), at 1346.

[11]N. Palmer, 'Conversion, Trespass and Title to Art Work', in: N. Palmer (ed.) *The Recovery of Stolen Art: A Collection of Essays,* London: Kluwer Law International 1998, at 34.

[12]According to Palmer, trespass exists in various forms, affecting land and persons as well as chattels; damage to a reversionary interest is mainly concerned with physical damage and is of subsidiary importance to stolen art; negligence is a general tort which has little direct bearing on the misappropriation of chattels. See Palmer, ibid. at 34; Frisby & Jones, *supra* note 8, at 12.

[13]Frisby & Jones, ibid., at 28–29.

[14]Ibid., at 29.

[15]Ibid.

[16]Palmer, *supra* note 11, at 39; National Coal Board v. Evans [1951] 2 K.B. 861.

[17]Lord Nicholls, Kuwait Airways v. Iraqi Airways Co (Nos. 4 and 5), [2002] UKHL 19; [2002] 2 AC 883.

can occur in many different circumstances.[18] Typical acts of conversion include taking, detention, and disposition of a chattel.[19] Given the large number of circumstances in which it can arise, it is difficult to give a comprehensive definition of conversion. The most common case law definition states: 'dealing with goods in a manner inconsistent with the right of the true owner amounts to a conversion, provided that it is also established that there is an intention on the part of the defendant in so doing to deny the owner's right or to assert a right which is inconsistent with the owner's right.'[20] Most legal historians believe conversion grew out of detinue, early common law's principal action for the protection of a claimant's interests in his chattels.[21] According to Simon Douglas, conversion owes much to fifteenth and sixteenth century plaintiffs' use of various tactics to counter the deleterious effects of a rigid pleading system. Detinue initially meant a misappropriation of a chattel. A misappropriation reveals two facts: 'first, it means that the owner has been excluded from his goods; second, it means that the defendant is using the goods as his own'.[22] An action of conversion can be based on either of these facts.[23] Conversion is a tort of strict liability; the basis of liability in conversion is the exclusion of the owner from his goods.[24] "It is enough that a

---

[18]Where the defendant possesses or controls the chattel, three possible forms of judgment are available: (a) an order requiring delivery of the goods and payment of any consequential damages; (b) an order requiring delivery of the goods but giving the defendant the alternative of paying damages by reference to the value of the goods, together with (in either alternative) payment of any consequential damages; or (c) damages. See section 3(2) of Torts (Interference with Goods) Act 1977. Although relief under section 3(2) is at the discretion of the court and the claimant may choose between the other two sections, in practice, the measure of damages in a successful claim is generally the market value of the chattel at the time of its conversion. For this reason the action has been described as the 'forced judicial sale of the chattel to the defendant.' Frisby & Jones, *supra* note 8, at 18; J. Ulph, 'Tracing and Recovering Stolen Art or the Proceeds of Sale', in: N. Palmer (ed.), *The Recovery of Stolen Art: A Collection of Essays*, London: Kluwer Law International 1998 at 74.

[19]S. van Erp & B. Akkermans (eds.), *Cases, Materials and Text on Property Law,* Oxford: Hart 2012, at 200.

[20]Lancashire & Yorkshire Ry v. MacNicoll, [1918] LJ(KB) 601 at 605.

[21]S. Douglas, 'The Nature of Conversion', *The Cambridge Law Journal* 68 (2009), no. 1, at 205–206.

[22]Ibid., at 206.

[23]In a recent case, three basic features of conversion are summarized. First, the defendant's conduct was inconsistent with the rights of the owner (or other person entitled to possession). Second, the conduct was deliberate, not accidental. Third, the conduct was so extensive an encroachment on the rights of the owner as to exclude him from use and possession of the goods. The contrast is with lesser acts of interference. If these cause damage they may give rise to claims for trespass or negligence, but they do not constitute conversion.' See Kuwait Airways v. Iraqi Airways Co (No. 3), [2002] 2 AC 883 at p. 1084 per Lord Nicholls; al see Douglas, ibid. at 206.

[24]Douglas, ibid. at 223.

defendant wilfully does an act inconsistent with the rights of the owner: there is no need for him to even know of any better 'rights' to the chattel".[25] Any person, however innocently, who obtains possession of the goods of a person who has been fraudulently deprived of them, and disposes of those goods for his own benefit, or for that of another person, is guilty of conversion.[26] Merely receiving goods under an unauthorized sale can amount to conversion. For instance, an innocent purchaser of a sculpture from a thief, or from a previous buyer from the thief, commits a conversion against the true owner by buying and taking delivery of the sculpture. But the buyer will not be liable in conversion if he gets a valid title under one of the statutory exceptions to the general principle of *nemo dat quod non habet* (You cannot give what you don't have). The seller himself (who may be no less innocent) commits a conversion by selling the object, and it makes no difference whether the buyer gets a valid title or not.[27]

The right to possess is one of the bundle of rights that make up property rights, so in this sense, trespass to goods by asportation overlaps with conversion. A principal difference between the two torts lies in the burden of proof in litigation: conversion is a tort of strict liability, but trespass requires the alleged tortfeasor to act deliberately or negligently. As a result, it is easier for the claimant to prevail when suing in conversion. In practice, most cases concerning misappropriation of works of art are brought in English courts in conversion.[28] Assuming the claimant sues in conversion in an English court for return of the Dunhuang manuscripts and the case is classified by the court as conversion, the next question arising is the qualification of the claimant, that is, whether the claimant is entitled to sue.

4.2.2 *Had the Claimant Acquired the Title?*

Palmer emphasizes that 'the mere fact that a person owns a chattel does not qualify him to sue for its conversion. The claimant must show either that he had possession of the goods at the material time or that he had an immediate right of possession'.[29] In the present case, the manuscripts were in the actual possession of the caretaker Taoist Wang, when the alleged misappropriation took place, and the claimant can only establish his right by proving that he had an immediate right of possession. 'A majority of the Court of Appeals has held that a person who relies on an immediate

[25] Frisby & Jones, *supra* note 8, at 13.

[26] Erp & Akkermans, *supra* note 19, at 199.

[27] Palmer, *supra* note 11, at 35.

[28] See Government of the Islamic Republic of Iran v. The Barakat Galleries Limited, [2007] EWHC 705, reversed by [2007] EWCA Civ 1374.

[29] Palmer, *supra* note 11, at 37.

right to possession in his action for conversion must show that the right is derived from some proprietary right in the goods'.[30]

The manuscripts were discovered by Taoist Wang in the sealed Library Cave in 1900 and Taoist Wang 'sold' the majority of the manuscripts to explorers from 1907 onwards (see Chap. 1).[31] In this case, how can the claimant show his immediate right of possession derived from some proprietary right in the manuscripts? In the 1900s, Qing law was in force in China, thus it is necessary to look into the Qing law regarding the ownership of treasure trove. Some might doubt the existence of civil law in traditional China which lacked the concept of a separation of civil law and criminal law.[32] In effect, ancient China did have civil law, even though it was considered less important than criminal law. The most important legal code in the Qing dynasty is The Great Qing Code, also known as Ta Tsing Leu Lee, which combined all laws in a single corpus.[33] As Jing Junjian observes, The Great

[30]Ibid., at, 37–38.

[31]The reasons for the sealing of the Library and its timing have long interested scholars. They have put forth various theories, and the most influential are the waste-repository hypothesis proposed by Sir Aurel Stein and the refuge hypothesis proposed by Paul Pelliot. On the basis of the fragments he found in the Cave, Stein held that the Cave contained scared waste collected from different shrines in Dunhuang. The absence of Xi Xia writings, as well as the chaotic piling up of documents, paintings, wall coverings, Buddhist statutes, and steles led Pelliot to conclude the Cave was sealed off in 1035 as a storage room when the Xi Xia invaded Dunhuang. Rong Xinjiang (1999–2000), at 247–250.

[32]Some scholars argue that civil matters were more societal than legal in nature in ancient China, because they were rooted in and protected by the social relationships of the parties. As observed by Chang Wejen, the Confucian tradition accepted that it was possible to claim as one's 'due', but not as 'right', 'entitlement', or 'share'. Anne Osborne also writes 'The surest guarantee of one's rights seems to have been their acknowledgement by the local community.' See W. Chang, 'Confucian Theory of Norms and Human Rights', in: W.T. de Bary & T. Weiming (eds.), *Confucianism and Human Rights*, New York: Columbia University Press 1998, at 132; A. Osborne, 'Property, Taxes and State protection of Rights', in: M. Zelin, J.K. Ocko & R. Gardella (eds.), *Contract and Property in Early Modern China*, Stanford: Stanford University Press 2004, at 156; also see J.K. Ocko & D. Gilmartin, 'State, Sovereignty, and the People: A Comparison of the "Rule of Law" in China and India,' *The Journal of Asian Studies* 68 (2009), no. 1, at 74; Zhang Jinfan, *Civil Law in the Qing Dynasty* (in Chinese), Beijing: Chinese University of Political Science and Law Press 1998, pp. 1–20.

[33]The Great Qing Code was based on The Great Ming Code, one of the most important law codes in Chinese history. As described by Jing, The Great Qing Code includes sections of 'terms and general principles', as well as statutes and sub-statutes regulating government personnel, population/household, rites, the military, and the punishment of crime. They include provisions concerning the imperial clan, government appointment, the civil economy, rites, military government, criminal penalties, public works, etc., of which the criminal statutes are the most important. The 'minor matters' included mainly stipulations in the 'household law' section under the major categories of debts, markets, land and houses, and marriage, and subcategories such as succession and family division. However, Jing argues this Code 'was not a code in the modern sense but rather a compilation of ethical values, enforced by criminal penalties, dealing with the relationship of the individual vis-a-vis the family and the state'. See J. Jing, 'Legislation Related to the Civil Economy in the Qing Dynasty' (transl. by M.H. Sommer), in: P.C.C. Huang (ed.), *Civil Law in Qing and Republican China*, Stanford: Stanford University Press 1994, at 42.

Qing Code contains many statutes and sub-statutes concerning disputes between private parties over property rights.[34] In addition to the Great Qing Code, other legislations like the *Daqing huidian (大清会典), Hubu zeli (户部则例),* also contains civil provisions.[35] These statutory civil provisions, together with customary law and case law constitute the main sources of the Qing civil law.[36]

Although The Great Qing Code was by no means a comprehensive civil code, it did contain provisions on the ownership of treasure trove. The second paragraph of Article 151 of The Great Qing Code provides: 'If someone digs up buried ownerless objects on public or private land, he is permitted to keep and use it. But if the objects are ancient relics that are not appropriate for ordinary people to possess, like bells, tripods, seals, or any rare or unusual object, he shall send the objects to the governments within thirty days. Otherwise, he shall be sentenced to 80 stokes of the heavy bamboo, and the items will be forfeited to the government.' Historically, many Chinese feudal codes contained similar provisions concerning the ownership of unearthed treasure trove since the Tang dynasty,[37] and contemporary Chinese law deals with the ownership of unearthed cultural relics in a similar way.[38] Under the Qing law, a finder does not have ownership of discovered treasure trove, and

---

[34]Ibid., at 43.

[35]Daqing huidian was the largest statute compilation of the Qing dynasty, and Hubu Zeli was first codified in the Qianlong period, amended every five years, which regulated on government functions, population, taxation, customs, treasuries, salt, currency, etc. See Zhang, J., *supra* note 32, at 18–20.

[36]Ordinary Chinese resorted to local magistrate courts to resolve intractable disputes. Disputes over property, family, and commercial affairs occupied a large proportion of the typical magistrate's docket (perhaps a third of all cases). Magistrates enforced contracts for land sales and commercial transactions as the economy boomed in the eighteenth and nineteenth centuries. Notably, on some issues the customary law was conflicting with statute law. It was not until The Draft Civil Code of the Great Qing of 1911 that the hierarchy of the various sources was specified, but this Draft never came into force because the Qing dynasty was overturned in 1912. This Draft provides that statutes take precedent of customary law, and customary law precedes judicial logic. Zhang Jinfan believes that the unspecified hierarchy of the sources of Qing civil law gave magistrates discretion in deciding which sources should be applied. The discretion caused uncertainty in legal practice and sometimes magistrates abused their discretion. In most of the cases, magistrates relied on both statute law and local custom. See Zhang, J., *supra* note 32, pp. 1-40.

[37]In ancient Chinese law, the unearthed objects are called Sucang wu (宿藏物). The Qing law inherited the provisions from the Ming law, which was the continuity of the Tang law and the Song law. See Article 447 of The Great Tang Code (Tanglv shuyi juan); *Vol.* 27 of the Criminal Statute of the Song dynasty (Song xingtong).

[38]The PRC's Property Law promulgated in 2007 contains similar rules on the ownership of the finding. In China's socialist legal system, property is classified into three distinct categories: private property, state property and collective property. Article 114 stipulates that, as regards the finding of a drifter or the discovery of an object buried underground or a hidden property, the relevant provisions on the finding of a lost-and-found property shall apply by analogy. Where there is any other provision in such laws as the law concerning the protection of cultural relics, such provisions shall prevail. The Law on Protection of Cultural Relics (amended in 2002) provides that cultural relics unearthed within the territories of the People's Republic of China, except where otherwise provided for by regulations of the state, are owned by the state (Article 5).

traditional Chinese legal practice establishes that treasure trove belongs to the state. Thus the claimant can argue that Taoist Wang did not acquire ownership of the Dunhuang manuscripts according to The Great Qing Code. Instead, the claimant is the rightful owner of the Dunhuang manuscripts based on the Qing law and succession.

Exclusion of Foreign Law

In English conflict of laws, the reservation of public policy has been regarded as a necessary general term to exclude foreign law, and it is now well settled that this doctrine 'should only be invoked in clear cases in which the harm to the public is substantially incontestable, and does not depend upon the idiosyncratic inferences of a few judicial minds.'[39] In addition to the doctrine of public policy, another well-established general principle to exclude foreign law is the non-enforceability of penal or revenue laws, or other public laws of another country.[40]

As regards to a foreign state's claim for property, whether English courts will recognize the title alleged by a foreign state depends on the way in which it has acquired ownership. Where the foreign state has acquired title under its law to property within its jurisdiction in a case not involving compulsory acquisition of title from private parties, English courts will recognize the title.[41] In contrast, if a state has acquired title under public law by confiscation or compulsory process from the former owner, it will not be able to claim the property in England from the former owner or its successors in title, unless it has had possession.[42] If it has taken the property into its possession then its claim will be treated as depending on recognition; if it has no possession it will be seeking to exercise its sovereign authority.[43] This means if a chattel is removed to England before it has been reduced to the possession of the foreign state, it is submitted that the foreign state has a valid but unenforceable title.

For instance, in the case New Zealand v. Ortiz and others, the New Zealand government sought to recover a valuable Maori carving which had been illegally exported from New Zealand and bought by Ortiz. Under a New Zealand statute historic articles exported without permission were forfeited to the Crown. In this case, the New Zealand government had never taken the carving into its possession, and the English Court of Appeals did not enforce the compulsory confiscation of

[39]Dicey (2012), at 99.

[40]Ibid., at 107–108.

[41]Ibid., at 120.

[42]Ibid., at 120–121.

[43]Ibid., at 121.

the New Zealand statute.[44] And the recent case between Iran and the Barakat Galleries shows that English courts would recognize state proprietary right in goods derived from legislation of another country.[45] In that case, Iran based its legal title on Iranian cultural property law (The 1979 Legal Bill), and the Court of Appeal recognized this. The Court distinguished between export restrictions and assertion of ownership. The former is clearly a public law and unenforceable absent another treaty obligation while the latter is justifiable. When a state owns property in the same way as a private citizen, there is no impediment to recovery.[46]

In the Dunhuang manuscripts case, the claimant would probably base the acquisition of title to the manuscripts on the Qing law. Although The Great Qing Code is of public law nature, the rules providing state ownership of treasure trove would be recognized by the English courts. But whether this claim would be enforced by the English courts depends on whether the claimant has had possession of the manuscripts before they were removed to England. Documents show that Taoist Wang reported the finds from the Library Cave to the local magistrates after the discovery, but it was not taken serious at first. In March 1904, the local magistrate came to check and made an inventory of the content of the Cave, and ordered Taoist Wang to take care of the site (see Chap. 1). The claimant can argue that it had been reduced to its possession because of the act of the local magistrate in 1904, and Taoist Wang was acting as a custodian.

4.3 The Deprivation and Its Effects

In this case, if Taoist Wang is deemed to be a custodian to take care of the manuscripts, could he give a valid title of the manuscripts to others in 1907? The answer to this question might vary depending on the application of law since this case involves Chinese law and English law. Here questions arise as to whether Chinese law or English law governs the transfer. This section will first look into the English choice of law concerning the involuntary transfer, and then analyze the applicable law in this case.

---

[44]In the first trial, the judge held that this New Zealand statute was not penal law, and there was no general category of non-enforceability of foreign public law. But the Court of Appeals reversed this decision on the ground that this statute was a public law which would not be enforced. New Zealand v. Ortiz and Others, [1982] Q.B. 349, reversed by [1984] A.C.1 (CA and HL).

[45]Government of the Islamic Republic of Iran v. The Barakat Galleries Limited, [2007] EWHC 705, reversed by [2007] EWCA Civ 1374.

[46]In this case the owner of the Barakat Galleries purchased some antiquities from the auction houses in France, Germany, and Switzerland for approximately $500,000. Iran asserted these antiquities were illegally exported between 2000 and 2004 and it had legal title based on The 1979 Legal. After being refused by Barakat to return the antiquities, Iran sued in London's High Court. The High Court held that, in the absence of explicit evidence, it could not establish Iran's title of the antiquities under Iranian law. Without title, Iran could not bring an action under the English law of conversion. But the Court of Appeal reversed the decision of the High Court.

4.3.1 Choice of Law

The UK has implemented the European private international law regulations: Rome I and Rome II.[47] These regulations have universal application, selecting both the law of Member States and non-member states alike. But the cause of action in the Dunhuang manuscripts case took place before the entry into force of these regulations, thus the case falls outside the scope of the Rome regulations.[48] Thus to determine the choice of law in this case, rules of the English conflict of laws would be considered. Under English conflict of laws, it is well settled that the validity of a transfer of chattels depends upon the law of the country in which the transfer takes place (*lex situs*).[49] In the case *Winkworth v. Christie*, Manson and Woods Ltd., the plaintiff had a collection of Japanese works of art, which were stolen from his estate in England and taken to Italy. The second defendant bought this collection in good faith in Italy, who delivered the objects to the first defendants in England for auction by Christie's on his behalf. The plaintiff then issued proceedings against the defendants founded in conversion and detinue, aiming at recovering the works and asserting his title.[50] In this case, the choice of law determines the ownership of the collection, because English law favors the original owner whereas Italian law protects good faith acquisition. That means under Italian law, the second defendant had obtained valid title of the objects; but under English law, the plaintiff's title will prevail. In the judgement, it is ruled that English law decides whether the theft in England gave the thief a valid title, but has no power to decide whether the thief (or some other person) could give a valid title to others if the goods were out of England. Whether the second defendant has acquired title is determined by Italian law because the transfer took place in Italy.[51]

Following this rule, the validity of the transfer of the manuscripts between Taoist Wang and Stein and its effect on the proprietary rights are governed by Chinese law, because the manuscripts were in China at the time of the transfer.

---

[47]Rome I governs the law applicable to contractual obligations, while Rome II defines the conflict-of-law rules applicable to non-contractual obligations in civil and commercial matters. Rome I was implemented in the UK with effect from December 17, 2009 (S.I. 2009/3064), and Rome II has been applicable in the UK since January 11, 2009 (S.I. 2008/2986).

[48]Rome I only applies to contracts that are concluded as from December 17, 2009, and Rome II shall apply to events giving rise to damage which occurs after its entry into force (January 1, 2009).

[49]See Dicey (2012), at 1336; The governing case for the lex situs approach is the decision of Cammell v. Sevell [1853] CExch, and this principle has been reaffirmed by many subsequent cases.

[50]Detinue is one of Forms of Action in the old common law, used to recover personal property from a person who refuses to give it up. Winkworth v. Christie, Manson and woods Ltd. [1980] 1 All E.R. 1121.

[51]Ibid.

Changes in Lex Causae

Once Chinese law is to govern the validity of the transfer and its effects, notably, Chinese law has undergone a dramatic transformation since the discovery of the Dunhuang manuscripts in 1900: from a feudal legal system in the Qing dynasty, to the six codes modelled after European legal codes by the Nationalist government, then to the socialist legal system after the CPC took power. In property law, specific rules on original acquisition, good faith acquisition, and extinctive prescription have changed drastically in the past 100 years. Under such circumstance, which Chinese law applies? This question concerns the changes in the content of the lex causae.[52]As stated by Morris, 'changes in the *lex causae* present much the most important and difficult problems of time in the conflict of laws, especially when the change purports to have retrospective effect'.[53]

There are three theoretically possible ways to solve the problems caused by the changes in *lex causae*: it could refuse to take any account of the change, or resort to its own rules of statutory interpretation, or leave the issue to the transitional law of the *lex causae*.[54] Morris opines that 'the overwhelming weight of opinion among writers is that the forum should apply the *lex causae* in its entirety, including its transitional rules. This is certainly the prevailing practice of courts on the continent of Europe'.[55] That means the third solution—leaving the issue to the transitional law of the *lex causae*- finds the favor with the writers and the courts in most countries as the 'most convenient, rational and in greatest harmony with the tenets of private international law'.[56] This is probably the prevailing practice in the English courts as well.[57] But Morris points out that public policy may occasionally induce the forum to refuse recognition to foreign retrospective laws.[58]

---

[52]Morris stresses that three different types of problem concerning the time factor in the conflict of laws have been identified by writers: changes in the conflict rule of the forum; changes in the connecting factor, and changes in the content of the lex causae (the law chosen by the forum to apply to determine substantive issues). In the Dunhuang manuscripts case, the English conflict rule and the connecting factor (place of the transfer) is not changed, so I do not discuss these two problems in this case study. See J.H.C. Morris, 'The Time Factor in the Conflict of Laws,' *The International and Comparative Law Quarterly* 15 (1966), no. 2, at 422; Dicey (2012), at 63–68.

[53]Morris, ibid., at 426–427; Dicey (2012), at 68.

[54]J.K. Grodecki, 'Conflicts of laws in Time', *British Year Book of International Law* 35 (1959), at 64.

[55]Transitional rules of law govern the reach of new laws backward and forward through time. Some take the form or rules or presumptions for construing statutes or judicial decisions if their intended temporal scope is not clear. Others, such as constitutional rules, limit the permissible temporal scope of legal rules. See Morris, *supra* note 52, at 427; Dicey (2012), at 68.

[56]Grodecki, *supra* note 51, at 64.

[57]But there is at least one case contrary to this general view: Lynch v. Provisional Government of Paraguay, (1871) L.R.2P.&D. 268. See Grodecki, ibid., at 64–82; Morris, ibid., at 427, 484; Dicey (2012), at 68.

[58]Morris, ibid., at 427, 484.

Therefore, when the English courts refer to the Chinese *lex causae*, the Chinese rules of statutory interpretation, the transitional law will also be included in its reference. As a general principle, the transitional rule in Chinese civil law is that: 'For cases accepted after January 1, 1987, if the civil conduct occurs before 1987, the laws and policies at the time of occurrence of the civil conduct shall be applied; if there is no concrete provision in the laws and policies then and there, the General Principles of the Civil Law may be applied by analogy'.[59] Accordingly, the Chinese law of the time when the transfer occurred shall first apply to determine the substantive issues of the Dunhuang manuscripts case. If the law of that time provides no rules or policies in this respect, the contemporary Chinese civil law is to be applied by analogy.[60]

4.3.2 Application of Chinese Law

The lack of concept of the separation of civil law and public law has been discussed in Sect. 4.2.1 of this chapter. In effect, traditional Chinese law used penal law to protect proprietary rights. It is held 'the most powerful evidence for the existence of strong rights of property lies in the imperial statutes relating to theft'.[61] Encroachment on property has been criminalized since the Pre-Qin period in China, but at that time all kinds of encroachment on property were called 'theft' or 'robbery' ('Dao'). After the Qin state gained control over the whole of China, the trade development stimulated the emergence of folk debit and credit, unjust enrichment, embezzlement, etc. The Qin Code for the first time in China's history criminalizes the act of taking possession of another's money or property under his custody and refusing to return it. The Qin Code also criminalises encroachment on public property by governmental functionaries through taking advantage of his office, including appropriating, stealing, swindling or by other means illegally

[59]Article 196 of the Opinion (For Trial Use) of the Supreme People's Court on Questions concerning the Implementation of the General Principles of the Civil Law of the People's Republic of China. In Mainland China, there is not a civil code yet. The General Principles of the Civil Law of the People's Republic of China 1986 provides the general rules on civil matter as indicated in its title, some specific rules have been amended by new legislations and interpreted by the People's Supreme Court. The judicial interpretations promulgated by the People's Supreme Court are of great weight in the practice of trials. The Opinion was adopted at the Judicial Committee of the Supreme People's Court on January 26, 1988.

[60]Also see Huang Jin & Du Huanfang, 'Chinese Judicial Practice in Private International Law: 2003', *Chinese Journal of International Law* 7 (2008), no. 1, at 240–242.

[61]M. Zelin, 'A Critique of Rights of Property in Prewar China', in: M. Zelin, J.K. Ocko & R. Gardella (eds.), *Contracts and Property in Early Modern China*, Stanford: Stanford University Press 2004, at 20.

taking public property into his own possession. The encroachment on public property by governmental functionaries was criminated as 'theft' in the *Qin Code*.[62] Since the Tang dynasty, theft of property had been treated as a major crime and defined very broadly.[63] The Great Tang Code systemised six forms of theft of property, called '*Liuzang*', including robbery, ordinary stealing, accepting property and subverting the law, accepting property without subverting law, accepting property from those under his administration, and embezzlement. In the Great Ming Code, the six forms of theft were altered to supervisors or guardians stealing money or supplies from granaries or treasuries, ordinary persons stealing money or supplies from granaries or treasuries, ordinary stealing, accepting property and subverting law, accepting property without subverting law, embezzlement.[64] The six forms of theft in the penal section of The Great Qing Code underlie the protection of property in the Qing law.[65] For example, the provisions on 'stealing', 'stealing property from the Imperial Treasury', 'theft of force', 'wrongful taking in the daytime', 'obtaining property from the government or an individual by deceit and cheating' and so on, all touch on this matter. It is suggested that the principle of protecting private property thoroughly permeated The Great Qing Code.[66] It regulates the theft of money or supplies by supervisors or guardians from granaries or treasuries in Article 264: 'Whenever a supervisor or guardian himself steals money, supplies, or similar things from a granary or treasury, do not distinguish between principal and accessory. Punish on the basis of all the illegally obtained property taken together.'[67] In the opinion of the Chinese scholar in Chinese legal history Zhang Jinfan, one of the features of protecting property by the Qing law is that the punishment of violation of government property is heavier than that of private property, because the title of government property concerned the economic interest of the state and constituted the source of income for the ruling class.[68]

[62]Zhang, J., *supra* note 32, at 107–108.

[63]Zelin, *supra* note 61, at 20.

[64]T. Cheng, 'From the Tang *liuzang* to the Ming *liuzang*' (in Chinese), *Fudan Xuebao* (Social Science) 1984, no. 6, pp. 91–95; Jiang Yonglin, *The Mandate of Heaven and The Great Ming Code*, Seattle: University of Washington Press 2011, at 198.

[65]Studies on the judgments ruled by the magistrates show that pure civil claims were dealt with as civil cases; a civil claim annexed to a criminal case was treated as a criminal case. Zhang, J., *supra* note 32, at 27.

[66]Jing, J., *supra* note 33, at 50.

[67]Stealing money or supplies by supervisors or guardians from granaries or treasuries was a grave crime in the Qing legal system. Either principals or accessories of the theft shall be found guilty and punished in proportion to the total amount of the theft, without paying any regard to their roles in the offense and shares of the property. A criminal shall be sentenced to death if the value of the stolen objects exceeds 40 taels of silver. W.C. Jones (transl.), *The Great Qing Code*, Oxford: Clarendon Press 1994, at 243.

[68]Zhang, J., *supra* note 32, at 107.

If the claimant is successful in establishing his title to the manuscripts, it is undoubted that Taoist Wang's disposal of the manuscripts constituted a crime under Chinese law, since stealing government property was a criminal offence in traditional Chinese law. But if Stein acquired the manuscripts in good faith, could he acquire a valid title to the manuscripts?

Good Faith Acquisition

Traditional Chinese law did not establish a general rule concerning good faith acquisition, though some scholars claim that in ancient China there was some thought of good faith acquisition. They claim that the recently unearthed *Shuihudi Qin Bamboo Texts* reflected the thought of good faith acquisition in ancient China. The Bamboo Texts record the Qin law and governmental documents, which included a case relevant to good faith acquisition. A thief stole a coat from an original owner, and then the thief sold the coat to a buyer at a reasonable price. The thief used the money from selling the coat to purchase a piece of cloth. When the thief was arrested, only the cloth should be returned to original owner; the coat purchased by the buyer was not returned. This case contained the thought of good faith acquisition in ancient Chinese law. In spite of this, it is generally agreed that a system of good faith acquisition was not established due to the underdeveloped civil law in ancient China.[69]

A purchaser could not obtain a valid title to stolen goods through good faith acquisition in the Qing dynasty. This point of view can be ascertained by one of the cases provided in The Great Qing Code. A boatman was hired to ship some grains for taxation for the government. The boatman did not fulfil his duty to ship the grains to destination but sold the grains to a third party on half way. When the government cracked this case, the boatman was punished in accord with Article 264, and the people working in the harbor were also penalized for not reporting the theft. The grains which had been sold to a third party were confiscated by the government, and the buyer did not get the title even if he was in good faith (Article 264.03). This boatman case is comparable to the Dunhuang manuscripts case. In these two cases, the subject matters—the grains and the Dunhuang manuscripts—were public property according to Qing law, and they were entrusted to individuals, who were not governmental functionaries. And the public property was sold to other parties by the trustees in both cases, without authorization of the rightful owners. In accordance with to the precedent set in the boatman case, the buyer could not get a valid title from the trustee, and the trustee and the buyer were both punished for breaking the Qing law. Thus in the Dunhuang manuscripts case, Taoist Wang's disposal of the manuscripts was considered to be a theft under Qing law and the defendant could not get a valid title to the manuscripts even if he was acting in good faith.

[69]The Draft Civil Code of the Great Qing 1911(Articles 1278 &1279) provides a system of good faith acquisition for the first time in Chinese history, but it never went into force. Yu Kongfen 'Study on Good Faith Acquisition' (in Chinese), *Nandu Xuetan* 2000, no. 1, at 68.

In fact, contemporary Chinese civil law has not yet established a rule whether stolen goods are subject to good faith acquisition.[70] In China, original owners of stolen goods mainly recover their goods from the judicial organs. For example, if an object is stolen from an original owner and then sold to a third person, the police or courts will restore the object to the original owner when the case is solved, even if the third person has acted in good faith. If the original owner could not be found, the goods would be delivered up to the national coffer.[71] Even though this practice has been criticized, there is no rule protecting the interest of bona fide purchaser of stolen goods in China. Moreover, if the stolen goods are state-owned property, no people can ever have a valid title to state-owned property. Last but not least, cultural relics are limited merchantable goods provided by Chinese law, the circulation of which is subject to administrative law.[72] The flow of cultural relics is

[70]Article 89 of the Opinion (For Trial Use) of the Supreme People's Court on Questions concerning the Implementation of the General Principles of the Civil Law of the People's Republic of China is also deemed a provision on good faith. But it is only dealing with the situation of joint ownership. Article 106 of the PRC's Property Law 2007 provides that: 'In case a person unauthorized to dispose a realty or chattel alienates the realty or chattel to an assignee, the owner is entitled to recover the realty or chattel. The assignee shall obtain the ownership of the realty or chattel if meeting all of the following conditions, unless it is otherwise prescribed by law: (a) to accept the realty or chattel in good faith; (b) to purchase the realty or chattel at a reasonable price; and (c) in case registration is required by law, the alienated realty or chattel shall have been registered, while in case registration is not required, the delivery thereof shall have been accomplished. In case, according to the preceding paragraph, an assignee obtains the ownership of a realty or chattel, the original owner may require the person unauthorized to dispose of the realty or chattel to compensate for his losses. In case a related party obtains any other form of real right in good faith, the preceding two paragraphs shall apply by reference.' And article 107 provides an exception to the good faith acquisition. If it is a lost property, the original can reclaim it within two years from the date when he knows or should know who the assignee is. If the assignee purchases the lost property through auction or from a qualified shop, the original owner shall pay the assignee the amount purchasing the property.

[71]This general rule does not apply to some cases which concerns fraudulence governed by the law of bills. See Xiong Bingwan, 'On the Good Faith Acquisition of Stolen Property and its Repossessing Right' (in Chinese), *Falv Kexue* 2008, no. 2, at 135–137.

[72]In contemporary Chinese civil law, goods are categorized into merchantable goods and limited merchantable goods. Merchantable goods can be freely circulated between different civil persons; but the circulation of limited merchantable goods are prohibited or limited by law. These limited merchantable goods at least include two categories: (1) property exclusively owned by the state, such as mineral deposits, waters and sea areas; (2) goods which are not exclusively owned by the state but their circulations are prohibited or limited, such as military explosives, firearms, ammunition, narcotics, drugs, gold, cultural relics, pornographic publications and audio-visual products, etc. Goods are deemed to be merchantable unless it is otherwise prescribed by law. In China circulation of goods between equal civil persons is subject to civil law (including contract law and property law); and properties exclusively owned by state are prohibited to be circulated, which is specified in General Principles of the Civil Law (Article 81). Citizens can be the owner of limited merchantable goods in the second category and the circulation of such limited merchantable goods are subject to administrative law. Legislations on limited merchantable goods are dispersed in various administrative regulations, in order to protect the public interest, state ownership and the right of the weak parties. See Wei Zhenying (ed.), *Civil Law* (in Chinese), Beijing: Beijing University Press and Higher Education Press 2006, at 125.

subject to the Law on Protection of Cultural Relics and other administrative regulations. As a general rule, only the private-owned cultural relics are subject to trade; exportation of all cultural relics have to be authorized by the Chinese custom authority.[73] To summarize, if Chinese law is applied to the Dunhuang manuscripts case, either the Qing law or the contemporary Chinese law, transaction of state-owned cultural relics can never be legal; no bona fide purchaser could have a valid title to the state-owned cultural relics.

4.3.3 Exclusion of Chinese Law

It has been discussed in the proceeding sections that a foreign law can be excluded by an English court due to the public policy or the unenforceability of the foreign law. In this case, because of the non-separation of criminal law and civil law in The Grate Qing Code, and the public law nature of the restriction of the free flow of cultural relics, there is a possibility that the English court would not apply the Chinese law to govern the deprivation of the manuscripts. Under such circumstances, English law would be applied.

'English law, unlike some civil law systems (notably France), start from the position that it is the claim of the original owner which has priority'.[74] English law did not develop a general exception to the *nemo dat* rule like the good faith acquisition. But to strike a balance between the original owner and the bona fide purchaser, English courts and the legislature create the exceptions to the *nemo dat* rule. 'The specific exceptions are quite considerable in scope, and therefore it would be wrong to suggest that good faith acquisition protection is all but lacking in

[73]The Law on Protection of Cultural Relics provides that citizens, legal persons and other organizations, except institutions for the collection of cultural relics, may collect cultural relics obtained through the following channels: (a) lawfully inheriting or accepting as gifts; (b) purchasing from cultural relics stores; (c) purchasing from auction enterprises engaged in auction of cultural relics; (d) mutually exchanging or transferring in accordance with law the cultural relics lawfully owned by individual citizens; or (e) other lawful channels prescribed by the State. Cultural relics, as specified in the preceding paragraph, which are in the collection of citizens, legal persons and other organizations, except the institutions for the collection of cultural relics, may be circulated according to law (Article 50). And Article 51 reiterates the inalienability of state-owned cultural relics, 'no citizens, legal persons or other organizations may purchase or sell the state-owned cultural relics, except ones with the approval of the State'. Due to the special feature of limited merchantable goods, it is generally accepted in Chinese judicial practice that limited merchantable goods including cultural relics are not subject to good faith acquisition.

[74]This rule has been subject to some criticism in its application to contracts for the sale of goods on the ground that it is commercially inconvenient in that it fails to protect buyers in all good faith, who are unaware of the seller's lack of title. See P.B.H. Birks (ed.), *English Private Law: Vol. II, Law of Obligations, Litigation,* Oxford: Oxford University Press 2000, at 235–236.

English law. It is there, but in a wholly unsystematic way'.[75] These exceptions stem from both the common law and statute, including estoppel, voidable title or voidable contract, market overt (abolished in 1995), seller or buyer in possession after sale, mercantile agent and so on.[76] All exceptions to the *nemo dat* rule—apart from the market overt rule—require that the transferor is in possession of the goods with the owner's consent. Where the owner has not consented to the possession of the transferor, all subsequent transactions are, in principle, defective.[77]

It has been observed that 'the law prefers the interest of the third party where the original owner took the risk, or is held to have assumed the risk, that the goods would be sold without his actual authority or was in some way at fault in relation to the sale of goods. Thus a non-owner can pass a valid title to a buyer if he has actual or apparent authority from the owner to enter into the sale or where, by his conduct, the owner is estopped or prevented from asserting his ownership of the goods.'[78] In the Dunhuang manuscripts case, if the defendant can prove that Taoist Wang had actual or apparent authority from his owner to dispose of the manuscripts, the claimant might have been estopped or prevented from asserting his ownership of the goods. According to Salomons, the estoppel is not invoked easily in practice.[79] Firstly, the appearance of authority must be based on a clear and unequivocal representation made by the owner to the third person, or the world at large to effect that he is authorizing the other to dispose of his property. Notably, merely giving another person possession does not amount to conduct that will give rise to an estoppel.[80] Last but not least, the transferee bears the heavy burden of prove (See footnote 79). Where the English law governs the deprivation and its effects, it is unlikely that Stein had got a valid title to the manuscripts through the transfer by Taoist Wang.

[75]A.F. Salomons, 'Good Faith Acquisition of Movables', in: A.S. Hartkamp, M.W. Hesselink, E. H. Hondius, C.E. du Perron & C. Mak, (eds.), *Towards A European Civil Code* (4th rev. and exp. ed.), Alphen a/d Rijn: Kluwer Law International 2011, at 1055–1056.

[76]Ibid.

[77]Ibid.

[78]Birks, *supra* note 74, at 236.

[79]Salomons, *supra* note 75, at 1055–1056.

[80]In the case Moorgate Mercantile Co Ltd v Twitchings, the owner of the goods and the buyer were finance companies and both were members of HPI (Hire Purchase Information), a company set up to keep a register of hire purchase agreements relating to motor vehicles offering additional services to members to reduce the risk of fraud and theft. The buyer received a proposal to buy the car from them, searched the HPI register, found no extant hire purchase agreement registered and bought the car to relate it on hire purchase. The car was subject to an existing hire purchase agreement. Contrary to the usual practice the owners had not registered the hire purchase agreement. In the court decision, it held that the owner owed no duty to the buyer despite the fact that both of them were members of HPI, and the claimant was not estopped. See Moorgate Mercantile Co. Ltd v. Twitchings, [1977], AC 890.

4.4 Has the Possessor Acquired the Title?

Even if Taoist Wang did not get a valid title to the manuscripts, it does not necessarily hinder the present possessor from acquiring a valid title.[81] In general, there are two possibilities for the present possessor to get a valid title to the manuscripts: by transfer, or by the lapse of time. It has been observed that where an object has passed through several hands, the *nemo dat* principle becomes less meaningful and the possibility of a limitation defense arises for the possessor. Here the relationship between Stein and the possessor matters in the acquisition by transfer.

In the *Handbook to the Collections of Sir Aurel Stein* published by the possessor, the collection history of the manuscripts has been described as follows. 'The British Library's Stein Collections have a complicated history resulting from the economics of exploration and the division of artifacts collected by Stein on his three expeditions to Chinese Central Asia. Financial support offered by the Trustees of the British Museum and by the Government of India was acknowledged in a division of his finds made largely on the basis of language, style, and type. All the material was first sent to London for division between the British Museum (various departments) and the Government of India'.[82] In Stein's personal narrative, his second expedition was undertaken under the orders of the Government of India. 'Their final sanction by the Government, with the approval of H.M. Secretary of State for India, was facilitated when the Trustees of the British Museum, accepting the former's suggestion, generously agreed to contribute two-fifths of the actual cost of the expedition, estimated by me at Rs. 36,000 (then £2400)'.[83] "It is a particularly gratifying thought that the large collection of antiques which I succeeded in bringing back as tangible 'archaeological proceeds', including hundreds of paintings of great artistic interest, manuscripts by thousands, etc., has made this share, even from the financial point of view, a very profitable investment."[84] Accordingly, two points can be summed up: first, Stein's expedition was partly funded by the possessor; second, the division of the finds by Stein was acknowledged before the expedition. Stein took the financial support as an investment for the supporters.

Based on the provenance description by the possessor and the personal narrative by Stein, the claimant can argue that Stein acted as an agent of the possessor. In this situation, there has been no successive conversion after the original deprivation, and the legal effects of the first derivation are attributed to the possessor. However, if the possessor has sufficient evidence to prove that Stein resold the manuscripts to the British Museum in England, under English conflict of laws, the legal effects of this

---

[81] A. Parkhouse, 'The Illicit Trade in Cultural Objects: Recent Developments in the United Kingdom', in: B.T. Hoffman (ed.), *Art and Cultural Heritage: Law, Policy and Practice,* New York: Cambridge University Press 2006, at 178.

[82] H. Wang and J. Perkins (eds), Hand book to the Collections of Sir Aurel Stein in the UK, London: The British Museum 2008, at 3.

[83] Stein (1921), *Vol.* I, at vii, viii.

[84] Ibid., at vii, viii.

transfer in England shall be governed by English private law. And if the possessor succeeds in proving that their acquisition of the manuscripts fall within the exceptions to the *nemo dat rule*, the possessor could have acquired a valid title to the manuscripts by transfer under English law. Even if the possessor did not acquire a valid title to the manuscripts by transfer, there is a possibility that the possessor might have acquired the title because of the lapse of time.

4.4.1 Effects of the Lapse of Time

In general, the lapse of time may have different effects on claims: it may lead to the acquisition of a right, or alternatively, to the loss of a right or action. Where the passage of time leads to the acquisition of a right, it is called acquisitive prescription. The loss of a right or action through the lapse of time is called extinctive prescription (limitation of actions), as it leads to the extinction of a right or action.[85] With regard to acquisitive prescription, it can be traced back to the ancient Roman law.[86] Marais finds that the earliest known form of prescription is found in the Twelve Tables, which later became known as usucapio. Initially, the Romans did not distinguish between acquisitive and extinctive prescription.[87] In the view of Jansen, as a result of the technicalities of Roman procedural law and the historical development of Roman prescription law, Roman lawyers confused the acquisitive prescription and extinctive prescription. It can be said that Roman law treated extinctive prescription as a special form of acquisitive prescription. This confusion has been and still is influential in European private law.[88]

Although the influence of Roman law is less significant on common law, English law also has long evidenced a desire to keep stale cases out of courts. But this policy has been applied in an uneven and erratic manner in both real property and personal actions.[89] Heriot states that a statute limiting the time for bringing an action to recover possession of land was first passed in 1207 during the reign of

---

[85]Erp & Akkermans, *supra* note 19, at 701.

[86]E.J. Marais, *Acquisitive Prescription in View of the Property Clause* (dissertation), Stellenbosch: Stellenbosch University 2011, at 17.

[87]As provided in Tabula 6.3, it was possible to acquire both movable and immovable objects through prescription. Two of the requirements for prescription are: (1) continuous possession or use of another's property; (2) for a certain period of time (two years for immovables and one year for movables). But stolen things were excluded from the effects of prescription; this was the case even if a bona fide third party obtained possession of stolen property. During the late republican and classical law periods, prescription finally became known as usucapio. The main difference between usucapio and prescription under the Twelve Tables is the fact that usucapio required the possessor to possess the thing bona fide and just (or valid title). See Marais, ibid., at 18–20.

[88]J.E. Jansen, 'Thieves and Squatters: Acquisitive and Extinctive Prescription in European Property Law', *European Property Law Journal* 1 (2012), no. 1, at 154.

[89]G.L. Heriot, 'A Study in the Choice of Form: Statutes of Limitation and the Doctrine of Laches', *Brigham Young University Law Review* 1992, no. 4, at 924–925.

Henry VIII. The policies behind the statute were that Parliament wanted to guard against the dangers of trying a case for which the relevant evidence had been lost or destroyed and to protect against the uncertainty that arises when potential defendants are left in limbo, not knowing whether or not they will be sued.[90] In equity law, the doctrine of laches addresses the same question. Numerous cases from the era of the statutes of Henry III and James I, in which the court dismissed the action for untimeliness, demonstrate the concern with which equity courts handled the issued. In the nineteenth century, equity courts decided the laches question according to the special circumstances of each case. Power was vested in the equity judge to do what was best.[91] Nevertheless, it is argued recent history has witnessed a near convergence between statutes of limitation and the doctrine of laches. In particular, through the use of discovery rules, many courts have transformed the statute of limitations into a near twin of the doctrine of laches.[92] In English law, the well-known doctrine of adverse possession is more or less the same as the concept of acquisitive prescription in civil law. Based on the statutes of limitation, the doctrine of adverse possession takes these statutes one conceptual step further by providing that the adverse possessor actually gains legal title, displacing the record owner. The notion is that after some extended period of time the law must finally recognize the validity of a long continuing reality.[93] But English law has not developed such acquisitive prescription rule concerning the acquisition of movable property. English law uses the statutes of limitation to exclude a stale case concerning movable property, thus some English lawyers claim that the English rules on limitation of actions perform a role similar to that of the rules of acquisitive prescription as to movables.[94]

Under the Limitation Act 1980, the limitation period applicable to a claim in respect of the conversion of a chattel, and any subsequent conversion of that chattel, is six years from the date of the original conversion. However, where the original conversion constitutes theft, time does not begin to run until the chattel is purchased in good faith (ss. 3(2) and 4).[95]

4.4.1.1 Theft Under English Law

The meaning of theft is not constant, and it changes from legal system to legal system and within the legal system over time.[96] Under Chinese law, Taoist Wang's disposal

---

[90]Ibid., at 925.

[91]Ibid., 927.

[92]Ibid., 967.

[93]L. Berger, 'Unification of the Doctrines of Adverse Possession and Practical Location in the Establishment of Boundaries', *Nebraska Law Review* 78 (1999), no. 1, at 2.

[94]See Frisby & Jones, *supra* note 8, at 130; Erp & Akkermans, *supra* note 19, at 702–703.

[95]The Law Commission, Limitation of Actions, (2001), 19–20.

[96]Prott & O'Keefe, *supra* note 428, at 368.

of the manuscripts has been deemed as theft. Under the Limitation Act 1980, theft includes: (a) any conduct outside England and Wales which would be theft if committed in England and Wales; and (b) obtaining any chattel (in England and Wales or elsewhere) by—(i) blackmail (within the meaning of section 21 of the Theft Act 1968), or (ii) fraud (within the meaning of the Fraud Act 2006) (Section 4(5)).[97]

There was no crime of embezzlement at common law. It was a statutory crime that evolved from larceny. In the *Bazeley's Case*, Bazeley (defendant) was a teller at a bank. In 1799, a customer deposited bank notes and cash for an account. Bazeley deposited most of what he received into the account, but placed one bank note in his pocket, which he later converted to his own use. He was prosecuted for theft. But the court deemed Bazeley's act to be a mere breach of trust but not a felony, because the bank never had possession.[98] This case caused the enactment on embezzlement in English law. The Larceny Act 1861 defines the embezzlement in this way: '[W]hosoever, being a clerk or servant, or being employed for the purpose or in the capacity of a clerk or servant, shall fraudulently embezzle any chattel, money or valuable security which shall be delivered to or received or taken into possession by him for or in the name or on the account of his master or employer, or any part thereof, shall be deemed to have feloniously stolen the same from his master or employer, although such chattel, money or security was not received into the possession of such master or employer otherwise than by the actual possession of his clerk, servant or other person so employed…(Section 68)'. The embezzlement by clerks or servants has been enacted as a form of theft ever since then. In the Dunhuang manuscripts case, if the claimant succeeds in proving that Taoist Wang was entrusted with the manuscripts and he was not authorized to dispose the manuscripts, Taoist Wang's disposal of the Dunhaung manuscripts has been embezzlement, a form to theft under English law.

4.4.1.2 A Purchaser in Good Faith

An action for conversion to recover the goods or their value may be brought at any time against the thief or any person whose possession of the stolen goods is related to the theft. The six-year limitation period will start to run from the date of the first good faith conversion.[99] That means a good faith possessor can rely on the

---

[97]Under the Theft Act 1968, a person is guilty of theft if he dishonestly appropriates property belonging to another with the intention of permanently depriving the other of it. Any assumption by a person of the rights of an owner amounts to appropriation; where property or a right or interest in property is or purports to be transferred for value to a person acting in good faith, no later assumption by him of rights which he believed himself to be acquiring shall, by reason of any defect in the transferor's title, amount to theft of the property.

[98]Rex v. Bazeley 168, Eng. Rep. 517 (1799).

[99]R. Redmond-Cooper, 'Time Limits in Actions to Recover Stolen Art', in: N. Palmer (ed.), *The Recovery of Stolen Art : A Collection of Essays,* London: Kluwer Law International 1998, at 148.

protection by the English limitation law. In this sense, good or bad faith plays a crucial role in the disputes over stolen goods.

'Good faith appears in a wide variety of contexts in English law but is not often defined, and where it is, the definition is not particularly helpful, even for the area or rule in question'.[100] In English law, the burden of proof is on the person who tries to show good faith. The unreported case *De Préval v. Adrian Alan Limited* shows how the courts look on art professionals who fail to carry out sufficient checks.[101] In this case, the plaintiff sought to recover a pair of nineteenth century candelabra which she claimed had been stolen from her in France in 1986. The defendant, an antique dealer, asserted that the disputed candelabra had been bought by its principal shareholder and director (Mr. Alan) from a reputable dealer in New York in 1984, some two years before the theft of the plaintiff's candelabra. The court held that the defendant must have acquired the candelabra between 1986 and 1989. The case turned on whether the plaintiff was barred from bring her claim because there had been a good faith purchase over six years previously. The judge found that given the dealer's expertise as an experienced antique dealer, he ought to have realized that the candelabra were rare and special. So he ought to have doubted the seller's title. The judge held that the defendant had failed to establish that the candelabra were acquired in good faith. This case demonstrates that the degree of good faith required of the possessor seems exaggerated high, and this has been criticized by dealers as imposing unreasonably high standard on them in relation to identifying 'suspicious' goods.[102]

In the Dunhuang manuscripts case where Stein was acting as the agent for the possessor, the possessor bears the burden of proof to show that Stein was acting in good faith during the acquisition. Judging from Stein's personal narrative, it is very

[100]J.F. O'Connor, *Good Faith in English Law,* Aldershot: Ashgate 1999, at 10. The US Uniform Commercial Code defines 'good faith' as 'Honesty in fact and the observance of reasonable commercial standards of fair dealing in the trade'. In French law, 'good faith' means: that the transferee has acquired the asset in the mistaken belief (and thus in good faith) that the transferor is the owner. The mistake of the acquirer must be 'common' in the same sense that any other person placed in the same circumstances would have made the same mistake. This is the objective approach. On the other hand, good faith is evaluated taking into account the intellectual capabilities and personality of the acquirer. This is a subjective approach. Good faith is presumed, but it can be rebutted if either the subjective or the objective approach leads to other conclusion. Article 7(2)(3) of the draft Uniform Law on the Acquisition in Good Faith of Corporeal Movables: 'The transferee must have taken the precautions normally taken in transaction of that kind according to the circumstances of the case'. 'In determining whether the transferee acted in good faith, account shall, inter alia, be taken of the nature of the movables concerned, the qualities of the transferor or his trade, any special circumstances in respect of the transferor's acquisition of the movables known to the transferee, the price, or provisions of the contract and other circumstances in which it was concluded.' For more information, see E.C. Ritaine,' National Report on the Transfer of Movables in France', in: W. Faber & B. Lurger (eds.), *National Reports on the Transfer of Movables in Europe, Vol. 4,* Munich: Sellier 2011, at 134.

[101]Quoted from Redmond-Cooper, *supra* note 527, at 149. For original source, see De Préval v. Adrian Alan Ltd, [1997], QBD.

[102]Redmond-Cooper, ibid., at 149.

unlikely that Stein was a bona fide purchaser. Stein described Taoist Wang and his restored temple before he saw Taoist Wang in this way: 'The first vague rumor had reached me of a great mass of ancient manuscripts which had been discovered by chance several years before hidden away in one of the cave-temple. There these treasures were said to have been locked up again by official order in charge of the Taoist priest who had come upon them.'[103] Stein reiterated this 'rumor' before he acquired the manuscripts. 'From statements heard by us at Tun-Huang it had appeared likely that, when the great find of manuscripts had been officially reported through the Tao-t'ai at Su-chou to the Viceroy of Kan-su, orders had been issued from the latter's Ya-men for the transmission of the specimens, and subsequently for the safe-keeping of the whole collection.'[104] Stein's statement provides strong evidence of his knowledge of the fact that Taoist Wang was ordered officially to safe-guard the manuscripts, and had no authority to dispose the manuscripts.

Furthermore, details show that the 'transaction' between Stein and Taoist Wang was conducted in a shady and suspicious atmosphere. 'It was to keep Wang Tao-shih (Taoist Wang) in a pliable mood and to prevent him from giving away to the nervous flutterings with which the chance of any intrusion and of consequent hostile rumors among his patrons intermittently filled him.'[105] "The Tao-shih in the end had summoned up courage to fall in with my wishes, but with the explicit stipulation that nobody besides us three was to hear what was being transacted, and that as long as I was on Chinese soil the origin of these 'finds' was to be kept entirely secret. He himself was afraid of being seen at night outside his temple quarters. So Chiang Ssu-yeh took it upon himself to be the sole carrier".[106] From many aspects, it is unlikely that Stein was a bona fide purchaser during the transaction of the Dunhuang manuscripts.

4.4.2 *Choice of Limitation Law*

If the Limitation Act 1980 governs the Dunhuang manuscripts case, it is very unlikely that the possessor's rights would be protected by the English limitation law. However, whether the Limitation Act 1980 is applicable in this case depends on the English conflict of laws as to limitation in space, and that in time.

4.4.2.1 Classification of the Limitation: Procedural or Substantive?

At common law, two kinds of statutes of limitation were distinguished: those which bar a remedy, and those which extinguish a right. Statutes that bar a remedy were

[103]Stein (1921), Vol. II, at 801.

[104]Ibid., at 803.

[105]Ibid., at 812.

[106]Ibid., at 813.

procedural, while the statutes that extinguish a right are substantive. This common law rule was well-established.[107] 'In general, the English law as to limitation of actions was regarded as procedural at common law, but ss. 3(2) and 17 of the Limitation Act 1980 were probably substantive since they expressly extinguish the title of the former owner'.[108]

The Foreign Limitation Periods Act 1984 adopts the general principle that the limitation rules of the *lex causae* are to be applied in actions in England, even if those rules do not lay down any limitation period for the claim. This general principle is subject to an exception based on public policy.[109] In accordance with this general principle, English limitation rules are not to be applied unless English law is the *lex causae.* A foreign limitation period is now regarded as a substantive matter rather than a procedural one, and it is irrelevant that under *lex causae* the limitation period would be regarded as procedural.[110]

In the *City of Gotha* case, a priceless painting of Dutch mannerism was taken from the City of Gotha to the Soviet Union in the 1940s. It was smuggled from Moscow to West Berlin in the 1980s, acquired by Mina Breslav in 1988 and received by Sotheby's in London on November 29, 1988. Cobert bought the painting from Mina Breslav in March 1989. The City of Gotha and Federal Republic of Germany claimed the return of the painting from Cobert. One of the key issues of this case is whether the claim has been time barred. Under German limitation law, the right to recovery is barred after period of thirty years, and the time begins to run when the claim arises. The claim was not statute barred under German law. Pursuant to the Foreign Limitation Periods Act 1984, the English High Court applied the German limitation law to govern the limitation issue, when it applied the German domestic law to trace the title to the painting.[111] In the judgment, the court went further to analyze the public policy in excluding foreign law. It is held the English law of limitation serves the purpose of providing protection for defendants from stale claims, encouraging claimants to institute proceedings without unreasonable delay and conferring on a potential defendant confidence that after the lapse of a specific period of time he will not face a claim. English law provides that time will not run in favor of a defendant who is guilty of deliberate concealment whenever that deliberate concealment takes place until the plaintiff has discovered the concealment or could with reasonable diligence have done so. Had the German law barred the claim, it would have been disapplied as being contrary to English public policy. It is held that there is a public policy in

---

[107]Dicey (2012), at 227.

[108]Ibid.; Section 3(2) of the Limitation Act 1980 provides: 'Where any such cause of action has accrued to any person and the period prescribed for bringing that action has expired and he has not during that period recovered possession of the chattel, the title of that person to the chattel shall be extinguished.'

[109]Ibid., at 229–230.

[110]Redmond-Cooper, *supra* note 101, at 318.

[111]City of Gotha and Federal Republic of Germany v. Sotheby's and Cobert Finance S.A., [1993] C 3428, [1997] G 185.

England that time does not run either in favour of the thief or in favor of any transferee who is not a purchaser in good faith.[112] Thus if the Dunhuang manuscripts case falls within the scope of the Limitation Act 1980 and the Foreign Limitation Periods Act 1984, the limitation rules of the *lex causae* would be applied.

4.4.2.2 Chinese Statue of Limitation

It has been generally agreed that traditional China lacked the systematic institution of prescription or statutes of limitation. The maxim that 'you have to pay what you owe' has been deeply rooted in Chinese mentality, and the limitation of actions is regarded to be contrary to traditional Chinese morality. The concept of prescription first appeared in the Draft Civil Code of the Great Qing 1911, which never came into force.[113]

Contemporary China establishes the statutes of limitation in its civil law. Statutes of limitation law functions like extinctive prescription in other civil law systems, whereas acquisitive prescription is still not accepted. It is said acquisitive prescription is conflicting with traditional Chinese values and social principles. In China statutes of limitation affect a party's right to win a lawsuit. That means what becomes 'extinct' is the claimant's right to win a lawsuit, but his substantive rights are not extinct. A court is not allowed to take the initiative to look into limitation law if the defendant does not invoke the limitation defense. Besides, if the defendant does not put forward the limitation defense in the first trial, his limitation defense in the second defense would not be supported by the courts.[114] In practice, a claimant can file a stale lawsuit at any time to Chinese courts, but the court will not decide in favor of the claimant if the defendant invokes the limitation defense after the appropriate time is confirmed to have elapsed. However, if the defendant agrees to pay the damages voluntarily, the courts will recognize it and the defendant will not be allowed to recover the damages he paid.

There are three types of limitation in Chinese civil law: general limitation, special limitation, and maximum limitation. The general limitation of actions is two years as of the date that the claimant knows or should have known that his rights have been infringed upon. Exceptions are made for disputes over contracts of

---

[112]Ibid.

[113]But some scholars disagree with this view. They argue that although there was not a systematic institution of prescription in the statutes, customary law connotes that local magistrates would apply the idea of prescriptions to rule cases. See Li Xiandong, 'Limitation Law in Ancient China' (in Chinese), *Journal of Huaibei Coal Industry Teachers College* (*Philosophy and Social Science*) 25 (2004), no. 3, pp. 52–56.

[114]See Articles 136, 138 of the General Principles of the Civil Law of the People's Republic of China; articles 3, 4 of Provisions of the Supreme People's Court on Several Issues concerning the Application of Statute of limitations during the Trial of Civil Cases, Judicial Interpretation No. 11 [2008].

international trade and the import/export of technology, for which the limitation of action is four years; and for claims for personal injuries, claims for sale of substandard goods, rent-related claims and claims for loss of or damage to property left in the care of another person, all of which expire after one year. The maximum limitation of actions is 20 years.[115] Nevertheless, it is not made clear whether all claims are subject to statute of limitations.[116]

Respecting the statute of limitations of recovering property, the Chinese Supreme Court makes it clear that: 'Claims regarding damage to state property which has not been delegated to citizens or legal persons to operate or manage are not subject to periods of limitation'.[117] Under contemporary Chinese law, only when the state property is delegated to operate or manage to Chinese citizens or legal persons, it is subject to periods of limitation, whereas in other situation the claims regarding state property are not subject to limitation periods. In Chinese civil law, the scope of 'to operate or manage' is limited to economic or commercial activities. As a general rule, cultural relics are limited merchantable goods, and state owned cultural relics are not allowed to be traded in economic activities. Apart from that, to dispose of state owned without authorization is penalized by Chinese criminal law.[118] Thus claims for recovery of stolen state property in cases like this are not subject to statute limitation. That means if Chinese statute limitation governs the Dunhuang manuscripts case, the claim is not statute barred under Chinese law.

4.4.2.3 Conflict of Limitation Laws in Time

It has been discussed that the claims for the Dunhuang manuscripts is not statute barred either under Chinese limitation law or contemporary English limitation law. The last issue to deal with in this case study is the conflict of statute of limitations in

[115] Articles 135–137 of the General Principles of the Civil Law of the People's Republic of China.

[116] Although the claim of rights relating to realty is subject to the extinctive prescription has been heatedly discussed, this issue is not addressed by the Property Law 2007. There are three theories in this respect. The first theory is that claim of rights relating to realty is subject to extinctive prescription, because the limitation rules are generally applicable to all kinds of claims and there are no exception rules on claims of right in rem until now. The second theory denies the application of extinctive prescription to claims of right in rem. The reason is that claim of rights relating to realty is a right of relief; if it is subject to limitation of actions, the protection of real right is at stake. The third theory is an eclectic doctrine that the claim of right in registered property is not subject to limitation of actions, while the claim of right in non-registered property is subject to limitation. See Wang Yi, 'Claim of Right in Rem and the Application of Action Limitation' (in Chinese), *Contemporary Law Review* 20 (2006), no. 1, pp. 74–81; M. Guo, 'Application of Limitation of Actions' (in Chinese), *Law Review* 2009, no. 9, pp. 72-80.

[117] Article 170 of the Opinion (For Trial Use) of the Supreme People's Court on Questions concerning the Implementation of the General Principles of the Civil Law of the People's Republic of China.

[118] See Section 4—Crimes of Disrupting Administration of Cultural Relcis—, of Criminal Law of the PRC.

time. As Preston and Newson observe, before July 1, 1940, the general law relating to the limitation of civil actions was embodied in a series of statutes. The most important statutes included the Limitation Act 1623, the Civil Procedure Act 1833, the Real Property Limitation Acts 1833 and 1874, and the Public Authorities Protection Act 1893.[119] These enactments were replaced by the Limitation Act 1939. The Limitation Acts 1980 repeals and consolidates the enactments regarding limitation of actions from 1939 to 1980.[120]

According to Preston and Newson, only since the Limitation Act 1939, it has been provided that the title of the original owner to the chattel in conversion actions shall be extinguished.[121] In other words, before the Limitation Act 1939 statute of limitations relating to conversion matters had been classified as procedural law. The principle that procedure is governed by the *lex fori* has been universally admitted.[122] In the Dunhuang manuscripts case, the original conversion took place in 1907, before the enactment of the Limitation Act 1939. It is highly likely that the English courts would apply the English limitation law before 1939 to govern the Dunhuang manuscripts case. The six-year limitation period originated in the Limitation Act 1623 had remained unchanged ever since. By the Limitation Act 1623, actions of trover (one of the old common-law forms of action for conversion) were limited to six years from the date of the cause of action. Moreover, the elements of 'theft' and 'good faith acquisition' began to be considered after the Limitation Act 1980. Therefore, the claim seeking the recovery of the Dunhuang manuscripts were probably barred by the six-year limitation period by the old English statute of limitations.

Furthermore, Preston and Newson write: 'If the case is one where the new law gives him a longer period to bring his action, it will not avail him if the action was already barred on June 30, 1940, under the law then in force, unless the action is one which can be revived by acknowledgment or part payment after the period has expired, and has in fact been duly so revived under the new law.'[123] The Limitation Act 1980 (s. 9(1) of Schedule 2) contains a transitional provision that 'nothing in any provision of this Act shall enable any action to be brought which was barred by this Act or (as the case may be) by the Limitation 1939 before the relevant date'. And the Limitation Act 1939 (s. 33(a)) provides a similar transitional rule. In other words, if the action had been statute barred before 1940 by the old English law, the

[119]C.H.S. Preston & G.H. Newson, *Limitation of Actions* (2nd ed.), London: The Solicitor's Law Stationery 1943, at 1.

[120]The Limitation Act 1939 and 1975 were wholly repealed by the Limitation Act 1980. Other enactments such as the Mental Health Act 1959, the Limitation 1963, the Fatal Accidents Act 1976, the Civil Liability (Contribution) Act 1978, and the Limitation Amendment Act 1980 were partially repealed. See ss. 40(3) of Limitation Act 1980.

[121]Preston & Newson, *supra* note 119, at 19.

[122]Dicey (2012), at 203.

[123]Preston & Newson, *supra* note 119, at 19.

new English limitation law cannot enable a case which has been barred. Consequently, although the new law renders more protection to the plaintiff, it cannot be invoked to enable a stale claim which had been barred by the old law. So it is very likely that the Dunhaung manuscripts case has been statute barred by the old English limitation law.

4.5 Conclusion

To answer the three questions outlined in this chapter's introduction, three points are concluded here. First of all, the claimant can trace the title to the Dunhuang manuscripts to The Great Qing Code which provides for the state ownership of the unearthed treasure trove. It is unlikely that this ownership provision would be excluded by the English courts, even though The Great Qing Code contains penal provisions. Based on the Qing law, the claimant can qualify himself to sue the possessors for the conversion. Secondly, under English conflict of laws, the validity of the transfer of the manuscripts between Taoist Wang and Stein and its effect on the proprietary rights are governed by Chinese law as the transfer took place in China. Under Chinese law, either the Qing law or the contemporary Chinese law, the original deprivation of the manuscripts is deemed as theft, and the buyer could not acquire a valid title to the manuscripts. If Chinese law is excluded to govern this issue, English law is unlikely to recognize the buyer's title acquired by transfer, because the transfer between Stein and Taoist Wang probably does not fall within the exceptions to the *nemo dat* rule. The last point to emphasize is the statute of limitations. In general, the limitation rules of the *lex causae* are to be applied in actions under contemporary English law. If the *lex causae* of Chinese law governs the substantive issues of this case, Chinese limitation rules also apply. Chinese statutes of limitations provide that an action to recover stolen public property will not be statute barred. The consequence of applying Chinese law in entirety is that the claimant will get back the Dunhuang manuscripts, which may be inconsistent with the public policy of English law. However, the rule of conflict of limitation laws in time is of crucial importance in this case. Before the Limitation Act 1939, limitation rules relating to conversion were considered as procedural law. When limitation law is deemed as procedural law, statute of limitations of the *lex fori* would govern the case. According to the transitional provision of the English statute of limitations, a stale case which has been barred by the old statute of limitations cannot be enabled by the new statute. The claim seeking recovery of the Dunhuang manuscripts was probably barred by the six-year limitation period by the old English statute of limitations. The limitation of actions turns out to be the biggest hurdle in restitution claims.

On the one hand, this case study reflects the complexity of finding legal answers to the questions that would arise in transnational civil litigation concerning stolen cultural property. Each case has to be considered separately in many aspects: characterization of dispute, proof of title, conflict of laws in time and place, public policy, limitation law and others. On the other hand, it indicates that a requesting party would probably lose a lawsuit if seeking for legal remedies for restitution of cultural objects deprived a long time ago through civil litigation.

Chapter 5
Cultural Identity: The Politics of Recognition

> *They are the symbol and the blood and the soul of Greek people... We have fought and died for the Parthenon and the Acropolis... When we are born, they talk to us about all this great history that makes Greekness... This is the most beautiful, the most impressive, the most monumental building in all Europe...*
>
> Melina Mercouri

5.1 Introduction

Today it is universally accepted that looted/stolen cultural objects should be restituted to their rightful owners. However, the rules protecting cultural are regulated in detail only since the 1954 Hague Convention and the 1970 UNESCO Convention have been adopted, but these conventions are of no retroactive effect to cultural objects that were looted or stolen before the entry into force of these conventions. As demonstrated in Chaps. 3 and 4, it is almost impossible for original owners or their successors to recover cultural objects which were stolen or looted long ago through judicial means, so it is safe to state that there is no sufficient legal protection of these objects pursuant to remedies provided by contemporary international and national law. By contrast, the demands for the restitution or return of cultural objects to countries of origin or cultural groups have been increasingly voiced in various international forums. On the one hand, hard law rules against the

---

This statement was made by the former Greek Cultural Minster, Melina Mercouri, when she fought for the return of the Elgin Marbles. The Greece officially ruled out taking legal action in its battle to reclaim the Elgin marbles in May, 2015, when it was advised to take this case to European Court of Human Rights by human rights lawyers. The Greek cultural minister Nikos Xydakis said the route to retrieving the treasures lay in diplomatic and political channels and not international courts where outcome were far from assured. See Helena Smith, 'Greece Drops Options of Legal Action in British Parthenon Marbles Row', *The Guardian*, (May 13, 2015) http://www.theguardian.com/artanddesign/2015/may/13/greece-drops-option-legal-action-british-museum-parthenon-marbles-row, viewed July 20, 2015.

Z. Liu, *The Case for Repatriating China's Cultural Objects*,
DOI 10.1007/978-981-10-0597-8_5

repatriation claims as such; on the other hand, the claims for repatriation are voiced in more forums. Noting the gap between the demands and the law, this chapter is set out to investigate these repatriation claims by analyzing their cultural and ethical considerations, and to evaluate the conflicting values of the parties involved.

In practice, countries of origin and cultural groups have repeatedly stated that cultural objects are an integral part of their identity, just as Melina Mercouri argues in the case of the Parthenon Marbles.[1] Does the thesis that cultural heritage is instrumental to people's cultural identity entail the repatriation of cultural objects to cultural groups/communities? By contrast, it is also argued that cultural heritage belongs to a common human culture, so every people is equally entitled to the enjoyment of cultural heritage. Do these two views conflict with each other? What are the human values and interests in these arguments? This chapter seeks to have a comprehensive examination of these two arguments—cultural identity and cosmopolitanism—in the repatriation claims by looking into their legitimacy and criticism.

To answer these questions, this chapter starts by exploring the interconnection between cultural heritage and cultural identity, physical access to cultural objects and constructing cultural identity, and the theories regarding ownership of cultural objects. In terms of the interconnection between cultural heritage and cultural identity, it is generally agreed that cultural heritage is an important element to the construction of cultural identity in scholarship and popular society. This section briefly examines the study of the construction and maintenance of identity, and notes that cultures provide sources for the construction of cultural identity. It also analyzes the need of physical access to cultural heritage to the enjoyment of cultural heritage, including the issues of authenticity and location. As to the ownership of cultural objects, traditionally, cultural objects were treated as just a form of property, but some commentators note that treating cultural objects as just a form of property might endanger the cultural values. Today's various ways of thinking of cultural objects would be considered. Attention will be drawn to the relationships between states and cultures that are illuminating for understanding the connection between countries of origin and cultural objects.

Following that, the human interest of cultural identity in the claims for the repatriation of cultural objects would be discussed. Various norms relating to cultural identity are addressed, including multiculturalism, the politics of recognition. It notes that in most cases cultural objects that countries of origin and cultural groups are claiming were removed through conquest, colonization, or imperialism. People who were victimized in these historical periods were not treated equally, and their cultures and cultural identity were not recognized. The legacy of this misrecognition or non-recognition is still haunting some people, and some repatriation claims are in a certain sense demands for recognition of their cultural identity. This section looks into the misrecognition felt by people who seek the return of their cultural objects, and the effects of misrecognition.

[1]See Merryman (1985), no. 8, at 1913.

A cosmopolitan view is elaborated after the analysis of cultural identity. The attitudes towards universal museums from the West and from the East are concerned. It notes that cosmopolitanism and the recognition of cultural identity share the common roots of egalitarianism. The display of some cultural heritage with controversial provenance by some universal museums is also a form of non-recognition, which does not promote understanding or tolerance. Rather, it goes against the spirit of cosmopolitanism. This chapter ends with the balance of the seemingly conflicting interests.

5.2 Cultural Objects as Instruments to Identity

Cultural heritage as an element of cultural identity is frequently mentioned in academic discourse. In the introduction to a collection of papers examining the interconnections between heritage and identity, Brian Graham and Peter Howard have observed that these two concepts are both important, but their interconnections are slippery and ambiguous.[2] According to Graham and Howard, the interconnections between heritage and cultural identity are articulated through a set of practices, such as naming, memorialization, musealization and the like.[3] Also these interconnections are interpreted through a significant number of disciplinary lenses, namely geography, history, museum and heritage studies, archaeology, art history, anthropology, and media studies. Thus the study on heritage and identity is clearly multi-disciplinary, which may bring different perspectives and methodologies to explore shared problems. For example, museum experts and archaeologists pay more attention to tangible heritage than to intangible heritage, whereas art historians are largely concerned with intangible aspects of high culture.[4]

Notably, cultural heritage as an element of cultural identity has been reiterated in many legal instruments on cultural heritage. In UNESCO's introduction of the Hague Convention of 1954 and its two protocols, it provides: 'The cultural heritage reflects the life of the community, its history, and identity. Its preservation helps to rebuild broken communities, re-establish their identities, and link their past with their present and future'.[5] The 1970 UNESCO Convention states in the preamble that 'cultural property constitutes one of the basic elements of civilization and national culture, and that its true value can be appreciated only in relation to the

---

[2]B. Graham and P. Howard, 'Introduction: Heritage and Identity', in: Graham and Howard (2008), at 1.

[3]Ibid., at, 9; Lucky Belder also writes, 'the instrumental approach to cultural heritage is apparent in the Western debate on cultural identity'. See L.P.C. Belder, *The Legal Protection of Cultural Heritage in International Law: And its Implementation in Dutch law* (doctoral thesis Utrecht University), Utrecht: Utrecht University 2013, at 39.

[4]See Graham and Howard, ibid., at 9.

[5]*Convention for the Protection of Cultural Property in the Event of Armed Conflict* (May 14, 1954), see unesco.org.

fullest possible information regarding its origin, history and traditional setting'. The Council of Europe also states: 'heritage is both an element of identity common to all Europeans and a factor for differentiation. It is a channel for knowledge and mutual recognition of diversity, stimulating dialogue between people and communities'.[6] This concept is stipulated in the conventions adopted by the Council of Europe, including the Faro Framework Convention on the Value of Cultural Heritage for Society of 2005,[7] the European Convention on the Protection of the Archaeological Heritage of 1995, etc.[8] Article 3 of the Faro Convention provides: 'cultural heritage is a group of resources inherited from the past which people identify, independently of ownership, as a reflection and expression of their constantly evolving values, beliefs, knowledge and traditions, and the ideals, principles, and values, derived from the experience gained through progress and past conflicts…'

Today it seems to be a truism that cultural heritage is an element of identity. However, there is no specific definition of 'culture', 'identity' in international law, even though there is an understanding and implication of these concepts. To understand the interconnection between cultural heritage and identity, a brief examination of these two concepts may help.

5.2.1 Culture and Identity

For legal theorists, the term culture is vague. As Yvonne Donders writes: 'It (culture) can refer to many things, from cultural products, such as arts and literature,

---

[6]Council of Europe, *The Role of Culture and Cultural Heritage in Conflict Prevention, Transformation, Resolution and Post-Conflict Action: the Council of Europe Approach* (document prepared by the Secretariat of the Directorate of Culture and Cultural and Natural Heritage), AT (2010)397 rev. 1., 18 January 2011, at 5.

[7]This Convention was done at Faro on October 27, 2005, and entered into forced on December 1, 2009. To date, 21 member States have ratified the Convention.

[8]The Convention is a revised version of London Convention of 1969 adopted in 1992 at Valetta, and entered into force in 1995. It regards archaeological heritage 'as a source of the European collective memory and as an instrument for historical and scientific study' (Article 1). 'Collective memory' was studied systematically for the first time by Maurice Halbwachs in the 1920s. In Halbwaches' eyes, groups such as families, social classes, associations, and religious communities all have their own distinctive memories. These memories have been constructed by their group members, often over long periods of time. But it is individuals who remember, not groups or institutions, although these individuals, being located in a specific group context, draw on that context to remember or recreate the past. Halbwachs distinguishes collective memory from history. For him, history is the objective facts while collective memory is constructed. Some scholars argue collective memory maintains a group identity. Like the Samoan poet and writer Albert Wendt assets, 'Memory is our only source of finding out who we are. If we had no memory, we wouldn't be conscious that we're alive. The self, really, is a trick of memory. We are what we remember, society is what it remembers. That is why we must control what we remember-history- and hand that on to our children.' See M. Halbwachs, *On Collective Memory* (ed., transl., introd. by L.A. Coser), Chicago: University of Chicago Press 1992.

to cultural literature, to cultural process or to culture as a way or life'.[9] It has been accepted that culture is a notoriously difficult term to define, and there was no agreement among anthropologists regarding the nature of culture in the early 1990s, despite a century of efforts to define the term.[10]

The most commonly used definition and understanding of culture in today's cultural and anthropological studies is attributed to Franze Boas and his students. Boas is considered both the founder of modern anthropology and the father of American Anthropology, and since Boas, the term culture has figured profoundly in the national and international discourse.[11] Boas rejects the idea that culture is a process from savage to civilized, but emphasizes the diversity and particularity of the many and varied cultures of different peoples or societies.[12] One of Boas's student, Ruth Benedict, developed Boas's concept of culture the farthest. In her work *Patterns of Culture*, Benedict writes 'a culture, like an individual, is a more or less consistent pattern of thought and action'.[13] As stated by Benedict, a culture is 'not merely the sum of all its parts, but the result of a unique arrangement and interrelation of the parts that has brought about a new entity'.[14] In other words, a culture is more than the sum of cultural traits; it is an interrelated organism, and it can be identified. Culture is considered to be important, as 'culture shapes all our thinking, imaging and behaviour... For groups and societies, culture is energy, inspiration and empowerment'.[15]

It appears that the usage of the term culture in the UNESCO instruments follows that in the Boasian anthropology. In the first international conference on cultural rights organized by UNESCO in 1968, culture is conceptualized as 'a human experience which is difficult to define'; it is recognized 'as the totality of ways by which men create designs for living'.[16] In the *Universal Declaration on Cultural*

---

[9]Y.M Donders, 'Do Cultural Diversity and Human Rights Make a Good Match?', *International Social Science Journal* 61, (2010), *iss.* 199, at 15.

[10]H.Spencer-Oatey (compiled), *What is Culture? A Compilation of Quotations*, viewed June 12, 2014 http://www2.warwick.ac.uk/fac/soc/al/globalpad/openhouse/interculturalskills/global_pad_-_what_is_culture.pdf, at 1.

[11]For an overview of Boas's contribution to the development of the concept of culture in anthropology, one can refer to G. W. Stocking, JR., 'Franz Boas and the Culture Concept in Historical Perspective', *American Anthropologist* 68, (1966), 867–882.

[12]In the nineteenth century, the term culture was used as a synonym for European civilization. In 1870 the British anthropologist Edward Tylor published *Primitive Culture*, in which Tylor argues that culture move from low to high, primitive to advanced. See Spencer-Oatey, *supra* note10, at 1.

[13]Benedict (1960), at 53.

[14]Ibid. In *Patterns of Culture*, Benedict compared the basic configurations of culture and personality of three cultures: the Pueblo and Plains Indians, the Dobu of Melanesia, and the Kwakiutl of the Northwest coast of America. And she portrayed the Pueblo Indians as 'Apollonian', the Plains Indians as 'Dionysian', the Dobuans as 'Paranoid', and the Kwakiutl as 'Megalomaniac'.

[15]UNESCO, *Our Creative Diversity: Report of the World Commission on Culture and Development*, (1995), 11.

[16]UNESCO, *Cultural Rights as Human Rights* (1970), SHC. 68/XIX.3/A, 105.

Diversity, adopted unanimously by Member States of UNESCO on 2 November 2001, it reaffirms that 'culture should be regarded as the set of distinctive spiritual, material, intellectual and emotional features of society or a social, and that it encompasses, in addition to art and literature, lifestyles, ways of living together, value systems, traditions and beliefs'. This *Declaration* has also noted that 'culture is at the heart of contemporary debates about identity…'.

Respecting identity, this term is even more slippery. As summarized by the American cultural anthropologist Richard Handler, in the human science, 'identity' is used in reference to three aspects of human experience: individual human person; collectivities or groups that are imagined to be individuated as human persons; and the relationship between the two.[17] However, Handler has criticized the usage of identity in scholarship. In his view, many scholars now agree that cultures and social groups are changing with time, and are not bounded in space. In his words, 'groups do not have essential identities; indeed, they ought not to be defined as things at all'.[18]

Systematic investigations of identity can be traced to psychologist Erikson's theoretical framework introduced in the 1950s. In Erikson's theory, 'the term identity points to an individual's link with unique values, fostered by a unique history of his people'.[19] He places identity both at the 'core' of the individual as well as his or her 'common culture'.[20] Further exploration has been made in the social identity approaches proposed by Tajfel and Turner. The social identity approaches highlight the value and emotional significance attached to group identity, and its close interconnectedness with self-identity and self-esteem.[21] Today it is widely agreed that self-definition does not occur in a vacuum, but in a world already defined. People all live and move in communities, and are members of these communities. An individual is an animated focal point of traits resident in a

[17]Handler (1994), at 28.

[18]Ibid., at 30.

[19]E.H. Erikson, 'The Problem of Ego Identity', in: M.R. Stein, A.J. Vidich and D.M. White (eds), *Identity and Anxiety: Survival of the Person in Mass Society*, Glencoe: Free Press 1960, at 38.

[20]Erikson's other work on identity include *Childhood and Society*, New York: Norton 1950; *Identity: Youth and Crisis*, New York: Norton 1968 and etc.

[21]In the late 1970s, the social psychologists Tajfel and Turner conducted a series of experiments and found that groups which people belonged to were an important source of pride and self-esteem. Groups give us a sense of social identity: a sense of belonging to the social world. In addition to how you view yourself, social identity also influences how people treat you. After Tajfel's death in 1982, John Turner and his colleagues sought to elaborate and refine the cognitive element of social identity theory, and these elaborations comprised a new and separate theory: self-categorization theory. In self-categorization theory, Turner and his colleagues returned to the categorization process that was considered fundamental to social identity theory. Social identity theory and self-categorization theory comprise the social identity approach. This approach originated in social psychology, but has been applied to a wide variety of fields and continues to be very influential. See H. Tajfel and J.C. Turner, 'An Integrative Theory of Intergroup Conflict', in: W.G. Austin and S. Worchel (eds), *The Social Psychology of Intergroup Relations?*, Monterey: Brooks/Cole 1979, pp. 33–47; J.C. Turner and M.A. Hogg, *Rediscovering the Social Group: A Self-Categorization Theory*, Oxford: Basil Blackwell 1989.

community that transcends him in both space and time.[22] Manuel Castells, one of the formost social theorists writing today, makes the statement that 'For those social actors excluded from or resisting the individualization of identity attached to life in the global networks of power and wealth, cultural communes of religious, national, or territorial foundation seem to provide the main alternative for the construction of meaning in our society'.[23] Castells emphasizes that the constitution of these 'cultural communes' is not arbitrary. It builds on raw materials from history, geography, language, and environments. They are materially constructed, around reactions and projects historically and geographically determined.[24] In the view of Castells and the like, people's identity is constructed and affected by cultural communities. These cultural communities provide sources for people's self-definition and a sense of belonging.

I think Benedict Anderson's concept of imagined communities offers insightful observation in understanding culture and cultural identity. In Anderson's idea, a community, e.g. a nation, is imagined, 'because the members of even the smallest nation will never know most of their fellow-members, meet them, or even hear of them, yet in the minds of each lives the image of their communion'.[25] But Anderson insists that imagining does not mean fabrication or falsity. 'Communities are to be distinguished, not by their falsity/genuineness, but by the style in which they are imagined'.[26] I agree with Anderson and I suggest seeing a culture as an imagined community, which is presented in reality as a shared way of living and thinking. Tangible and intangible elements such as history, religion, ethnicity, geography, language, which are 'raw materials' in Castells's words, are contributing factors in the shaping and evolving of people's way of thinking and living. The personification of a culture is cultural identity. Cultural heritage is the legacy inherited from previous generations, which is an expression and representation of history, systems of value, beliefs and tradition of a social group. Cultural heritage can be used to identify and reify a culture, and reinforce people's cultural identity or a sense of who we are as a people.

5.2.2 *The Power of Possession: Authenticity*

Cultural objects are instruments to people's cultural identity. But it appears unclear whether physical access is required for the enjoyment of cultural objects and the constitution of people's cultural identity. In the famous case of the Parthenon Marbles, the Greeks maintain that the Parthenon has been a symbol of Athenian

[22]See Mead (1971), no. 1, pp. 1–14, Friedman (1992), no. 4, pp. 837–859.

[23]Castells (2010), at 68–69.

[24]Ibid.

[25]Anderson (2006), at 6.

[26]Ibid.

national identity since the fifth century BC. Elgin's removal of the Marbles took away a part of Greek identity in the days of disrespect for other cultures, and that was a cultural crime or cultural deprivation. But Merryman argues that the British removal and display of the Marbles is not cultural deprivation. Merryman bases his argument on the ground that the British had never attempted to 'appropriate the identity of the Marbles, disguising or misrepresenting their origin'.[27] Rather, the British have presented the Marbles openly and candidly as the work of Greek art from the beginning; and the Greek cultural heritage has been preserved and enhanced by the British acquisition and exhibition.[28] In Merryman's view, since the Marbles have been admired as great Greek art, the British are not depriving the Greeks of their cultural identity. Additionally, Merryman doubts whether the enjoyment of cultural value requires possession of the Marbles. In his view, the information and images of Marbles are very well accessible to the Greeks through other alternatives, e.g. books, photographs, reproductions. The authentic Marbles have many times the market value of the reproductions, but it is not clear whether the cultural value can only be acquired through originals.[29] With regard to cultural deprivation or cultural appropriation, there has been controversy over whether it is possible to steal the culture or cultural identity of another.[30] Some reject the idea of cultural appropriation and value the absolute freedom of imagination. In their opinion, only with exchange of cultures and freedom of imagination can the greatest art be created.[31] By contrast, some emphasize that cultural appropriation is a serious issue, because 'we have a new need for authenticity'.[32]

In the discussion of authenticity of cultural heritage, it concerns two aspects. The first aspect deals with the authenticity of the object itself; in other words, it is about the distinction between originals and reproductions. In the 1930s, the German cultural critic Walter Benjamin explored the difference between 'originals' and 'reproductions' in his famous essay 'The Work of Art in the Age of Mechanical Reproduction'.[33] Benjamin argued that even the most perfect reproduction lacks the presence of space and time. The time element can only be brought out by chemical or physical analysis of originals, and the space element of an object has to be studied from the location of the originals.[34] Benjamin captures the uniqueness of original works of art with the term 'aura', a word that shrinks in an age where the

---

[27]Merryman (1985), at 1913.

[28]Ibid.

[29]Ibid., at 1913–1914.

[30]Brown observes that the expressions used to describe the flow of cultural elements from indigenous societies to the larger world progressed from the clinical 'cultural appropriation' to 'biopiracy' and 'ethnocide', and then to 'cultural genocide' and 'the new vampires'. See Brown (2003), at 3.

[31]Coombe (1993), at 249–251.

[32]Ibid.

[33]See Benjamin (2008).

[34]Ibid., at 5.

work of art can be reproduced by technological means.[35] In Benjamin's theory, 'the uniqueness of the work ('aura') is identical with its embeddedness in the context of tradition'.[36] The oldest works of art came into being in the service of some ritual-magic, typically religious; that means ancient works of art were originally created for the purpose of 'worship'. This magic power inherited in works of art from which 'aura' is generated, Benjamin identified as the 'cultic' value of works of art. Along with cultic value, works of art have been recently given 'display' value for profit and economy. As Benjamin framed it, absolute weight was placed on cult value of the objects in primitive times, but more attention is paid to exhibition value today.[37]

In agreement with the 'aura' thesis, I think Merryman's analysis of the enjoyment of the Marbles through reproductions is not persuasive. For ordinary people, it is self-evident that access to original masterpieces and those reproductions makes a huge difference in psychological feeling and experience. There is a village in Shenzhen called Dafen that reproduces the largest mass (some 60 percent) of old masterpieces in the world. People in South China can easily order reproductions of a Van Gogh, or a Dali, or a Rubens, or a Lichtenstein from the Dafen village.[38] Some of the reproductions are of very high quality, and non-professionals cannot recognize the subtle difference. However, instead of flooding to Dafen to appreciate the greatest reproductions of masterpieces, millions of people make the long journey to Europe to worship the authentic works of art. Cultural objects are unique and irreplaceable, and the enjoyment of originals cannot be substituted by that of reproductions.

The other aspect of authenticity regards the interconnection between cultural heritage and its cultural and historical context. Cultural objects are linked to the idea of bounded and objectified cultures. In practice, some cultural objects may be exhibited in galleries, as examples of a human creative ability that transcend the limitations of time and place, representing the highest point of human achievement; and they might be exhibited in museums as the authentic works of a distinct collectivity, as integral to the harmonious life of an ahistorical community and incomplete outside of 'cultural context'.[39] Still some cultural heritage can only have the fullest meaning and be appreciated sacredly in the 'authentic' cultural contexts. This can be best illustrated in the case of the Kaaba Shrine. To the world's Muslims, the Kaaba shrine is the holiest place on earth. Can one remove the Black Stone of Kaaba, and display it in British Museum or one of the other great museums in the world? Technically, it is possible. But people will not do so if we want to respect the Muslim world. In essence, Mecca is the only 'authentic' place for the Kaaba Shrine and the Black Stone. Islam was born in Mecca; every year millions of

---

[35]Ibid., at 6–7.

[36]Ibid., at 10.

[37]Ibid., at 10.

[38]See for example the commercial website dafenart.com, viewed May 14, 2014.

[39]Coombe (1993), at 257–258.

pilgrims from all over the world gather to circle Kaaba during the Hajj. Only in Mecca does the presence of Kaaba with the Black Stone have the fullest meaning. Numerous examples, such as Mogao Grottoes and Dunhuang, the Terracotta Army and Xi'an, the statues in the Notre Dame and Paris, confirm the close interconnection between cultural contexts and cultural heritage.

Due to the intimate interconnection between cultural heritage and its authentic cultural context, some argue that cultural heritage is inalienable wealth for a cultural group; and they introduce inalienable possessions of cultural heritage.[40] As Weiner puts it, 'persons and groups need to demonstrate continually who they are in relation to others, and their identities must be attached to those ancestral connections that figure significantly in their statuses, ranks, or titles. To be able to keep certain objects that document these connections attests to one's power to hold oneself or one's group intact. For to give up these objects is to lose one's claim to the past as a working part of one's identity in the present'.[41]

5.2.3 Who 'Owns' Cultural Objects?

Over the issues of possession and ownership of cultural objects, some theses have been developed. Traditionally, cultural objects were treated as no more than a form of property in law. In recent decades, scholars have reiterated that tangible cultural heritage is of two potentially conflicting aspects: culture and property. Culture embodies group-oriented notions of value, whereas 'property' traditionally focuses on legal rights of individuals to possession of objects. From a property law perspective, a material object can be the subject of property. Some lawyers including Jeremey Waldron, Eric Posner, and others, emphasize that private ownership of tangible cultural heritage shall be prioritized. They argue that cultural objects are just a form of property, and should not be merited special treatment.[42] On the opposite, scholars like Joseph Singer, Jack Beermann, Peter Welsh, Michael Brown, and others, defend the cultural aspect of cultural heritage, and argue that culture transcends individual ownership.[43] These two contrasting critiques are referred to as 'a view from the marketplace of goods' and 'a view from the cultural commons'.[44]

[40]See Weiner (1985), pp. 210–227, Weiner (1992), Welsh (1997), no. 3, pp. 12–18.

[41]Weiner, ibid., (1985), 210.

[42]J. Waldron, 'Property, Justification and Need', *Canadian Journal of Law and Jurisprudence* 6 (1993), at 185,188, Welsh (1997), no. 3, pp. 12–18, Posner (2007), no. 1, at 222.

[43]J.W. Singer and J.M. Beermann, 'The Social Origins of Property', *Canadian Journal of Law and Jurisprudence* 6 (1993), no. 2, at 217, 244; Brown (2003), 582.

[44]Carpenter et al. (2009), at 1039–1044.

In the article 'In Defense of Property', Carpenter, Katyal, and Riley criticize the association of 'property' with a narrow model of individual ownership.[45] They depart from the individual rights paradigm, and situate indigenous cultural property claims in the interest of 'peoples' rather than 'persons'. In terms of peoplehood or stewardship, they argue that cultural properties are integral to indigenous groups' identity or peoplehood, and deserve particular legal protection.[46] I share their views that protecting cultural objects as property does not necessarily endanger the cultural values. Regarding the ownership of cultural objects, Merryman identifies two ways of thinking about cultural property in a seminal article published in 1986: cultural internationalism and cultural nationalism.[47] Cultural internationalism is shorthand for the concept of cultural property 'as components of a common human culture, whatever their places of origin or present location, independent of property rights or national jurisdiction'.[48] Another attitude—cultural nationalism—is to see cultural property 'as part of a national cultural heritage'. This attitude gives nations a special interest, and it implies the attribution of national character to objects, independently of their location or ownership. It legitimizes national export controls and demands for the 'repatriation' of cultural property. In Merryman's conception of 'cultural nationalism', the attachment of cultural objects to their home countries is highlighted.[49] He concludes that both views have their legitimate places, and have something important to contribute to the formation of policy, locally, nationally, and internationally, concerning pieces of humanity's material culture. But where choices have to be made between the two ways of thinking, then the values of cultural internationalism—preservation, integrity, distribution, and access —seem to carry greater weight, because the firm, insistent presentation of the those values in discussions about trade in and repatriation of cultural property will in the longer run serve the interests of all mankind.[50]

---

[45]Ibid., at 1022.

[46]Ibid., at 1022–1124.

[47]Merryman (1986), at 831–853.

[48]In Iriye's Cultural Internationalism and World Order, cultural internationalism entails a variety of activities undertaken to link countries and peoples through the exchange of ideas and persons, through scholarly cooperation, or through efforts at facilitating cross-national understanding. This use of cultural internationalism is different from Merryman's. See Iriye (1997).

[49]Generally, the term nationalism is used to describe two phenomena: the attitude that the members of a country when they care about their national identity, and actions to achieve self-determination. Cultural nationalism in some literature has been defined as a form of actions to achieve self-determination, contrasted with ethnic nationalism and liberal nationalism. Ethnic nationalism, rooted in an ethnic conception of 'the nation', defines membership in the nation in terms of descent. Civic nationalism, by contrast, is a kind of nationalism compatible with values of freedom, tolerance, equality, and individual rights. A 'civic nation' in this sense, need not be unified by commonalities of language or culture. But Merryman's reference of cultural nationalism concerns about national identity, rather than actions to self-determination. See Nielsen (1999), pp. 119–130, A. Stilz, 'Civic Nationalism and Language Policy', *Philosophy and Public Affairs* 37 (2009), no. 3, at 257.

[50]Merryman (1986), 852–853.

Merryman's article is highly influential and has been cited in almost all the papers relating to law and cultural heritage. As Stamatoudi observes, the 'tale' of cultural property law is very much a 'Tale of Two Cities': nationalism and internationalism. But the views of these two opposing camps are becoming less rigid, as both camps are borrowing arguments from each other. However, she contends that the arguments advocating antiquities are best preserved in countries which have the means to preserve and exhibit them have lost ground, because they 'divide the world further into those who 'can' and those who 'cannot' instead of shifting the discussion to those who can help and those who cannot'.[51] Chinese scholars Wang Yunxia and Huang Shuqing insist that as a general rule, the rights of people from countries of origin should be respected first; only when a state fails to protect cultural heritage or destroys cultural heritage intentionally, should cultural internationalism prevail.[52] They maintain that cultural nationalism does not necessarily hinder cultural exchange. Cultural exchange generates respect and appreciation of a culture, but it should be conducted in a lawful way and respect the will of the people from the countries of origin. Taking the Terracotta Army as an example, cultural nationalism can promote both the preservation and exchange of culture effectively.[53] A Chinese expert on cultural heritage, Xie Chensheng, argues that the nature of cultural objects is comparable with that of intellectual property: the knowledge should be shared by all the people in the world, but the intellectual property right can only belong to a legal person. The overemphasis of international ownership of cultural objects is equated to the legalization of looting cultural objects. In other words, it would be legal to take or loot all cultural objects, if these cultural objects belonged to all people.[54]

I think Merryman's two ways of thinking about cultural property are important in conceptualizing the ownership of cultural objects, but these two ways do not accurately reflect today's law, policy making, as well as claims for the repatriation of cultural heritage. As Francioni indicates in an article published in 2011, there are more than just two ways of thinking about cultural property. Cultural property can be seen as part of national identity, territory, environment, tradition; it can also be regarded as objects of personal property, human rights and communal property, and others.[55] In the discussion of the ownership of cultural property, in particular its

[51] I.A. Stamatoudi, *Cultural Property Law and Restitution: A Commentary to International Conventions and European Union Law*, Cheltenham: Edward Elgar 2011, at 253–254.

[52] Yunxia and Shuqing (2008), pp. 41–47.

[53] Since it was discovered in 1974, the Terracotta Army has been exhibited for more than a hundred times in over forty countries. Increasing amount of visitors come to the place of discovery to admire the Terracotta Army. In the year 2011 alone, a recorded number of more than four million Chinese and non-Chinese visitors went to the Terracotta Army museum. Ibid., at 46–47.

[54] Xie Chensheng, 'We Shall Prevent Four Wrong Tendencies in Understanding Cultural Relics' (in Chinese), *Liaowang,* February 4, 2013, viewed May 3, 2013, chinanews.com/cul/2013/02-04/4544503.shtml.

[55] Francioni (2011), no.1, at 9–10.

relationship between people, I think, it is necessary to have a look at the interconnection of cultures and states.

5.2.3.1 States and Cultures

The terms 'state', 'country', and 'nation' are often used interchangeably in English; for example, the expression 'throughout the nation' simply means 'throughout the country' in the United States. Seton-Watson, author of the influential work Nations and States, argued that 'no scientific definition of the nation can be devised; yet the phenomenon has existed and exists'.[56] Seton-Watson defines a nation 'a community of people, whose members are bound together by a sense of solidarity, a common culture, a national consciousness'; but defines a state as 'a legal and political organization, with the power to require obedience and loyalty from its citizens'.[57] In my view, it is important to distinguish 'a cultural or ethnic group' from 'a political entity' in dealing with ownership of cultural objects, so I make a distinction between 'state' and 'nation' in this chapter, following Seton-Watson's definitions of 'nation' and 'state'. In the opinion of Seton-Watson, a nation exists when a significant number of people in a community consider themselves as forming a nation, or behave as if they formed one. It is not necessary that the whole of the population should feel that connection, or behave in the same way. Nor is it possible to fix an absolute minimum percentage of a population which is so affected. When a significant group holds this belief, it possesses 'national consciousness.[58]

In Seton-Watson's description, a state can exist without a nation, or with several nations; and a nation can be coterminous with the population of one state, or be included together with other nations within one state, or be divided between several states.[59] Seton-Watson's definition of nation is bound by 'common culture', so the relationship between a state and a nation is comparable to that between a state and a culture. However, in Gellner's view, there is no obvious relation between a state and a culture in the modern world. Gellner maintains that in the modern world the role of culture in human life was totally transformed by economic and scientific changes, which have transformed the world since the seventeenth century when nationalism was introduced. Nationalism creates nations, not the other way around. Thus nationalism is, essentially, the general imposition of a high culture on society; the nation is a product of the process of modernization.[60] By contrast, Gellner's student Smith holds an opposite argument on nationalism. Smith emphasizes the importance of myths, memories, traditions, and symbols of ethnic heritage in the

[56]Seton-Watson (1977), at 5.

[57]Ibid., at 1.

[58]Ibid., at 5.

[59]Ibid.

[60]Gellner (1983), at 3–4, 56–57, Gellner and Smith (1996), no. 3, at 367–368.

formation and persistence of the modern nation state. These cultural and historical elements also form the basis of competing claims to territory, patrimony, and resources.[61] The debate between Gellner and Smith highlights the complex relationship between 'states' and 'nations' or 'cultures' in the modern world.

The well-known political philosopher, Will Kymlicka, notes that most of the world's states are multinational or multicultural countries.[62] In other words, a state is a federation of various cultures. But as Kymlicka points out, in multinational or multicultural countries, there typically is a majority national group, and then one or more national minorities. 'However, historically, virtually all liberal democracies have, at one point or another, attempted to diffuse a single societal culture throughout all of its territory'.[63] 'Societal culture', according to Kymlicka, is 'a culture which provides its members with meaningful ways of life across the full range of human activities, including social, educational, religious, recreational, and economic life, encompassing both public and private spheres'.[64] Promoting integration into a common societal culture—a common citizenship, a common language—has been seen as essential to social equality and political cohesion in modern states. Some minorities have accepted integration into the common societal culture, while others have strongly resisted integration. For some national minorities, the imposition of the majority language threatens their existing culturally distinct society.[65] To take China as an example, the Han Chinese are the majority ethnic group native to China. In addition to Han Chinese, there are another fifty-five minority ethnic groups with distinctive cultures. Also among the Han Chinese, there is considerable genetic, linguistic, cultural, and social diversity mainly due to the long history of immigration and assimilation. When we speak of 'the Cantonese' as opposed to 'the Chinese' or 'the Sichuanese', and even something as broad as 'the North' or as 'the South', it can be sufficiently meaningful for some purposes.[66] For social cohesion, the Chinese government promotes a common culture, which is mainly based on Han culture, over mainland China. However, the promotion of the Chinese societal culture has encountered with resistance by some minorities,

[61]Smith (1999), at 8–10. Anderson also criticizes Gellner's formulation of nationalism. In Anderson's view, Gellner is so anxious to show that nationalism is under false pretences, and Gellner assimilates 'invention' to 'fabrication' and 'falsity', rather thatn to 'imaging' and 'creation'. See Anderson (2006), at 6.

[62]The 200 countries and regions contain over 600 living language groups, and some 2,500 ethnic groups and multitude of religions in the world today. See Kymlicka (1995a), at 1, 76, Kymlicka (1997), at 19, 29.

[63]Kymlicka (1997), at 19, 28.

[64]Kymlicka (1995a), at 19, 28.

[65]Kymlicka (1997), 28–32.

[66]See H.D.R. Baker, 'Review. Tao Tao Liu and David Faure (ed.), *Unity and Diversity: Local Cultures and Identities in China*', *Bulletin of the School of Oriental and African Studies, University of London* 61 (1998), no. 2, at 381.

notably the Tibetan and Uighur.[67] Besides, Chinese culture or Han culture is not limited to mainland China. For instance, Singapore is also a society populated predominantly by cultural and ethnic Chinese.[68]

Overall, states and cultures are interlinked but different concepts; the extent of a culture and the boundaries of a state are not necessarily congruent. In the international community, a state operates as the legal representative for its people and cultures. In some countries, the promotion of a societal culture or national identity is designed to bridge a culture and a state, but interests of a culture might conflict with that of a state, especially the minority culture in multicultural states.

5.2.3.2 Countries of Origin and Cultural Objects

Given the complex relationship between states and cultures, the lack of distinction between a 'culture' and a 'sovereign state' in the 'cultural nationalism' thesis has drawn sharp criticism from many commentators, such as James Cuno. Cuno, the former curator of the Art Institute of Chicago, argues that cultural objects have no obvious relation to nation-states in the book *Who Owns Antiquity?*. In Cuno's view, the relationship is no more than a historical accident: 'they happen to have been found within its modern borders'.[69] Cuno studies the cases of Turkey and China. In the China's case, Cuno distinguishes the notions of 'culture' and 'national culture' by contrasting 'Xinjiang minority culture' against 'Chinese national culture'. National culture, in Cuno's eyes, is a 'political construction', while culture is 'a porous, constantly evolving and dynamic human creation, the result of numerous and endless influences from generations of contact with foreign people'.[70] China is multicultural, but China is trying to officially include its minority cultures within the majority culture that is of the elite and ruling people. Cuno asserts that Chinese national culture is not the 'culture of every ethnic or linguistic group within modern China'.[71] Looking back to the historical development of Xinjiang, Cuno finds that the Xinjiang region is and always has been a borderland; it was not always under the control of China. People living in Xinjiang have their own Uighur cultural

---

[67]Also within Han Chinese, there are also voices to preserve their local culture. It is reported that some Cantonese speakers protest the increase of the amount of local television broadcast in Mandarin. On the other hand, promotion of societal culture does not necessarily contradict with the local cultural identity, as a people can have multiple identities. The identity of being Chinese and that of being Cantonese are in most of the cases in harmony. See A. Ramzy, 'Protesters Stand Firm on Cantonese Rights', *Time*, August 2, 2010, viewed May 6, 2014, content.time.com/time/world/article/0,8599,2,008,060,00.html.

[68]The distinguished historian Tu Wei-ming put forward the concept of 'cultural China' against political China. The boundaries of political China, as an independent state, are not congruent with cultural China. See Tu Wei-ming (2005), no. 4, pp. 145–167.

[69]Notably, by Cuno's definition, 'nation' refers to both the 'sovereign authority' and the 'group of people', equated to nation-state in the book. Cuno (2008), at 17.

[70]Ibid., at 92.

[71]Ibid., at 92.

identity, which is formed by the people's history as frontier or border people and is different from the Han identity. Though Uighurs have the Chinese citizenship, Uighur identity is the most important identity for Uighurs.[72] Cuno states 'it is hard to imagine, when driving the long, straight, recently paved road from Urumqi to Turpan, that many people there cared about the Old Summer Palace sculptures when they were looted in the 1860 or 'saved' for China and the Chinese in 2000'.[73] From another approach, the famed scholar David Lowenthal insists that the past is another country. For Lowenthal, the idea that nations and tribes are enduring entities with sacred rights to time-honored legacies is mistaken. Nobody 'owns' a past. The history we study is never our own; it is always the history of people who were in some respects like us and in others different. The national, tribal, and local retention and restitution claims are flawed in logic, untenable in fact, lethally divisive in practice. These claims endure because they are embedded in long-standing notions of cultural property- even of natural and intangible legacies, and because global agencies and scholarly bodies lend them moral standing.[74]

Moreover, 'nationalism' has been frowned upon in Europe after the world wars, as Kymlicka states. The image of 'nationalism' has been shaped to be culturally xenophobic, ethnically exclusionary, anti-democratic, territorially expansionist, and prone to violence in Europe. In the discussion of the Quebec nationalism, partly to avoid the negative connotations of nationalism, some defenders of enhanced powers for Quebec avoid the language of nation and nationalism. Instead they talk in the language of community, culture and identity. Kymlicha cites Webber as an example, who proposes that people should avoid the language on nationalism when discussing Quebec.[75]

Therefore, linking cultural objects to 'country of origin' have been thought to be problematic or flawed by many scholars. In their opinion, cultural objects are of no nationality. I share Cuno's view on the relation between minority culture and majority culture in a state. Uighurs probably do not care about the bronze sculptures looted from the Old Summer Palace, but Cuno has not elaborated on whether Uighurs care about their own Uighur cultural objects. If a great Uighur palace was destroyed and plundered, would the Uighurs care about those looted objects? If Cuno explores this issue from the perspective of the Uighur cultural identity instead of Chinese national identity, would he come to the same conclusion?

As Graham and Howard point out, 'the idea of present-centeredness is a recurrent theme in the recent literature on cultural heritage'.[76] It means that the study of

[72]Ibid., at 106–111.

[73]Ibid., at 112–113.

[74]D. Lowenthal, 'Why Sanctions Seldom Work: Reflections on Cultural Property Internationalism', *International Journal of Cultural Property* 12 (2005), no. 3, pp. 403–411, Lowenthal (1985). Some scholars like Sidney E. Mead and Jonathan Friedman hold an opposite opinion to Lownthal's view. In their view, self-determination does not occur in a vacuum, but in a world already defined. The past is always practiced in the present; constructing the past is an act of self-identification. See Mead (1971), at 4–5, 13; Friedman (1992), at 837, 853, 856.

[75]See Kymlicka (1997), at 14–15.

[76]See Graham and Howard (2008), at 2.

heritage does not involve a direct engagement with the study of history; instead, 'the contents, interpretations, and representations of the heritage resource are selected according to the demands of the present and, in turn, bequeathed to an imagined future'.[77] In brief, it is now largely agreed that most heritage has little intrinsic worth, but it is the people that place values upon artefacts or activities. People view heritage through a whole series of lenses: religion, ethnicity, class, wealth, gender, personal history. Meanings of cultural heritage are 'marked out by identity, and are produced and exchanged through social interaction in a variety of media; they are also created through consumption'.[78] In line with this, it is the people that place values upon cultural objects. Another important scholar, Kwame Anthony Appiah, put forward the idea that 'the connection people feel those objects that are symbolically theirs, because they were produced from within a world of meaning created by their ancestors—the connection to art through identity—is powerful'.[79] As in the case of the Vikings, whose cultural identity is tied up with lineage and locality, most cultural patrimony was produced before the modern state Norway came into being. Some wonderful gold and iron work made by the Viking ancestors are displayed in the national museum in Oslo; if a Viking was told that those objects belonged not to the Viking descendants but to the state, they would be astonished.[80]

In reality of course, some people feel strong connections to their countries or to their cultural background (morality, religion, nation, or tradition).[81] Cultural objects, as elements of identity, are represented and interpreted in different ways by different people. Accordingly, cultural objects are referred to as national treasures for a country, sacred items for a religion or a tribe, and symbols of collective memory for a community. A sovereign state is empowered to enact domestic legislation and sign international conventions on cultural issues. In some repatriation actions, a country of origin is the legal representative for its cultural groups in the global society. However, the assertion that 'cultural heritage belongs to the country of origin' is not tenable in all cases.[82] First of all, border lines of states have changed and can be

[77]Ibid.

[78]Ibid.

[79]Appiah (2007), at 134–135.

[80]Ibid., at 118–121.

[81]Charles Taylor claims what people see themselves defined by their cultural background is not just that they are strongly attached to this background. Rather it is the cultural background that 'provides the frame within which they can determine where they stand on questions of what is good, or worthwhile, or admirable, or of value'. See Taylor (1989), at 27.

[82]In has been pointed out in the ICOM Study of 1979 that: the notion is often ambiguous. 'It can in fact indicate the country in which the work was created, the country of which its author is a national or the last country to hold the object prior to its removal. Due to the course of history, the changing of national boundaries and State succession, the three elements do not always coincide and contemporary events show the partitioning of State still take place.' See ICOM, 'Study on the Principles, Conditions and Means for the Restitution or Return of Cultural Property in View of Reconstituting Dispersed Heritages,' Museum International 31 (1979), no.1, at 65.

changing, so in some cases, it is very problematic to identify the country of origin for some cultural objects. Suppose that a cultural object was looted from the former Yugoslavia, which has dissolved into six countries (if Kosovo is included, the number would be seven), and now these countries are claiming this object. How to identify the country of origin? A most recent case of such disputes concerns a collection of Crimean cultural objects loaned by the Allard Pierson museum in Amsterdam. Russia annexed Crimea a month after the exhibition was opened in Amsterdam, and the loaned artefacts came from five museums from Ukrain, four of which are now under the control of Russia. While the Netherlands does not recognize the annexation of Crimea, it refused to return the artefacts to the four museums in Crimea. Now these four museums are suing the Allard Pierson museum for the return of the treasures.[83] In this case, is Russia or Ukraine the country of origin of the Crimean treasures exhibited in the Allard Pierson museum? Furthermore, some cultural objects were exported legitimately through cross-border trade or cultural communication in history. For example, Chinese porcelains have been exported to Europe since the 16th century, and some cultural objects were offered as gifts to other countries in history. Among the disputes over cultural heritage, some cultural objects which were removed against the will of the original owners, in particular those stolen or looted in periods of colonialism or imperialism, might be symbolic of the recognition of people's cultural identity, in my opinion.

5.3 Recognition of Cultural Identity

It has been noted by Nancy Fraser and Axel Honneth, the two most important contemporary theorists of recognition, that "'recognition' has become a keyword of our time".[84] According to Fraser, the term recognition comes from Hegelian philosophy, and it 'designates an ideal reciprocal relation between subjects in which each sees the other as its equal and also as separate from it'.[85] In effect, much contemporary in the political theory of recognition was undoubted fueled by Charles Taylor, whose essay 'The Politics of Recognition' is often regarded the 'single most influential work' or the classic expression of the theory of recognition.[86]

---

[83]See 'The Netherlands Told to Keep out of Crimean Court Case', *Dutch News.nl,* April 8, 2015, http://www.dutchnews.nl/news/archives/2015/04/the-netherlands-told-to-keep-out-of-crimean-gold-court-case/ viewed April 14, 2018.

[84]Fraser and Honneth (2003), at 1.

[85]Ibid.

[86]C.M. Taylor, 'The Politics of Recognition', in: A. Gutmann (ed.), *Multiculturalism: Examining the Politics of Recognition*, Princeton: Princeton University Press 1994, pp. 25–73. After Taylor published this essay, he vacated the field. In the meantime Honneth and Fraser have become the two most important theorists of recognition. For a general overview of the development of the theories of recognition, see Burns and Thompson (2013), at 6–8.

5.3.1 *The Politics of Recognition and Multiculturalism*

In Taylor's theory, people's identity is partly shaped by recognition or its absence, often by the misrecognition of others. Therefore a person or group of people can suffer real distortion, if the people or society around them mirror back to them a confining or demeaning or contemptible picture of themselves.[87] To illustrate this thesis, Taylor cites the arguments made by some feminists as an example. Because of the misrecognition, women have considered themselves inferior to men, and they suffer the pain of low self-esteem. Their self-depreciation becomes the source of their own oppression.[88] According to Taylor, in hierarchical societies, people's identity was largely fixed by his or her social position in the earlier. That means a person's place in society to a large extent was determined by what other people recognized that person. With the decline of social hierarchies, the seeds of liberalism were sown. Taylor identifies two important notions underlying liberalism. The first notion is the ideal of authenticity, and it is about new understanding of individual identity which has emerged since the end of the eighteenth century. It emphasizes the value of 'being true to myself' and 'my own particular way of being'; it becomes crucial in modern consciousness: 'each of our voices has something unique to say'.[89] And the second notion is the 'politics of equal dignity, which is based on the idea that all humans are equally worthy of respect. These politics were shaped by Rousseau and Immanual Kant in Western civilization, now used in a universalist and egalitarian sense.[90] However, Taylor notes that the politics of equal dignity ignores the importance of different cultural backgrounds which are crucial in the construction of individual identity. Hence, Taylor proposes the 'politics of difference'. For Taylor, the politics of difference is 'full of denunciations of discrimination and refusals of second-class citizenship', and it 'gives the principle of universal equality a point of entry within the politics of dignity'.[91] Today most theories of recognition assume that people depend on the feedback of others in the society to construct their identity; people who experience non-recognition or misrecognition will find it difficult to embrace themselves and to have successful relationships with others.[92]

The politics of recognition is closely associated with the idea of multiculturalism, which has developed since the 1960s. Trudeau, the former Prime Minister of Canada, defended the multiculturalism policy to the House of Commons on 8 October 1971. His speech perfectly summarizes the notion of multiculturalism: 'there cannot be one cultural policy for Canadians of British and French origin, another for the original peoples and yet a third for all others. For although there are

[87]Taylor, ibid., at 25.

[88]Ibid., at, 25–26.

[89]Ibid., at 28–30.

[90]Ibid., at 27.

[91]Ibid., at 38–39.

[92]See Ibid., at 25–26.

two official languages, there is no official culture, nor does any ethnic group take precedence over any other. No citizen or group of citizens is other than Canadian, and all should be treated fairly… Canadian identity will not be undermined by multiculturalism. Indeed, we believe that cultural pluralism is the very essence of Canadian identity. Every ethnic has the right to preserve and develop its own culture and values within the Canadian'.[93]

The central idea of multiculturalism is that every cultural group is equal and should be treated fairly. Liberal theories of multiculturalism dominate the field in the rich literature. Robert Goodin suggests that although liberals have argued from different perspectives, 'all of them share an affinity with 'protective multiculturalism' in representing minority cultures as against the majority rather than as benefiting the majority'.[94] Protective multiculturalism highlights the right to minority cultures, which concerns the issue of cultural imbalance between the majority culture and minority culture in some multicultural states. It is generally agreed on that cultures provide the options for living a life. Thus protection of minority cultures is not only beneficial to minorities, but also makes the options available to other peoples.[95] In Kymlicka's eyes, protecting the group-differentiated rights or collective rights of the ethno-cultural groups is an approach to solve the conflicts between different peoples.[96] Responding to the fear that protection of collective rights is inimical to individual rights, Kymlicka distinguishes two kinds of claims that an ethnic or national group might make.[97] The first involves intra-group relations, e.g., the decision of individual members not to follow traditional practices; internal restrictions may raise the danger of individual oppression. The second involves inter-group relations—that is, the ethnic or national group may seek to protect its distinct existence and identity by limiting the impact of the decisions of the larger society. External decisions may raise certain dangers of unfairness between groups; an extreme example is South Africa under Apartheid.[98] Kymlicka posits that liberals can and should endorse certain external protections, where they promote fairness between groups, but should reject internal restrictions which limit the right of group members to question and revise traditional authorities and

---

[93]P.E. Trudeau, 'Multiculturalism', *Canada History*, October 8, 1971, viewed May 8, 2014, http://www.canadahistory.com/sections/documents/Primeministers/trudeau/docs-onmulticulturalism.htm .

[94]R.E. Goodin, 'Liberal Multiculturalism—Protective and Polyglot', *Political Theory* 34 (2006), no. 3, at 290.

[95]Appiah (2005), at 70.

[96]Kymlicka (ed.) (1995), at 3.

[97]As stated by Kwame Anthony Appiah, for a long time, the great liberal struggle was to get the state to treat its members as individuals only, without favoring or disfavoring particular ethnic or religious or gender identities. If the state is in the business of advantaging and disadvantaging particular identities in ways, it will encroach upon individual's freedom to shape his or her life. Appiah (2005), at 70.

[98]Kymlicka (1995a), at 35–36.

practices. In sum, certain 'collective rights' of minority cultures are consistent with liberal democratic principles.[99]

I think, in essence, both the politics of recognition and the multiculturalism policy concern human dignity and equality. The people from less-favored groups, cultures demand respect and equal treatment of their collective identities in a society, as the denial or misrecognition of these collective identity might affect their individual dignity and rights. The demands of the repatriation of cultural heritage, in a sense, can be seen as demands of the recognition of cultural/national identity. I will interpret this view by looking into claims of the restitution of colonial cultural heritage.

5.3.2 Interpretation of Recognition of Cultural Identity in Disputes over Colonial Heritage

In periods of colonization, some cultures have been disrespected or oppressed. Reiterating their own cultural identity and unique culture in the post-colonization period is in its truest sense striving for recognition of their cultural identity. Also cultural identity serves the foundation of independence. For example, the Declaration of Intergovernmental Conference on Cultural Policies in Africa of 1975 declares: 'Cultural identity serves as a foundation for the independence and the construction of modern African nations; African culture remains a decisive weapon in struggle for liberation and in the continuing fight against colonialism, racism and apartheid; it is a basic manifestation of the feeling of unity and solidarity inspiring contemporary Africa…'.[100] Repatriating cultural objects removed from a colonial context is part of the campaign demanding recognition of their cultural identity, because the displacement of these cultural objects from their original cultures symbolizes non-recognition and disrespect of their cultural identity.

In most repatriation cases, the loss of cultural objects took place at a time when people did not have the capability to protect their lives and cultural heritage. It should be pointed out that attitudes toward colonialism or imperialism have varied greatly from time to time and from place to place. Edward Said has shown how

---

[99]Ibid., at 37. Other distinguished liberal political philosophers, e.g., John Rawls, Joseph Raz have also contributed to the theory of multiculturalism.

[100]The conference was organized by UNESCO with the co-operation of the Organization of African Unity in Accra between 27 Oct. to 6 Nov. 1975. The Russian scholar Vladimir Kartashkin observes that countries under colonial domination are intensely aware of the need to establish and assert a national identity on the basis of cultural values which often need to be revised and adapted to present conditions. Cultural identity contributes to liberation, for it provides a justification for independence movements and resistance to colonialism. V. Kartashkin, 'Economic, Social, and Cultural Rights', in: K. Vasak (ed.), *The International Dimensions of Human Rights*, Westport: Greenwood Press 1982, at 129.

Europeans divided the world into the East (Oriental) and the West, or uncivilized and civilized in the thought-provoking book Orientalism. According to Said, for Europeans, the Orientals had been seen as non-human beings, and the Eastern societies had been characterized as static, uncivilized, and undeveloped.[101] In the revised edition of Imagined Communities, Anderson confirms such Orientalist imaginings of the nineteen-century colonial states, by looking into institutions of the census, maps and museums. Anderson argues that museums exhibiting colonial objects serve the purpose of dominating. As in the cases of Burma, the contemporary natives were thought to be no longer capable of repeating their putative ancestors' achievements. Exhibition of monuments in rural poverty told the natives: 'Our very presence shows that you have always been, or have long become, incapable of either greatness or self-rule'.[102] At the beginning of the twentieth century, some people defended colonization by 'social efficiency', which assumed the Western European nations represent the most socially efficient nations, and some other nations as being weaker.[103] They argued that human progress requires the efficient nations to rule the non-efficient nations, because the earth has to be peopled, governed and developed.[104] In the mid-twentieth century, some equated imperialism with free trade, namely John Gallagher and Ronald Robinson. In their influential article 'The Imperialism of Free Trade', Gallagher and Robinson have written that 'it is necessary to revise our estimate of the so-called 'imperialist' era'.[105] By contrast, people victimized by colonization and imperialism generally have a grievance of the 'invasion' by colonial powers or imperialists. This grievance comes from being treated as second-class people, and their culture being considered undeveloped. For instance, Chinese people would consider imperialism as conquest, inequality, exploitation and hegemony.

Nowadays, people generally despise the practice of colonization. However departing from their cultural objects involuntarily are still thorns for some people. Seeing those objects displayed in foreign museums might keep refreshing people's memory of the history of being colonized, conquered or mistreated. This memory has nurtured resentment, misunderstanding and conflicts, and it is still haunting some people.[106] This experience might cause 'crisis of cultural identity'– people

[101]Said (1994).

[102]Anderson (2006), at 181.

[103]J.A. Hobson, *Imperialism: A Study*, London: George Allen and Unwin 1902, at 154–156.

[104]Ibid.

[105]In their opinion, political annexations or imperial hegemonies was the unavoidable consequence when other means of securing free trade were exhausted. Thus they suggest, 'the historian who is seeking to find the deepest meaning of the expansion at the end of the nineteenth century should look not at the mere pegging out of claims in African jungles and bush, but at the successful exploitation of the empire, both formal and informal, which was then coming to fruition in India, in Latin American, in Canada and elsewhere.' See J. Gallagher and R. Robin, 'The Imperialism of Free Trade', *The Economic History Review* 6 (1953), no. 1, pp. 1–15.

[106]See Alfred (2005), Alfred (2011), pp. 79–96.

feel not knowing who they are.[107] In Alfred's view, the spiritual crisis that colonized people are undergoing is a terrible experience for them. To solve this problem, those people have to gain recognition and respect; they have to regenerate themselves and take back their own dignity.[108]

5.4 A Cosmopolitan View

Even though repatriation of cultural objects has implications of recognition of people's cultural identity, some defend the collections of looted or colonial cultural heritage from a cultural internationalist perspective—taking cultural heritage as components of a common human culture. Cultural internationalism originates from the concept of cosmopolitanism.[109]

In the essay 'Toward Perpetual Peace', Kant identifies three definitive articles as guiding principles to protect people from war. Namely, the civil constitution of every state shall be republican; the right of nations shall be based on a federation of free states; and cosmopolitan right shall be limited to conditions of universal hospitality.[110] In Kant's theory, no one originally has any greater right than any other to occupy any particular portion of the earth; thus a stranger shall not be treated as an enemy when he arrives on someone else's territory. Kant stresses that the idea of 'a cosmopolitan right is a necessary complement to the unwritten code of political and international right, transforming it into a universal right of humanity'.[111] Although some scholars have argued that Kant's scheme for perpetual peace has been undermined by the subsequent course of history of numerous wars, Kant's vision is regarded as 'the single most important philosophical source for

[107]Taylor suggests that an identity crisis is a painful and frightening experience. People experiencing an 'identity crisis' lack a frame or horizon, 'within which things can take on a stable significance, within which some life possibilities can be seen as good or meaningful, others as bad or trivial'. See Taylor (1989), 27–28.

[108]Alfred (2011), 90–96.

[109]The term cosmopolitan, 'citizen of cosmos', was first coined in the fifth century B.C., when asked where he came from, Diogenes of Sinope said, he said 'I am a citizen of the world.' and it has been repeated by many philosophers since then. The cosmos referred to the world, not in the sense of earth, but in the sense of universe. Talk of cosmopolitanism originally signalled, then, a rejection of the conventional view that every civilized person belonged to a community among communities. See Diogenes Laertius, *Lives of Eminent Philosophers, Vol. 2* (transl. by R.D. Hicks, ed. by E. Capps a.o.), London: William Heinemann 1926, at 65; P. Kleingeld and E. Brown, 'Cosmopolitanism', *Stanford Encyclopedia of Philosophy* (ed. Fall 2013), July 1, 2013, viewed October 14, 2012, http://plato.stanford.edu/entries/cosmopolitanism/.

[110]I. Kant, 'Toward Perpetual Peace: A Philosophical Sketch', in: I. Kant, *Political Writings* (2nd ed.), Cambridge: Cambridge University Press 1991, at 3–9.

[111]Ibid., at 9.

contemporary normative theories of international relations'.[112] Furthermore, it has recently been argued that there is a change today which implies cosmopolitanism is becoming a legal-political reality. The change includes the developing cosmopolitan conscience, the inter-dependent global market, and the shared global risks.[113]

5.4.1 Universal Museums

Kant's idea of cosmopolitanism has been embraced by a number of contemporary theorists to address the relocation of cultural heritage, such as Merryman, Cuno, Lowenthal, and Appiah. To my mind, the artist Day worded this beautifully: 'art is a language of wider than national comprehension, and seems, therefore, just the one form of expression which can and should be cosmopolitan'.[114] Some art historians claim cultural internationalism to be a foundational belief in the discipline of art history in many ways. Art history rests on the assumption that it is possible for someone to look at art from a time and place not her own and understand it. Taken to extremes, this assumption can erase cultural, social, and historical differences.[115] Esner argues, 'art knows no fatherland'.[116] To support her argument, Esner cites a remark by Thoré-Bürger, a French art critic: 'When the art of all countries, each with its own indigenous qualities, has moved closer together, when (artists) have got into the habit of reciprocal exchange, art will take on a new quality; it will be infinitely enriched without, however, sacrificing the particular genius of each people…'.[117]

Cosmopolitanism also provides the philosophical source for universal museums. The foremost curators of the British Museum, MacGregor and Williams, argue it is not the extensive collections but the privileged interpreter of a set of universal cultural values that underlies in the universal museums. For universal museums, cross-cultural comment and interpretation is necessary; it is believed that most

---

[112]P. Cheah, 'Introduction', in: B. Robbins and P. Cheah (eds), *Cosmopolitics: Thinking and Feeling Beyond the Nation*, Minneapolis: University of Minnesota Press 1998, at 23. It is conceived that there are two streams of cosmopolitanism that occurred between Kant and Marx. The Communist Manifesto of the Communist Party (1848) famously claims that 'the bourgeoisie has brought its exploitation of the world market given a cosmopolitan character to production and consumption in every country' and that, through this process, the proletariat was becoming the truly universal class. See Colás (2011), no. 5, at 1053–1056.

[113]Lourme (2014), 1–2.

[114]See Brockington (ed.) (2009), 1–2. Léonce Bénédite made a similar statement that 'In the domain of art, there are, properly speaking, no more diverse nations speaking different languages; at the very most there are neighboring provinces, which can tell apart only by the local accent.' See Esner (2001), at 360.

[115]Niedzielski-Eichner (2005), no. 2, at 192–193.

[116]Esner (2001), at 357–373.

[117]Ibid.

objects hold many meanings.[118] Defending the collection of the British Museum, its former director, David Wilson, lists a number of reasons why they cannot contemplate the return of any part of their collections to countries of origin. In addition to the local conditions of insecurity, atmospheric pollution, political instability, the most important defense is on good philosophical grounds. In Wilson's view, the British Museum was founded as a universal museum and has remained true to the idea. The British Museum is designed to present as complete and integrated a picture, thus political, emotional, nationalistic or sentimental influence on the collections shall be inhibited.[119] Wilson's idea has been endorsed by other universal museums, notably the Declaration on the Importance and Value of Universal Museums.

Nevertheless, as Dr. Mark O'Neil, head of Glasgow Museum, points out, the credibility of the idea of universal museums is undermined by its being deployed chiefly as a defense against repatriation claims. A way of refusing to engage in dialogue around the issue of repatriation is as likely to confirm prejudice.[120] In contrast to upholding the idea of universal museums in the West, people requesting the return of cultural objects to their countries of origin criticize the Declaration issued by the universal museums in 2002. In an article, Opoku, a scholar from Ghana, suggests that the idea of universal museum is the invention by Western museum curators to defend their past dubious acquisitions. He writes with sarcasm: 'they are busy preaching that these objects are part of the heritage of mankind that they are keeping for all, at a time when most Western countries have made it almost impossible for Africans and Asians to enter their territories. It makes one wonder whether the museum directors know the implications of what they are preaching. Or are they simply living in another world, far from the realities of racial politics in international relations? There is hardly anyone in the non-Western world who does not view the so-called great museums as fortresses for looted artefacts of others'.[121] Therefore, as Curtis notes, the challenge for universal museums is to develop a real universal ideal: one that is available outside Europe and the US where all the signatories to the Declaration are based.[122]

Similarly, the Indian scholar, Kingh, has elaborated on how Western museums are seen outside the West. In line with her findings, Western museums are seen as 'terrifying places with insatiable appetites' by those people.[123] These museums are considered not just as cultural institutions, but as the arms of more powerful states.

---

[118]MacGregor and Williams (2005), no. 1, at 59.

[119]D.M. Wilson, *The British Museum: Purpose and Politics*, London: British Museum Publications 1989, at 115.

[120]O'Neill (2004), no. 3, at 190, 200, G. Abungu, 'The Declaration: A Contested Issue', *ICOM News* 2004, no. 1, at 5.

[121]K. Opoku, 'Reflections on the Cairo Conference on Restitution: Encouraging Beginning', *Modern Ghana* May 16, 2010, viewed October 24, 2013. http://www.modernghana.com/news/275930/1/reflections-on-the-cairo-conference-on-restitution.html.

[122]Curtis (2005), at 54.

[123]K. Singh, 'Universal Museums: The View from Below', in: Prott (ed.) (2009), at 125.

In spite of their apparent good intentions, Western universal museums are often viewed 'with resentment and suspicion in the non-West'.[124] She says telling people that universal museums promote tolerance and mutual respect in some places would provoke anger or derision. However, she feels that the universal museums are worth preserving, because those museums are a significant cultural phenomenon. In the future, universal museums are not likely to proliferate as the historical conditions for these museums are unlikely to be repeated.[125] It seems people from countries outside the West are skeptical about the universal museums, which can be seen from an incident between Bangladesh and The Guimet Museum in Paris. The Guimet Museum scheduled to display priceless archeological items loaned from Bangladesh in 2007. However, this exhibition generated huge protest in Bangladesh due to the lack of transparency of the exhibition. In an open letter to French government and citizens undersigned by artists, archeologists and other concerned citizens of Bangladesh, it states that "Musee Guimet is one of 18 museums that have jointly signed a separate Declaration on Importance and Value of Universal Museums, which opposes returning art works, especially ancient ones, to their original owners. This is in direct opposition to the UNESCO (UNITROIT) Convention on Stolen and Illegally Exported Cultural Objects (1995)... Bangladesh was identified as one of the three most vulnerable countries to such threats (theft). Kwame Opoku's recent statement 'Musée Guimet in Paris which incidentally also holds thousands of stolen/illegal objects from China and the rest of Asia' has increased citizen debate about the lending... While we were originally open to the idea of showing the work at Musee Guimet provided the transparency issues were addressed, the recent actions of the museum has removed any semblance of trust in the organisation, and we are no longer willing to loan our prized possessions to an organisation with such standards of behaviour..."[126] Finally France accepted Bangladesh's decision not to go ahead with the display of the items and cancelled the exhibition in Paris.[127]

I share O'Neill's view that the credibility of universal museums has been undermined by its being deployed chiefly as a defense against repatriation claims.

---

[124]Ibid.

[125]Ibid., at 126. In effect cultural internationalism does not shape current museum acquisition policies. Robert Hallman suggests that an internal push for reform and great external pressure has made a cultural internationalist agenda untenable, and museums are no longer willing to stand up with art dealers. The temporary exchange of cultural property through international loan exhibitions has proven to be the only form of international exchange in cultural property that the museum community broadly and openly endorses. The application of cultural internationalism within the museum community is largely confined to defending against restitution claims. See Hallman (2005), no. 12, at 202–203, 217.

[126]Quoted from K. Opoku, 'Bangladesh Protests against Parisian Musee Guimet', January 6, 2008, viewed March 16, 2015, http://www.afrikanet.info/archiv1/index.php?option=com_content&task=view&id=837&Itemid=0.

[127]See 'France to return artifacts, cancels Guimet exhibition', bdnews24, 27 December 2007, viewed October 14, 2014, http://bdnews24.com/bangladesh/2007/12/27/france-to-return-artefacts-cancels-guimet-exhibition1.

When Chinese people visit the objects looted from the Old Summer Palace displayed in Western museums, they would probably think of the destruction of the Old Summer Palace, which is still a sore point in their collective memory. And they probably feel another thing: *luohou jiuyao aida*, that means 'if you are backward, you will be attacked'. The situation is comparable with that when the people of Benin see the Benin Bronze. In this sense, the great universal museums might deepen misunderstanding and intolerance, instead of promoting understanding and tolerance. The memories of departing from their treasures might hamper people to appreciate the great art from various civilizations, which goes against the good philosophical foundation of the universal museums.

5.4.2 Balance of the Interests

In my view, the value of cosmopolitanism shall be upheld, and the truest value of cosmopolitanism is that all human beings and cultures should be treated equally. We share some common nature, common conditions of existence, and common difficulties. At the same time, we grow up in different cultural backgrounds from which we construct our identities. Parekh is right in stating that 'by acknowledging their universality and particularity, we are acknowledging the obligation to respect both their shared humanity and cultural difference'.[128] The world is comprised of cultures, and it is true that a culture does not know the political boundaries constructed by people. But in reality, some cultures are backed more strongly by powerful political entities, whereas some cultures are vulnerable and almost marginalized. The idea of multiculturalism is to assure that all cultures are treated equally. Thus in this sense, multiculturalism and cosmopolitanism share the common egalitarianism root.

In the process of globalization, some people are apprehensive about the effects of the loss or marginalization of smaller cultures. In accordance with Castell, data has shown time again that the more the world becomes global, the more people feel local.[129] The unprecedented globalization has caused fear that all cultures might be assimilated, thus in this context, people would like to embrace their identity and difference. Concerns have been expressed about the survival of local cultures. Some people consider that local cultures are transformed or absorbed by a dominant outside culture; cultural autonomy is lost.[130] In this context, increasing attention has been paid to cultural diversity, as part of the global battle against the cultural

---

[128]Parekh (2000), at 124.

[129]Castells (2010), at xxiii.

[130]See C. Barker, *Cultural Studies: Theory and Practice*, (3rd ed.), London-Los Angelos: SAGE 2008, at 159–160.

homogenization and commercialization of culture.[131] UNECSO has organized numerous conferences, round tables, colloquiums, seminars and other meetings, as well as reports, publications, and studies on cultural diversity.[132] The *Universal Declaration on Cultural Diversity* is the result of the global concern for the preservation of cultural diversity, which raises cultural diversity to the level of 'the common heritage of humanity', 'as necessary for humankind as biodiversity is for nature' and makes its defense an ethical imperative indissociable from respect for the dignity of the individual.[133] It makes it clear that each individual must acknowledge not only otherness in all its forms but also the plurality of his or her own identity, within societies that are themselves plural. Only in this way can cultural diversity be preserved as an adaptive process and as a capacity for expression, creation and innovation.[134] After this Declaration, the Member States wished to adopt a legally binding instrument on cultural diversity, the product of which is the *Convention on the Protection and Promotion of the Diversity of Cultural Expressions* of 2005.[135] This Convention has been characterized as a 'sheep in wolf's clothing' or legally speaking as a 'hard legal instrument' with a 'soft legal content'.[136] But it is also noted that 'its legal content has been and will be capable of influencing and steering future developments in international law in general'.[137]

On the other hand, research has suggested that overemphasis on attachment to a culture might also cause violence.[138] It has been proposed that a cultural identity strongly based in collectivism and in fundamentalist adherence to religious or cultural principle is a contributory factor to terrorism.[139]

As the rise of religious extremism is threatening the security of the global community, how to strike a balance between maintaining defending heritage of

---

[131]S. von Schorlemer and P.T. Stoll, 'Introduction', in: S. von Schorlemer and P.T. Stoll (eds), *The UNESCO Convention on the Protection and Promotion of the Diversity of Cultural Expressions*, Berlin: Springer 2012, at 1.

[132]For an overview until 2010, see *UNESCO*, 'Reflections on cultural diversity', 2010, viewed June 8, 2014, http://www.unesco.org/en/cultural-diversity/reflections-on-cultural-diversity/.

[133]K. Matsuura, 'Cultural Diversity: A Vision', in: K. Sténou (ed.), *Universal Declaration on Cultural Diversity* (document for the World Summit on Sustainable Development, Johannesburg 2002), Paris: UNESCO 2002, at 3.

[134]Ibid.

[135]The Convention was adopted at the 33rd session of the General Conference of the UNESCO, and entered into force on March 2007. By 11 November 2013, 133 states have become Contracting Parties to the Convention. It contains 35 articles and one annex, and addresses a large number of concerns related to 'cultural and trade problems'

[136]R.J. Neuwirth, 'A Critical Analysis of the Provisions', in: T. Kono and S. van Uytsel (eds), *The Convention on the Protection and Promotion of the Diversity of Cultural Expressions*, Antwerp: Intersentia 2012, at 69.

[137]Ibid.

[138]Sen (2007).

[139]S.J.Schwartz, C.S. Dunkel, A.S. Waterman, 'Terrorism: An Identity Theory Perspective', Studies in Conflict and Terrorism, 32 (2009), pp.537–559.

vulnerable native communities without blocking the open communication essential to the life of pluralistic democracies is important in today's society. Brown has kept repeating this view throughout the book *Who Owns Native Culture?*.[140] However, in the debate of the repatriation of colonial or looted cultural heritage, we should take into account the fact that the legacy of some unfortunate historical events are hindering people from striving for a cosmopolitan society, as well appreciating their own cultural identity. Some of them still feel being stigmatized due to the historical wrongs that were done to them. The large scale of looting and theft of cultural heritage from the original cultural communities to colonial states is one of the legacies that is still haunting people. To defend the collections with dubious provenance from 'cosmopolitanism' perspective by universal museums is to some extent not respecting the value of this great idea. For some people, displaying looted cultural heritage is really hurting their dignity and feelings, which is a non-recognition of their cultural identity. Can the people of Benin or China be convinced of the high value of cosmopolitanism by seeing the looted cultural heritage displayed in the great universal museums? For some of them, to defend the colonial collections by using theories of cosmopolitanism is an invention of the powerful countries to legitimize the acts of confiscating their treasure. Some might take cosmopolitanism as another form of hegemony.

From a legal point of view, it has been observed that a new branch of international law—the international law of recognition—has been emerging since the end of the Cold War. This new branch of law has its legal manifestations in the areas which relate to cultural diversity, right to cultural identity and reparation of historical wrongs.[141] The human value and interest of the norms of recognition have been addressed in the previous sections. In brief, it is a matter of equality and human dignity. I think, the issue of the repatriation of cultural objects that were looted or stolen in periods of imperialism and colonization concerns all the three areas mentioned in the emerging law of recognition. In a sense, the return of cultural heritage to a culture might help to maintain the vitality and integrity of a culture, thus it promotes cultural diversity in the world. Also cultural heritage is regarded instrumental to cultural identity; if right to cultural identity is recognized, right to cultural heritage should be granted. The large scale of deprivation of cultural heritage from its original country has been deplored by people from these countries. The restitution of cultural objects to some extent is seen as a reparation to the historical wrongs. That is why this issue has got constant attention in the international society since the 1960s, and it is becoming more apparent in the field of human rights law.

The Universal Declaration of the Rights of Peoples of 1976, known as the Algiers Declaration states: 'Every people has the right to the respect of its national and cultural identity' (Article 2), and 'every people has the right to its artistic, historical, and cultural wealth' (Article 14). The African Charter on Human and People's Right

---

[140]Brown (2003) 582.

[141]Tourme-Jouannet (2013), no. 2, pp. 667–690.

of 1981 also provides: 'All people shall have the right to their economic, social, and cultural development with due regard to their freedom and identity and in the equal enjoyment of the common heritage of mankind (Article 22, para.1)'.[142] In Shaheed's report submitted to the UN Human Rights Council in 2011, the extent to which the rights of access and enjoyment of cultural heritage form part of international human rights law is investigated. One of Shaheed's findings is that the rights of access to and enjoyment of cultural heritage form part of international human rights law. According to Shaheed, its legal basis lies in the right to take part in cultural life, the right of members of minorities to enjoy their own culture, and the right of indigenous people to self-determination and to maintain, control, protect and develop cultural heritage.[143] Thus some scholars observe that culture, cultural identity, and access to cultural heritage have become some inalienable 'rights'. As Sahlins has written, before, culture was just lived. Now it has become a self-conscious collective project. Every struggle for life becomes the struggle of a way of life.[144] Isar also suggests that 'culture' is now proclaimed as an inalienable 'right', conceived of as a value in itself, and justified as an inherited 'tradition'.[145] According to news reports, Turkey had intended to file a lawsuit for the return of sculptures that are currently held by the British Museum, at the European Court of Human Right in 2013. It is reported that the petition is likely to put on the ground of Article 1 of Protocol *no.* 1 to the European Convention on Human Rights: 'Every natural or legal person is entitled to the peaceful enjoyment of this possessions'. This challenge is described as 'a test case for the repatriation of art from one nation to another, a potential disaster for the world's museums'.[146]

5.5 Conclusion

This chapter has elaborated on the issue of cultural identity that is reiterated in the international conventions and soft-law instruments protecting cultural heritage. To approach to this issue, the interconnection between cultural objects and identity is

[142]This Charter, also known as Banjul Charter, is an international human rights instrument that is intended to promote and protect human rights and basic freedom in the African continent.

[143]Shaheed (2011), at 19.

[144]M. Sahlins, 'A Brief Cultural History of Culture' (unpublished), paper for World Commission on Culture and Development (UNESCO) 1994.

[145]Y.R. Isar, 'Cultural Diversity', *Theory, Culture and Society*, 23 (2006), no. 2–3, at 373.

[146]D. Alberge, 'Turkey Turns to Human Rights Law to Reclaim British Museum Sculptures', *The Guardian*, December 8, 2012, viewed July 14, 2014, http://www.theguardian.com/culture/2012/dec/08/turkey-british-museum-sculptures-rights. I contacted the Turkish embassy in Beijing in September 2014 for information about the case. I was told that there have been some discussions to apply to the European Court of Human Rights for the return of cultural property. One academic in particular was propagating this idea but in fact such a step was not taken as it was not found appropriate to follow this route. Thus in effect, for the return of cultural heritage other steps are taken and the European Court of Human Rights is not involved yet.

first investigated. Cultures provide sources for self-definition and orientation for individuals; some cultural objects, as symbols of cultures and links between past and future, are irreplaceable instruments to identity for peoples. In multicultural countries, some cultural objects might not directly link to the common national identity, but they are valued by people from the cultural communities. The thesis that cultural heritage is instrumental to cultural identity has been recognized in the international instruments of UNESCO and other international organizations. From a public international law perspective, countries of origin represent the claims on behalf of their cultural communities in dealing with disputes over cultural objects. For some people, access to authentic cultural objects is significant for their cultural life and is needed to share common cultural identity. Furthermore, the meanings of some cultural objects are only fully achieved when they are situated in their original location due to the characteristics of the place.

The main finding of this chapter is that the demands for the repatriation of cultural objects by countries of origin/cultural groups are in essence demands for the recognition of their cultural identity. Recognition of cultural identity is a matter of equality and human dignity. As a legacy of some historical wrongs, such as conquests and colonization, some peoples still endure unhappiness and misrecognition. For people who lost their cultural heritage involuntarily, acts such as displaying looted cultural objects or sensitive items like human remains in museums or selling them in public auctions, and shutting down channels of negotiation are taken as forms of misrecognition or non-recognition of their cultural identity. The effects of these acts are negative and dangerous. They provoke misunderstanding and resentment between different peoples. The seemingly conflicting value of cosmopolitanism held by the universal museums shares the common root of egalitarianism of the politics of recognition. In some cases, defending the collection of dubious provenance from cosmopolitanism not only undermines the credibility of the museums, but also undermines the good philosophical foundation for universal museums.

The respect of cultural identity is one of the pillars of the international conventions to protect cultural heritage. Also the rights to cultural heritage and the rights to cultural identity have been included in several legal instruments of human rights, but the codification of these rights does not necessarily imply the repatriation of looted or stolen cultural objects to their countries of origin or cultural groups. Although the existing conventions are not retroactive, the spirits and human interests underlying these international conventions and soft-law instruments shall not be ignored, since they concern human dignity.

Chapter 6
Why Lost Cultural Relics Matter in China

> As symbols of identity of a nation or people, cultural property represented a valuable asset of human civilization. Illicit appropriation of and trafficking in cultural property was a sacrilege. Protecting cultural heritage and promoting the restitution of such property to countries of origin were inalienable cultural rights of people in all such countries.[1]

6.1 Introduction

I have described interconnections between cultural objects and cultural identity in Chap. 5. In this chapter, I seek to figure out Chinese perceptions of their loss of cultural relics in modern Chinese history. 'Chinese culture', dealt with in this chapter, refers to culture in 'China proper' (or 'Inner China', 'agrarian China'), which is termed the 'Chinese cultural sphere', the 'Sinic world', or the 'Sinosphere'.[2] Being aware of the problems of defining 'Chinese',[3] I mainly rely on

[1]This statement was made by China's permanent deputy representative to the United Nations in Geneva, Liu Zhenmin, at the meeting of the Sixty-fourth General Assembly of the United Nations. See GA/10888, 'General Assembly Considers Drat Text on Return, Restitution of Cultural Property', November 16, 2009, viewed April 12, 2014, http://www.un.org/press/en/2009/ga10888.doc.htm.

[2]See E.O. Reischauer, 'The Sinic World in Perspective', *Foreign Affairs*, (1974), Vol. 54, no. 2, at 341; Thorp and Vinograd (2006), at 18. Within the Sinosphere, each major region is distinguished from others by its own dialect, landscape, native crops, cuisine history, famous persons, heritage sites, regional customs and characteristics. David Yen-ho Wu suggests that any expert on ethnic studies today will notice that the difference between two Han groups can, in some cases, be more pronounced than that between a Han and a minority nationality group. For instance, the regionally defined groups of Han-Cantonese, Shanghaiese, and Taiwanese, including those living overseas have obvious ethnic differences in speech, dress, customs, religious beliefs, and so on. See Wu (1991), no. 2, at 167.

[3]Some scholars are critical about the distinctiveness of 'Chinese identity' or the so called 'Chinese-ness'. Some even argue that the 'Chinese' as a singular thing does not exist. For a critical perspective, see the collection of essays in Sinophone Studies (S. Shih, R. Chow, I. Ang and A. Chung (eds.), Sinophone Studies, New York: Columbia University Press 2013).

Z. Liu, *The Case for Repatriating China's Cultural Objects*,
DOI 10.1007/978-981-10-0597-8_6

a hermeneutic approach that views culture as a historically shaped, socially shared set of symbols, concepts, and ways of organizing them. The major concern of hermeneutic works is interpretation, a common theme of which is cultural identity.[4]

This chapter is divided into two sections. I will first deal with Chinese regards on their cultural relics. It is an introduction to Chinese attitudes and feelings towards cultural heritage and lost cultural relics. For a better understanding of this issue, some observations on Chinese history and traditional Chinese culture have to be made.

The second section discusses the perceptions of the loss and repatriation of cultural relics. The loss of cultural relics is closely associated with the weakness of Chinese national power in modern Chinese history when China was confronted with foreign powers. Here modern Chinese nationalism will be touched upon. As to repatriation of lost Chinese cultural relics, I will look into the motivation and implication of repatriation the Chinese government and the Chinese people, and interpret this issue in the theories of the recognition.

6.2 Approaches to Chinese Cultural Relics

In China, cultural relics are often linked to two concepts: history and culture. In effect, Chinese history and Chinese culture are two important elements to understand Chinese cultural identity. As proposed by a great Chinese historian, Qian Mu, to understand Chinese culture, one must look back to Chinese history. In Qian Mu's view, a culture is closely related to its history. Without knowing its history, it makes no sense to discuss a culture.[5] Because of the close interconnection with Chinese history and culture, culture relics are considered to be instrumental to Chinese cultural identity.

6.2.1 Symbolizing and Decoding Chinese History

As Henry Kissinger, an American diplomat and political scientist, writes, 'No other country can claim so long a continuous civilization, or such an intimate link to its ancient past and classical principles of strategy and statesmanship. Other societies, the United States included, have claimed universal applicability for their values and institutions. Still, none equals China in persisting—and persuading its neighbor to

[4]This approach is qualified by Yu Ying-shih in 1991; another approach is the positivist approach. See 'Clio's New Cultural Turn and the Rediscovery of Tradition in Asia', keynote address by Yu Ying-shih at the Twelfth Conference of the International Association of Historians of Asia, University of Hong Kong, June 24–28, 1991. Quoted from Nathan (1993), no. 4, at 924–925.

[5]For detailed introduction of Qian Mu's view on history, cultures, and nation, see Wong, W. *National Self-Survival: Qian Mu's View on History and Culture*, (dissertation), Singapore: National University of Singapore, 2004.

acquiesce—in such an elevated conception of its world role for so long, and in the face of so many historical vicissitudes'.[6] It is a truism that history plays a crucial role in the construction of Chinese cultural identity. In Chinese history, the states were first brought together in a united empire by the First Emperor, Qin Shi Huang, in 221BC. Following that, there was a pattern of dynastic rise and fall, which has been often reflected in historical accounts, poetry, and other literature of China. The theme of dynastic rise and fall resonates especially in the dynasties of Han, Tang, Song, Ming and Qing. These dynasties were separated from each other by periods of disunity and weakness, with several states in rivalry with other, or with tribes from the north and west conquering Chinese territory.[7] In the long history of China, abundant cultural relics have been created and handed down. Now these cultural relics are regarded as witnesses to Chinese history. The National Museum of China published an eight-volume work titled *Chinese History in Cultural Relics* in 1970.[8] This series presents Chinese history from the prehistoric age to the Qing dynasty by exploring stories contained in cultural relics. For example, some rice grains in a pottery jar provide evidence of the rice cultivation in China 10,000 years ago; a title deed which had been cut into the insole shape by a housewife yields original information of the land system of dynasties of Song and Yuan. It suggests that as historical remains, each cultural relic contains historical information. Cultural relics are witness to history, and offer a way of decoding history.[9]

To study the information contained in cultural relics, ancient China had developed a branch of learning called *jinshi-xue* (the study of bronze and stone) that has been regarded as the embryo of the modern archaeology and the study of cultural relics in China. *Jin* means ancient bronze objects in the Chinese language, and *shi* means stone tablets and stone statues.[10] Scholars of *Jinshi-xue* studied the inscriptions on unearthed bronze wares, classical bronze statues, inscriptions of the stone tablets and statues, jade, inscribed bones, and other relics.[11] However, *jinshi-*

[6]Kissinger (2011), at 2–3.

[7]Seton-Watson notes the temptation to pay more attention to the continuity than to the breaches in it is almost irresistible. The Chinese is the only one of the great empires which imposed a single culture on the vast majority of its subjects and maintained, with only a few short intervals of confusion, its sovereignty over the same territory for 3000 years up the present time. See Seton-Watson, *supra* note 608, at 275, 286.

[8]The most recent version of this work was published in 2011, see Xu, W. (2011).

[9]Ibid.; Li Ben, 'Witness to History by Cultural Relics', (in Chinese), April 21, 2004, viewed August 8, 2013, gmw.cn/03pindao/shuping/2004-04/21/content_15944.htm.

[10]Li Xiaodong, *An Introduction to the Science of Cultural Relics in China* (in Chinese), *Hebei Renmin Chuban She* 1990, at 17.

[11]The research methods of jinshi-xue included description and evidential research. Jinshi-xue developed into a systematic discipline in the Song dynasty and reached a peak in Qing dynasty under the influence of Jiaqian school, the most remarkable academic school in textology at that time. Statistics show that 906 kinds of literature of Jinshi-xue were recorded in the 200 years in Qianlong period (1711–1799). Some characteristics made jinshi-xue of the Qing period outstanding: delicate authentication, detailed evidential research, extensive range of research subjects (including coins, seals, jades). See ibid., at 17–21.

xue declined with the collapse of the Qing dynasty, and was replaced by archaeology. Also the term *jinshi* was replaced by the terms of antiquities and cultural relics.[12] In fact, either archaeology or *jinshi-xue* is focused on the historical information of cultural objects. The profound Chinese scholar, Wang Guowei, proposed applying dual evidence method in historical research at the beginning of the twentieth century. The dual evidence refers to classics works of narratives history and cultural relics.[13]

It is known today that cultural objects and archaeological sites provide sources to separate chronological facts from historiographical legends. Some of the legends are mentioned in the Book of History (*Shangshu*), believed to be compiled by Confucius. For instance, the Xia ruins excavated at Dengfeng in the 1980s have been confirmed as the remains of 'Yangcheng' of the early Xia dynasty.[14] The most well-known case is the oracle bones, the mystery and value of which have been gradually made known to the world in the past century.[15] The archeological excavations at Yin-xu in 1928 organized by the Chinese Academy of Sciences confirmed that the oracle bones were part of the Shang royal archive. That means this archeological discovery confirmed the existence of the Shang dynasty. Before that, historical evidence on the Shang history was limited to the legends mentioned in classics from the Zhou period. The later study of the oracle bones confirmed the accounts given in works of historical narrative about the Shang dynasty, even validating the names and orders of succession of the Shang kings.[16] Up to now, about 130 thousand pieces of oracle bones have been discovered. The inscriptions contain genealogical, calendrical, meteorological, and astronomical data, including the earliest records of a solar eclipse and a comet. The decoding of the inscriptions yield a mass of varied information giving a vivid insight into the lives of the Shang people relating to politics, the military, culture, and social customs.[17] Furthermore, being the earliest known specimens of the Chinese scripts, the oracle bone

---

[12]Ibid., at 17–21.

[13]Scholars after Wang Guowei further the dual evidence method into a tri-evidence method. Jao Tsung-I, Ye Xianshu, Huang Xianfan, and Shen Congwen all have proposed their own 'tri-evidence method'. But taking historical documents and cultural relics as historical research material is the common element they all share.

[14]Fei, X. (1988), at 175.

[15]It is submitted that the Shang rulers kept these inscriptions sacred because they were records of confirmed decisions or judgments and because they provided important precedents to the Shang rulers for future deliberations. There is practically no mention of the oracle bones in the abundant accounts of antiquity recorded from the Zhou dynasty to the Han dynasty. The absolute secrecy of the whereabouts of oracle bones until its being discovered is astounding. See ibid., at 178; Cui, B., 'On the Philological Value of Jiaguwen' (in Chinese), *Tushu yu Qingbao* 2007, no. 4, at 127.

[16]Liao Jing, 'A Historical Perspective: The Root Cause for the Underdevelopment of User Services in Chinese Academic Libraries', *The Journal of Academic Librarianship* 30 (2004), no. 2, at 109–110.

[17]Cui, B., *supra* note 15, at 127–128.

inscriptions are of fundamental importance for the study of Chinese paleography, such as the methods of character-building.[18]

In the case of the Dunhuang manuscripts, one of the premier scholars of Dunhuang studies Rong Xinjiang argues that the Dunhuang manuscripts have provided unprecedented insight for researchers on the history and civilization of China and the world.[19] In Rong Xinjiang's view, the value of the Dunhuang manuscripts lies in their originality and antiquity. These manuscripts help scholars to break away from the confines imposed by traditional historians, so scholars can have an independent look at history. The overall majority of historical materials, on which traditional Chinese historiography relies, were produced by elite literati who served as part of the bureaucracy. However, the Dunhuang manuscripts offer a body of primary material which had never before been organized, edited, or distorted by historians. By studying the Dunhuang manuscripts, researchers can often scrutinize an event through material that is contemporary with that event, and even reveal things that had been concealed by medieval historians.[20] Moreover, according to Rong Xinjiang, Dunhuang manuscripts offer authentic first-hand material to write about a history that has never been written. Traditional Chinese histories were all compiled from the perspective of the central administration, and in most cases recorded events concerning the imperial family and the limited group of top officials. The Dunhuang manuscripts provide rich information on various strata of society; they also include many unknown texts written in non-Chinese languages, such as Tibetan, Uighur, Khotanese, Sogdian and Sanskrit. These texts reflect the state of affairs of the different peoples in Dunhuang and the surrounding regions, as well as the relationship between the Guiyijun regime (a military outpost set by the Tang empire) and its population. These texts record the historical events of Central Asian people using their own language and script, which makes them more authentic and at the same time more valuable than records written in Chinese.[21] Based on the manuscripts, Chinese scholars have discovered more about the social institutions of the Tang dynasty, including equal land reallocation, taxation and corvee labor, land lease, documents on monastic economy and legal administration, the clan system, the military system, the history of the Guiyijun and more.[22]

In addition to the philological value of the Dunhuang manuscripts, the manuscripts also provide source to study the 'manuscripts culture' which aims at mapping out how knowledge was created, reproduced, and transmitted in medieval China (220–906). By studying the Dunhuang manuscripts of the Book of Han, which records the history of the Western Han dynasty, Chinese scholars, such as Yu Xin, try to find out the deeper connotation behind the manuscripts. In Yu Xin's

---

[18]About six thousand different characters have been recorded from the inscriptions, of which some two thousand can be identified with modern versions. See ibid.

[19]Rong, X. (2013), 341.

[20]Ibid., at 6.

[21]Ibid., at 6–7.

[22]Ibid., at 4.

research, he finds that the attitude towards knowledge reveals the holistic view of the world of a specific community; and the transmission of knowledge reflects the operation of power and social order. That means the value of the Dunhuang manuscripts is not limited to the philological texts; they reflect the transmission of knowledge, faith, and social culture.[23] Chinese cultural relics symbolize the long history of China and provide information to decode the history; also Chinese cultural relics are representation of Chinese culture.

6.2.2 Representing Chinese Culture

In terms of Chinese culture, some Western scholars use the term 'culturalism' to distinguish the Chinese civilization from others, to explain why China remained distinct from the rest of the world.[24] James Harrison notes two elements contributed to the construction of culturalism in ancient China: the belief that China was the only true civilization, and strict political adherence to Confucian principles.[25] In the eyes of the ancient Chinese, the land where they lived was the only piece of land for human beings. So they called this land *tianxia* (all under heaven). Gradually, *tianxia* turned into a cultural concept. People at that time believed that only *tianxia* was the true culture, and people living outside *tianxia* were barbaric. The seventeenth-century Chinese thinker Gu Yanwu draws a distinction between *guo* (state) and *tianxia*. In the view of Gu Yanwu, state is a political concept, whereas *tianxia* is a cultural notion, which refers to Chinese cultural tradition and heritage. For Chinese people, the change of dynasties or government is not as profound as the ruin of Chinese cultural values.[26] Similarly, according to the prominent historian of Asia Wang Gungwu, for those within (China), the early history of China as *tianxia* gave a sacral quality to the dynasties from the Xia and Shang to the Zhou; it was followed up by the unified empire of the Qin and Han. By that time, a larger cluster of 'proto-states' were ruled by people culturally identified as *zhuxia* (Chinese). For centuries, the meaning of being Chinese seemed simple and definite: a sense of belonging to a great civilization and performing properly according to the intellectual elites' norm of conduct.[27] Interestingly, although China had existed for

[23]Zhang Zhaoguang notes that the students'primers, text-books, and notebooks present the average intellectual level of the public; the examination papers contain information on the ideology and its influence on thinking. See Yu Xin, *Mapping the Extraordinary: Knowledge, Faith and Manuscript Culture in Medieval China* (in Chinese), Shanghai: Shanghai Guji Chuban She 2011, at 70–73.

[24]See Harrison (1969), pp. 2–15; Townsend (1992).

[25]Harrison, ibid., pp. 3–14.

[26]See Lu and Dellios (1998), no. 1, at 20.

[27]G. Wang, 'On Tianxia', Lecture delivered in September 2012 at the Australian Centre on China in the World, viewed August 4, 2014, http://www.thechinastory.org/2013/08/wang-gungwu-%E7%8E%8B%E5%BA%9A%E6%AD%A6-on-tianxia-%E5%A4%A9%E4%B8%8B/.

millennia, it was not until the twentieth century that Chinese historians have meticulously used source materials on foreign cultures to explain how what is understood as 'Chinese culture' came into being. They studied foreign cultures in order to understand Chinese culture.[28] For example, the Chinese philosopher Liang Shuming, who is regarded as the last Confucian, compares Chinese culture with other cultures. Liang Shuming defines 'culture' as a 'mode of life of a people'. Specifically, it is the way people resolve the contradictions between the will's demands (something like desires) and the obstacles presented by the environment. Life is the never ceasing volition or 'will' together with the ceaseless dissatisfactions and satisfactions. Liang Shuming puts forward the view that cultural differences lies in the differences of the 'direction' of the will, and the way the will attempts to deal with environmental obstacles. He identifies three cultural systems in the world by comparing the different modes of life. The first type, represented by the West, is the regular or normal direction of the will; people struggle to get what is desired and try to change the environment in order to fulfill the will. The second mode of life is represented by China. The basic direction of the will is to harmonize the will with the environment, in order to strike a balance between the two. In the third type of culture, the will turns backward into itself and seeks its own negation, represented by India.[29]

As part of traditional cultural legacy, Chinese art is often presented as an expression of Chinese culture. For example, in the work Chinese Art and Culture, two American leading art historians, Robert Thorp and Richard E. Vinograd, present Chinese art as a cultural expression of social, political, economic, and religious events or institutions in a chronological order.[30] According to another prominent art historian of Chinese art, Wen Fong, art has intentionally been accorded a vital and central treatment in the Chinese culture and society.[31] In Fong's view, the creation of art served to the political adherence to Confucianism in imperial China, because of the Neo-Confucian dictate that art must serve the Tao that was ineluctably represented by the state. Another reason is that in Chinese culture the pursuit of art was a valid way of cultivating one's moral self.[32] Among the forms of Chinese art,

[28]In the view of Wang Gungwu, traditional Chinese way of looking at 'culture' is rather more holistic, which covers religion, philosophy, politics, music, art, and all other branches of knowledge. See G. Wang, 'China's Quest: A New Cultural Identity', Lectures delivered in DU's 2009-10 Bridges to the Future Series on April 28, 2010, viewed August 3, 2014, https://www.youtube.com/watch?v=4R9HITn7HBw.

[29]See Liang, S. (2006), at 31; Alitto (1986), at 82–83; 612. Liang summarized some characteristics of traditional Chinese culture: vast territory with a large population; multi-national integration; long history; an unnamed power for the preservation of culture; immobile social status and culture; almost no religious life; emphasis on clan system; no scientific-orientation in academia; no democracy; priority of morality in the social structure; precocity; indifference to military; emphasis on filial piety; and the existence of hermits. See Liang, S. (2005), pp. 10–24.

[30]Thorp and Vinograd, (2006).

[31]Fong (1992), at 3.

[32]Ibid.

Chinese calligraphy and painting can never be neglected.[33] Chinese people believe painting and calligraphy share the common source; both the written ideographs and pictorial representation functioned as graphic signs that expressed meaning.[34] Thus, painting has been studied as documents with historical information, and some argue Chinese art is history.[35] Furthermore, painting is considered as a medium of consciousness, and it embodies boundaries, cultural axioms, epistemic awareness, and social interest.[36] In the case of the Admonitions Scroll, the painting illustrates a political parody by Zhang Hua (232–300). From the Han dynasty, Confucianism became orthodoxy in Chinese society. In Confucianism, a wife should submit to her husband. Zhang's parody takes a moralizing tone, attacking the excessive behavior of the empress Jia (256–300), who made a name for herself on account of her tyranny and cruelty in Chinese history. The parody aimed at providing advice to women in the imperial court, and Zhang used the painting as an allegory of the misconduct of the governmental officials. The creation of the Admonitions Scroll was to spread the teaching of Confucianism.[37]

Moreover, in ancient Chinese society, literary elites were thought to represent Heaven. Frederick W. Mote, an American Sinologist and historian, has observed in a remarkable article 'A Millennium of Chinese Urban History: Form, Time and Space Concepts in Soochow' that the real Chinese past is a past of the mind; 'the only truly enduring embodiments of the eternal human moments are the literary ones'.[38] As stated by Fong, art was produced almost exclusively by amateurs, usually aristocrats and scholar-officials, who had the leisure time necessary to perfect the

[33]The appreciation of painting and calligraphy has a long history in China. In the South-Qi dynasty, the great art critic, Xie He, had put forward the 'six principles of Chinese painting': spirit resonance, the way of using the brush, proper representation of objects, application of color, good composition, and transmission of the old masters by copying them. The six principles marked the theoretical framework of Chinese painting. In the Song dynasty, calligraphy and painting were adored in imperial court. Emperor Huizong was a great painter, poet, and calligrapher; he endeavored to search for great art. He managed to collect an unprecedented amount of masterpieces. Emperor Huizong also organized the compilation of Xuanhe Painting Catalogue and Xuanhe Calligraphy Catalogue. The painting catalogue recorded 6390 paintings by over 230 painters, and the calligraphy catalogue recorded 1198 pieces of calligraphic works by over 190 calligraphers of different styles. See Li, X., *supra* note 10, at 21–24.

[34]The fifth century scholar Yen Yen-chih believed that there were three kinds of signs: the magical hexagram of the Yijing (The Book of Changes), which represented nature's principles; the written ideographs, which represented concepts; the pictorial representation, which depicted nature's form. See Fong (1996), at 28.

[35]See Fong (2003), no. 2, pp. 258–280; Shi Shouqian, *Style in Transformation: Studies on the History of Chinese Painting* (in Chinese), Beijing: Peking University Press 2008.

[36]Hay (2005), at 117.

[37]See H. Wu, 'The Admonitions Scroll Revisited: Iconology, Narratology, Style, Dating', in: S. McCausland (ed.), *Gu Kaizhi and the Admonitions Scroll*, London: The British Museum Press 2003, at 89–91.

[38]F.W. Mote, 'A Millennium of Chinese Urban History: Form, Time, and Space Concepts in Soochow', in R.A. Kapp (ed.), *Four Views of China* (Rice University Studies 59, no. 4), Houston: Rice, at 51.

technique and sensibility necessary for brush work.[39] The term *biji* or *moji* (trace of brush or trace of ink) expresses the idea that these works of art represent the physical presence of the maker.[40] Because most of the greatest works of art in ancient China were created by literary elites, these works of art are symbolic of eternal spirit of the greatest Chinese literary in Chinese society. *Biji* of great literary men, as material proof of geniuses and their immortality, have been worshiped in Chinese elite society. Notably, calligraphic works by Wang Xizhi, Wang Xianzhi, and Wang Xun of the Jin dynasty have always been the most valued treasures throughout Chinese history.

6.2.3 Instruments to Chinese Cultural Identity

Because of the intimate relationship with Chinese history and culture, cultural relics are considered to be instruments to Chinese cultural identity, as history and culture provide significant sources for Chinese self-definition.[41] However, in the past two centuries, the Chinese society has undergone dramatic changes. Some might argue that ancient cultural relics have no interconnection with modern Chinese cultural identity. In terms of modern Chinese cultural identity, I will look into this issue from the Chinese sense of history and China's struggle with its tradition since the commencement of modern Chinese history.

6.2.3.1 Chinese Cultural Identity

Many Chinese people are very proud of their long history. Ask a Chinese how long Chinese history is, and you will probably get an answer that 'China has a 5000-year long history'. Regardless of the preciseness, belonging to a long history has been instrumental to Chinese sensibility. In Tu Wei-ming's view, the idea of being Chinese is reinforced by a powerful historical consciousness informed by one of the most voluminous veritable documents in human history. The chronological annals have flowed uninterruptedly since 841 BC in China. This cumulative tradition is preserved in Chinese characters, a script separable from and thus unaffected by phonological transmutations. The continuity of the long history in the same land and the people there found the Chinese civilization standing in East Asia, setting it aside from any other in human history.[42] In China, the past or, more precisely, notions of the past have assumed a unique centrality and exerted a powerful

[39]See Fong (1992), at 3.

[40]Fong (1996), at 28.

[41]See Zhu, C. (2007), no. 3, pp. 81–85; Mei, H. et al. (2009); etc.

[42]Tu,W. (2005), no. 4, at 147.

influence over philosophy and morality.[43] Since the dawn of Chinese civilization, history has been placed in a very high position by people. Confucius was believed to have composed the first history in China: Spring and Autumn Annals (*Chunqiu*). For Confucius, history and classics were two instruments to express his ideas. The equivalence between history and classics, as perceived by Ming and Qing scholars, suggests that in traditional China, history was not only knowledge about the past, but also a repertoire of ancient wisdom readily available for the needs of the present.[44]

The Chinese historian, Ge Jianxiong, states that Chinese people probably pay the most tribute to their history; the worship of history in ancient China went far beyond people's imagination.[45] There is even a saying that history is the religion for Chinese, as history functioned like a religion in ancient China. At that time people believed their ancestors would continue to live in another world and blessed their posterity.[46] In the Zhou dynasty, people began to accept the view that their gods of ancestors or the sages never blessed their posterity blindly; they would only bless their posterity if they behaved virtuously. The idea that Heaven is just came into being. Chinese gradually believed that successes or failure are the ultimate result of the act of ancestors. Success and honor are 'proof' of the greatness of one's forebears; and personal successes and virtues would ensure the same for descendants. On the other hand, people, especially emperors, feared that their evils would be rewarded with evil results or cursed by their posterity, so they acted with strong scruples toward history and historians. The painstaking care and scrupulousness to history made every newly-established dynasty in history give priority to the compiling and revising of the history of the former dynasty, seizing the initiative to interpret the Mandates of Heaven by writing history.[47]

Along with the strong perception of history, traditional Chinese spiritual culture is also significant in the construction of Chinese cultural identity, which can be

[43]S. Pearce, 'Form and matter: Archaizing reform in sixth-century China, in: S. Pearce, A. Spiro and P. Ebrey (eds.), *Culture and Power in the Reconstitution of the Chinese Realm 200–600*, Cambridge: Harvard University Press, 2001, at 151.

[44]E. Wang, *Inventing China Through History: The May Fourth Approach to Historiography*, Albany: SUNY Press 2001, at 28.

[45]Jianxiong (2008), no.9, pp. 11–13. Because of the important role that history plays in China, history is often sources of conflict and debate. As Callahan writes, 'history' is often seen as a security issue in East Asia international relations, and history is also an important security issue in Chinese texts. See Callahan (2006), no.2, at 183–185.

[46]No systematic mythology developed in ancient China; the heroes that made great contributions to their tribes and the emperors (later the representatives of Heaven) were adored as Gods. The characters of 'Di' (emperor) and 'God' in oracle bones refer to 'the ancestors of the primitive tribes'. Historians in ancient times not only recorded historical events around the emperors, but also acted as the bridges between Heaven and the people by recording the Will of Heaven and the astronomical phenomena faithfully. These historical records provide the only source for understanding the Will of Heaven to the posterity. In this sense historians in ancient China in effect were like priests or sorcerers in other religions. Ge, J., ibid., at 11–12.

[47]Ibid., at 13.

approached from the concept of Tao. Tao is a metaphysical concept originating with Lao Tzu. According to Yu Ying-shih, Tao and history constitute the inside and outside of Chinese civilization.[48] Yu Ying-shih suggests that the crystallization of Chinese culture into its definitive shape took place in the time of Confucius, when 'a hundred schools of thought' flourished in China. All these schools and their teaching did not come from life experience or from their studies, but they came spontaneously from the source of Tao. Chinese philosophies shared the common belief that Tao is hidden and yet functions everywhere in the human world.[49] As one way to express Tao, Confucianism gradually became the most influential thought and dominated Chinese society for two millennia. The Emperor Wu of Han adopted the principles of Confucianism as the state philosophy and code of ethics. From then on, Confucianism had infiltrated all fields of life of the Chinese people and had far-reaching influences on the development of Chinese history. Persons who wished to be candidates for official positions should study Confucianism. Confucianism reached the highest level it had ever had in China.[50] Still, traditional China also absorbed cultures from outside, such as Buddhism.[51] Neo-Confucianism was developed in the Song dynasty, which was an attempt to create a more rationalist and secular Confucianism by rejecting superstitious and mystical elements of Taoism and Buddhism that had influenced Confucianism during and after Han dynasty. At the same time, Neo-Confucianism borrowed concepts from Taoism and Buddhism.[52]

---

[48]Y. Yu, 'Address of yu Yingshih on the Occasion of Receiving the John W. Kluge Prize at the Library of the Congress', *Library of Congress*, December 5, 2006, viewed December 5, 2013, http://www.loc.gov/today/pr/2006/06-A07.html.

[49]Ibid. The major schools in the 'hundred schools of thought' included Yin-Yang school (originated in the official astronomers), Confucianist school (originated in Ministry of Education), Mohist school (originated in the Guardians of the Temple), School of Names (originated in the Ministry of Ceremonies), Legalist school (originated in the Ministry of Justice), and Taoist school (originated in the official historians). See Fung, Y. (1948), at 30–35.

[50]Fung, Y., ibid., at 197. According to Liang Shuming, Confucianism is focused on earthly life. Before the adoption of Confucianism, Chinese people also had their own 'religious' lives by worshiping totem, objects and gods. Gradually the ancient religions were replaced by Confucianism, and this process has been called the 'moralization of social relations by Confucianism. Only the tradition of worship for gods (heaven) and ancestor dating back to antiquity have been inherited until today. In Chinese culture, the emphasis on earthly life overrides 'religious' life. Liang, S., (2005), at 85–102.

[51]The influence of Buddhism in China reached its peak during the Tang dynasty and Buddhist arts flourished in that period. Chan Buddhism (commonly known as Zen) is a combination of the most subtle and delicate aspects of both the Buddhist and Taoist philosophies, which exercised a great influence later on in Chinese philosophy, poetry, and painting. Chan Buddhism became the dominant Buddhist school of China during the Tang and Song dynasties. Fung, Y. (1948), at 212.

[52]Neo-Confucianism, the synthesis of Taoist cosmology and Buddhist spirituality around the core of Confucianism, predominated in the intellectual and spiritual life of China, Korea, and Japan to the modern period. In Taoism, Chan Buddhism and Confucianism, the object of spiritual practice is to 'to become one with Tao' or to harmonize one's will with Nature. See Huang (1999), at 5.

However, in the second half of the nineteenth century, Chinese intellectuals began to struggle with the disposition of the Chinese tradition and Western modernization.[53] At the first stage, the ruling elites subscribed to traditional Chinese values and strengthened the empire by adopting modern Western management and technology, known as the 'spiritual China-material West' dichotomy. But the First Sino-Japanese War proved this movement to be a failure. Following that, some modern radical intellectuals including Lu Xun promoted that China must transform its old cultural identity into a completely new one in order to survive in the modern world. They blamed the evil Chinese tradition for China's loss in the modern world, thus Chinese had no choice but to abandon their past entirely.[54] The radical thoughts were intimate to the New Culture Movement, which called for a new creation of Chinese culture based on global and western standards. This movement exerted strong influence on the Chinese society and its young followers, notably Mao, and has been conceptualized as 'totalistic iconoclasm'.[55] It should be noted that there were some voices in preserving the Chinese tradition, like the camp of the *Xueheng Journal*, but those propositions were considered to be old fashioned.[56]

Following the foundation of the PRC, traditional Chinese culture continued to be negated. In the Cultural Revolution, Chinese tradition, especially Confucianism, experienced the darkest age ever.[57] After the Cultural Revolution, Chinese

[53]Alitto (1986), at 82.

[54]Hummel (1930), at 55; Tonglin Lu, 'Destruction, Revolution and Cultural Nihilism', in: R. Bogue and M. Cornis-Pope (eds.), *Violence and Mediation in Contemporary Culture*, Albany: State University of New York Press 1996, at 144.

[55]Mao was an avid reader of the New Journal of the New Cultural Movement. In Mao's later political life, he emphasized the function of ideology and believed in its ability to change the social reality. This was believed to have originated from the radical thoughts of the New Cultural Movement. Mao was insistent on opposing traditional Chinese culture; it was the unchanging theme of his thoughts. See Lu, T., ibid.

[56]The Xueheng Journal, begun in 1922, aimed to conserve the quintessence of native Chinese culture and blend it with Western knowledge. In effect, the Xueheng Journal was the literary headquarter of modern Chinese conservatism, attracting old-types scholars of all ages and from all fields of study together around Xueheng. The Xueheng scholars had close association with Babbitt. Babbit was profiled as a modern saint by Mei Guandi and he supervised Wu Mi at Harvard University. Wu Mi and his colleagues endeavored to introduce Babbitt's thought in the journal of Xueheng, especially the ideas of new humanism. Babbitt told his Chinese students that 'China needs to absorb the positive elements from the Western civilization and science. But it is more important to maintain the core values of humanism of the Chinese tradition. China should not abandon its tradition for pursuing progress. See X. Kuang, 'Xuehang Pai and the New Humanism' (in Chinese), *Journal of Peking University (Philosophy and Social Sciences)* 1994, pp. 90–99.

[57]A great deal has been written on this subject during the past four decades. It is generally agreed that the Cultural Revolution had its root in Mao's attempt to find an alternative path to socialism other than the Soviet one; and that it resulted in the total destruction of the common belief and value system of several generations of Chinese communists and intellectuals. After the Cultural Revolution, the Chinese government opened a door for total denigration of Cultural Revolution. It has been telling the Chinese people and the people over the world that the Cultural Revolution was 10 years of calamities, and that China's economy was brought to the brink of collapse during that period.

traditional culture was also regarded as backward in the mainstream of Chinese society in the 1980s.[58] The negative image of Chinese traditional culture began to disappear in the 1990s in China, and the Chinese state leaders borrow a lot of political norms from Confucianism, like 'ruling the country by virtue (*Yide zhiguo*)' by Jiang Zeming, and the notion of the 'harmonious society (*Hexie Shehui*)' by Hu Jintao.[59] In academia, scholars argue the resurgence of New Confucianism has been an eminent development since the late 1970s. New Confucianism has been termed as the third epoch of Confucianism.[60] Traditional Chinese culture is also coming back to popular society. University teachers, giving lectures on Confucianism on national television channels become 'star scholars' overnight; classics recital classes for children are sprouting up in many parts of the country; books on Confucianism or traditional culture are becoming popular. The ominous image of Chinese tradition as a stumbling block to Chinese modernity is almost gone in China today.[61]

Today's Chinese scholars regard Chinese cultural relics as objects instrumental to Chinese cultural identity, which are of spatial and temporal presence. The spatial presence concerns the geographic locality to which an object is related, and the temporal presence emphasizes how a cultural relic has witnessed and transcended the passage of time.[62] They argue that cultural objects are important mediums for

---

[58]The River Elegy shown on China's central television took a sharply critical stance on traditional Chinese culture. It asserted that China's land-based civilization was defeated by the maritime civilizations backed by modern science. The revival of China must come from the flowing blue seas which represent the explorative, open cultures of the West and Japan.

[59]The CPC announced to inherit and promote the refined traditional Chinese culture at its fourteenth Congress in 1992. After that, to promote traditional Chinese culture has been highlighted in its subsequent congresses. See Ai (2009), no. 61, pp. 689–701; Bell (2007), no. 2, pp. 20–28.

[60]It is held that New Confucianism has gone through three generations. The first generation, from 1920 to 1949, labored to make Confucianism relevant in a time of national crisis. Important representatives are Liang Shuming, Feng Youlan, Xiong Shili and Helin. The second generation, from 1949 to 1970, includes philosophers such as Tang Junyi, Mou Zongsan, Xu Fuguan. These four philosophers jointly published 'A Manifesto on Chinese Culture to the World' in 1958, announcing that Chinese culture, including Confucianism was not dead and that a reformed Confucian contribution to world civilization was not only possible but was to be applauded. See U. Bresciani, *Reinventing Confucianism: The New Confucian Movement*, Taipei: Ricci Institute for Chinese Studies 2001; Yao Xinzhong, *An Introduction to Confucianism*, Cambridge: Cambridge University Press 2000, at 6–7.

[61]See Wang Ruichang, 'The Rise of Political Confucianism in Contemporary China', in: R. Fan (ed.), *The Renaissance of Confucianism in Contemporary China,* Dordrecht: Springer 2011, at 33. There are several observations of the coming back of Chinese traditions. Some argue that the promotion of Chinese tradition serves the CPC's governing of China, because the attempt to replace family ties with ties with to the state during the Cultural Revolution proved to be a failure. Confucianism values still inform ways of life, especially regarding family ethics. By contrast, some attribute the revival of Chinese tradition to its 'intellectual cross-fertilization and rivalry'. See Bell (2007), at 23; Makeham (2008), at 331.

[62]Zhu, C. (2007), no. 3, pp. 81–85.

cultural transmission and inheritance; cultural objects can generate a sense of belonging to a culture or to a country, and store people's cultural memory.[63] In their view, tangible cultural relics materialize intangible cultural values and collective memory, thus cultural relics are symbols of cultures and instruments of cultural identity. The interpretation of cultural objects must be associated with the original cultural tradition; the signs in cultural relics are symbolic and have deeper meanings. For instance, in traditional Chinese culture, dragon designs are symbols of emperors, fish designs connote prosperity; horses mean success and so on. The cultural meanings and stories of cultural objects constitute its sole. Otherwise, it is an empty shell.[64]

6.3 Approaches to the Loss of Chinese Cultural Relics

It should be acknowledged that cultural relics and art have been appreciated by many Chinese people in the long history of agrarian China, except for some iconoclastic periods like the Cultural Revolution. Since the Opium Wars, Chinese cultural heritage has suffered irreparable damage from outside and inside. In view of the great amount of cultural relics lost in modern Chinese history, the Chinese government, some institutions and persons are endeavoring to recover the lost Chinese cultural relics (see Chap. 1). However, these recovering activities have encountered different voices. Responding to the treasure hunting trip sent by the Yuanmngyuan Administration in 2009, some show a sympathetic attitude to Chinese people for their loss of cultural objects, and they contend that everything looted should be returned. By contrast, some react to China's recovery program with a sneer or anger. Most of them share the opinion that these cultural treasures would not have survived the notorious Cultural Revolution if they had stayed in China. They argue that the credibility of their reclaimation is undermined by the Chinese cultural policy to their minorities. They take China's recovery claim as ideological propaganda and say that 'Chinese want to portray themselves as victims of colonial aggression'.[65] In the spring of 2013, I had a short academic tour in Beijing and consulted some experts of Chinese cultural relics and history from National Museum of China, Chinese Academy of Cultural Heritage, Peking

---

[63]Yan Haiming, 'Cultural Heritage and Cultural Identity' (in Chinese), *Chinese Cultural Relics Information*, October 18, 2013, viewed November 14, 2013, ccrnews.com.cn/plus/view.php?aid = 48361.

[64]See Shen Congwen, *Material Cultural History*, (in Chinese), Taiyuan: Beiyue Wenyi Chubanshe 2002, at 5–10; Zhang Guotian, 'The Semiotic Feature of Cultural Relics' (in Chinese), *Beifang Wenwu* 29 (1992), pp. 97–101.

[65]The media report of this trip has triggered a lot of reactions. For more information of the public reactions, see Chiarch, 'Reactions to the Chinese Mission to Inspect Chinese Antiquities in Foreign Museum Collections', in *A Big Job: Protecting China's Archaeological Heritage*, December 18, 2009, viewed July 2, 2014, chiarch.wordpress.com/tag/cultural-relics/.

University, China University of Political Science and Law. I asked about their opinions of the view that if those cultural objects had stayed in China, they would not have survived the Cultural Revolution. One of them told me that the Cultural Revolution has been a tragedy for all Chinese, and Chinese have kept re-examining the Cultural Revolution. But Cultural Revolution should not be used as a justification of the looting and theft of cultural objects that took place long before the Cultural Revolution. In the following text, I will discuss about how Chinese think of the loss and repatriation of cultural relics, and I will try to bring them into a coherent interpretation.

6.3.1 Loss of Cultural Relics as National Tragedy

To understand some Chinese feelings about their lost cultural objects, we can start from looking into the reactions of the auctions of the bronze heads from the Old Summer Palace. These auctions stirred up the Chinese national feelings. The Chinese experts and governmental officials kept warning the Chinese not to fall in the trap of patriotism.[66] Many Chinese consider the public auctions of looted cultural relics as brutal offenses to China. They complain about that Western people are still showing no respect to Chinese culture and Chinese people. Some Chinese urge boycott of the auction house; some describe it as adding salt to their wounds. It is true that the Old Summer Palace has become a mark of national bitterness for many Chinese. As expressed by some commentators, the burning of the Old Summer Palace was a fatal blow to traditional Chinese culture; Chinese highest culture had been ignored and smashed into pieces violently by the Western powers. There is a saying that the legacy of the destruction of the Old Summer Palace remains everywhere in China. Chinese pupils learn about the story of the Old Summer Palace from their textbooks, TV programs, and movies. The destruction of the Old Summer Palace symbolized the most barbaric rape of Chinese culture. The intentional destruction has caused much resentment and misunderstanding to Chinese for over one and a half centuries.[67]

The Chinese bitterness of the destruction of the Old Summer Palace probably reflects a general attitude towards the loss of the large number of cultural relics in modern Chinese history. Many Chinese regard the loss of Chinese cultural relics as a national tragedy or stigma. In Chinese discussion of the loss of cultural relics, words such as grievance, pain, national disaster, and cultural tragedy are commonly used. They mainly attribute the loss of cultural relics to the weakness of China in modern Chinese history, and such loss has been an unavoidable consequence of the

[66]It has been reported that when the auctions of the bronze heads from the Old Summer Palace proceeded in 2009, the Sino-French relationship dropped to the bottom.

[67]Zang (2010); Ye Tingfang and Wang Rongzu, 'A Paradise Lost: Memorial of the Destruction of the Old Summer Palace', (in Chinese) *Zhonghua Dushu Bao,* September 22, 2010, viewed July 23, 2014, http://epaper.gmw.cn/zhdsb/html/2010-09/22/nw.D110000zhdsb_20100922_1-17.htm.

decline of China. An old saying in China is used picture this situation: 'no eggs can remain unbroken when the nest is destroyed'.[68] The loss of cultural relics was one of the broken eggs when the nest of China was encroached upon.

As in the case of the Dunhuang manuscripts, the most highly quoted statement is made by the Chinese scholar Chen Yinke: 'The loss of Dunhuang manuscripts is a most tragic incident in the history of Chinese scholarship'.[69] The foreign explorers who acquired the manuscripts are still considered 'robbers' or 'thieves' in China. It is said Chinese scholars of Dunhuang studies have bitter feelings towards the loss of manuscripts, and they felt even worse when they realize the underdevelopment of Dunhuang studies in China. There was a time when scholars outside China used to say that 'Dunhuang is inside China, but Dunhuang studies are conducted only outside China'.[70] They have considered the loss of Dunhuang relics as a stigma, and worked very hard to erase this stigma. According to Rong Xinjiang, patriotism had been the major motivation for Chinese scholars to engage in the Dunhuang studies for decades. Some Dunhuang scholars hold the view that it is wrong for Chinese to fall behind in the Dunhuang studies, because those manuscripts are from China, and most of them are about Chinese stories and written in Chinese languages. The motivation to retrieve China as the research center of Dunhuang studies has generated great enthusiasm among Chinese scholars for Dunhuang studies, and Chinese scholars achieved a lot in the studies. However, the overemphasis on retrieving China to the research center of Dunhuang studies has become an impediment for Chinese scholars. It makes Chinese scholars reluctant to communicate with non-Chinese scholars, especially with Japanese. This has narrowed the horizon of Chinese scholars, and has limited the development of the Dunhuang studies.[71] Under such circumstances, in 1988 the preeminent Chinese scholar of Dunhuang studies, Ji Xianlin, put forward the idea that 'Dunhuang is in China, but Dunhuang studies are in the world'.[72] This cosmopolitan view of Dunhuang studies proposed by Ji Xianlin is of great significance for the Chinese scholars to break through the limits of nationality and locality. Scholars are of their own nationalities, but research and

---

[68]See Zhang Zicheng, *A Memorandum of A Century's Loss of Cultural Relics in China* (in Chinese), Beijing: Zhongguo Lvyou Chubanshe 2001; Wu Shu, *Who is Collecting China* (in Chinese), Taiyuan: Shanxi Renmin Chubanshe 2008; Lu Jiansong, *A Memorandum of Tragedies of Cultural Relics* (in Chinese), Chengdu: *Sichuan Renmin Chubanshe* 2002; etc.

[69]Chen Yinke's statement is in Chinese "敦煌者,吾国学术之伤心史也". Today inside the Mogao Grottoes there is a museum that displays photos of the loss of Dunhuang manuscripts. In the dooryard of the museum, there is a big stone statue engraved with '敦煌者吾国学术之伤心史也'. People will see the engraved stone statue when they enter the museum.

[70]Quoted from Tan Chung, 'Introduction', in: Tan Chung (ed.), *Dunhuang Art: Through the Eyes of Duan Wenjie,* New Delhi: Indira Gandhi National Centre for the Arts 1994, at 34.

[71]Rong, X. (2005), no. 4, pp. 173–175.

[72]Ibid., at 175.

cultures is not. Rong Xinjiang states that this might be straightforward for Western scholars, but it has taken Chinese a long time to realize this.[73]

Some might attribute the Chinese sentiments of their lost cultural relics to the political agenda of CPC so as to legitimize its ruling authority.[74] But it should be noted that some of these feelings had existed before the CPC took power over China. For example, the statement that Chen Yinke grieved at the loss of Dunhuang manuscripts was made in the 1920s. In my view, the Chinese sense of grievance about the loss might originate from the affection for the culture, and the rise of modern Chinese nationalism. In the past century, numerous excellent Chinese intellectuals and artists have come to Dunhuang and made their homes there: Liang Sicheng, Zhang Daqian, Ji Xianlin, Chang Shuhong, Duan Wenjie, Fan Jinshi, etc. For example, Fan Jinshi, the present president of the Dunhuang Academy, who is more widely known as the 'daughter of Dunhuang', has spent over half a century in Dunhuang on promoting and preserving its culture.[75] Also out of the affection for the culture, generations of intellectuals have been deeply concerned about the return of Dunhuang cultural relics. When Fan Jinshi was interviewed, she said: 'Foreign explorers made use of the ignorance of Taoist Wang and robbed Dunhuang of the invaluable cultural treasures in a despicable way. More importantly, the Gansu provincial government ordered to preserve the relics in Mogao Caves. According to (Chinese) law, the Taoist and the foreign explorers were not allowed to dispose of the cultural relics. Whoever took the relics broke the law, and they were thieves. The foreign institutes should not have turned down the restitution requests, and they should return the cultural relics back to Dunhuang.'[76] Besides, I would suggest understanding of emotions from the perspective of the rise of modern Chinese nationalism.

---

[73]Ibid.

[74]See Chiarch, *supra* note 65.

[75]According to newspaper report, Fan Jinshi arrived at Dunhuang in 1963 as a graduate student from Peking University when her parents were living in Shanghai and they were reluctant to allow their daughter to work so far away. At that time getting to Dunhuang was an ordeal. No planes, and few trains went there. The academy's headquarters had neither electricity nor running water. It is said despite the harsh conditions, Fan fell in love with Dunhuang and was determined to preserve its beauty. At the age of 76, she is still working as hard as ever. See H. Cotter, 'Buddha's Caves', *The New York Times*, July 6, 2008, viewed July 13, 2014, http://www.nytimes.com/2008/07/06/arts/design/06cott.html?pagewanted=all&_r=0; 'Researcher Fan Jinshi Honored for Preserving the Dunhuang Grottoes', womenofchina.cn, 1 March 2014, viewed September 14, 2014.

[76]'Fan Jinshi: A Watcher of Dunhuang' (in Chinese), September 14, 2010, viewed September 14, 2014, http://fashion.ifeng.com/art/interview/detail_2010_09/14/2510278_0.shtml. When I was at Dunhuang in September 2014, I happened to meet Fan Jinshi, while she was taking a walk after lunch; and she was greeted with high respect by the crowds. After she left, according to her colleagues, Fan Jinshi once said that her greatest wish is to recover the Dunhuang cultural relics lost abroad. She would organize to build one of the best museums at Dunhuang to house the Dunhuang manuscripts if they could come home.

6.3.1.1 Chinese Nationalism

It has been submitted that Chinese have very broad generalization about their own history: they think in terms of 'before the Opium Wars' and 'after the Opium Wars'.[77] This broad historical view and the subjugation experience after the Opium Wars have shaped the Chinese view of the world order. According to Kaufman, most Chinese elites' view of the international system today start from the implicit premise that today's international system has not changed in its essence from the nineteenth century. 'The world is composed of strong and weak nation-states that vie for the dominance on the global stage'.[78] Scholars note that the experience of subjugation in modern Chinese history has become an important element of Chinese identity today. For example, some claim that 'Chinese nationalism is not just about celebrating the glories of Chinese civilization; it also commemorates China's weakness.'[79]

Most scholars share the view that Chinese nationalism was the result of its confrontation with the Western powers. Before that the very Chinese sense of unity has meant belonging to a civilization rather than to a state or a nation.[80] The premiere Chinese sociologist Fei Xiaotong argues that the formation of the Chinese people into a single nation has been the result of a historical process of millennia, but only when the Chinese were confronted with the Western powers in the nineteenth century, were they aware of themselves as a national entity.[81] After a series of defeats in its modern history, a recurring theme in China has been the nationalist quest for China's regeneration to blot out the humiliation at the hands of imperialists. The slogan of 'rejuvenation of China' was started by Sun Yat-sen, and responded by the subsequent leaders like Jiang Jieshi, Mao Zedong, Deng Xiaoping and Jiang Zemin. Having accepted the norm of the modern nation-state system, these leaders no longer thought of China as the centre of the world and Chinese culture as a universal set of values. But they have shared a strong sense that China should be restored to its rightful status as a great power as they believed China's

---

[77]Kaufman (2010), no. 1, at 2.

[78]Ibid., at 1.

[79]Ibid., at 3. Notably, some scholars have strongly criticized the consumption of national humiliation in China, e.g. Wang, Z. (2012).

[80]Liang Qichao was believed to be the first person to introduce the term minzu (nation) to China in 1899. The term nation was adopted from the writings of Meiji Japan and associated with nationalistic writings warning the Chinese people of the danger of annihilation under Western invasion at the turn of the twentieth century. See Fei, X. (1988), Zhao (2000), Levenson (1968), Hsü (1960).

[81]In Fei Xiaotong's view, as a general rule, the name of an ethnic group is first applied by outsiders and then gradually becomes accepted by the group itself. People living in the same social community would not develop the consciousness of their ethnic entity without contacts with people outside their community. For example, the people known as Qins and Hans called themselves by these names only after they were referred to in this way by ethnic groups outside the Central Plain. A people acquires its specific name long after it has begun its existence as an entity, instead of becoming an ethnic entity because it is called by that name'. See Fei, X. (1988), at 167–217.

decline was a mistake of history, and they should correct it.[82] In today's Chinese society, nationalism and patriotism are still influencing the Chinese people, which can be seen from the conflicts during the Beijing Olympic Torch Relay in 2008, and the anti-Japanese demonstrations in 2012. According to Wang Zheng's, in societies like China, historical memory has already become a constructed social norm in the national 'deep culture' and will influence people's thoughts and actions. Chinese historical memory of a century of humiliation in China's modern history is powerful in shaping the Chinese national identity.[83]

To some extent the humiliations the Chinese feel in modern Chinese history have become part of their national identity. In a way, the tragic loss of cultural relics in this period is part of the Chinese cultural loss, part of their national humiliation. In such situation, some objects are thought to be of less cultural or artistic value, but are imposed with symbolic meanings due to the historical events, such as the bronze heads from the Old Summer Palace. These objects have become symbols of the national stigma and tragedy. So when the bronze heads are auctioned in the market, China feels provoked. Similarly, in the case of the Admonition Scrolls, some art historians claim that its status is created by transferring focus on the historical and aesthetic context of its production and reception to antipathy toward the Qing dynasty and regret for the many losses and humiliations suffered by China.[84]

6.3.2 *Repatriation of Lost Cultural Relics as Recognition of Identity?*

There are various interpretations of the repatriation of the lost Chinese cultural relics. It is apparent that different stakeholders have different attitudes towards the repatriation issue. From a political point of view, Richard Curt Kraus, a political scientist, regards Beijing's drive to recover elite art as part of China's broader cultural ambitions in the article 'The Repatriation of Plundered Chinese Art'.[85] In the opinion of Kraus, China has become one of the world's greatest exporters of art through the low-cost production to Western consumers. However, this facet of China's place in the international cultural economy is profitable, but unglamorous. In Kraus's view, the repatriation of elite art is a symbolic issue, with deep emotional resonance. On one hand, the glories of the Chinese past contribute to the glories of its civilization of today. On the other hand, the repatriation activities distract

[82]See Zhao (2004), at 12.

[83]Deep culture here refers to the unconscious framework of meaning, values, norms, and hidden assumptions that we use to interpret our experience. See Wang, Z. (2012), at 11–12.

[84]See C. Wang, 'The Qing Imperial Collection, circa 1905-25: National Humiliation, Heritage Preservation, and Exhibition Culture', in: H. Wu (ed.), *Reinventing the Past: Archaism and Antiquarianism in Chinese Art and Visual Culture,* Chicago: The Center for the Art of East Asia, University of Chicago 2010, at 236.

[85]Kraus (2009), at 837.

attention from less glamorous realities of China's participation in the global cultural economy. So Kraus sees repatriation of plundered objects as a part of a complex cultural policy linking China to the world.[86] It is true the Chinese government is eager to extend its cultural influence to the world with the growth of its economic power, and to recover the elite Chinese art, to some extent, might contribute to showing the glamour of the Chinese culture to the world. But nonetheless, I think, Kraus's analysis of Beijing's motivations to recover cultural heritage neglects the Chinese demands for respect or recognition of their culture and identity.

For some Chinese intellectuals, they believe that to return looted or stolen cultural objects is a gesture of showing respect to a culture. A Chinese writer, Feng Jicai, wrote an article titled 'For the Sake of Dignity of Civilization: Regarding Return of Dunhuang Cultural Relics' at the centennial of the discovery of the Library Cave.[87] In that article, Feng Jicai describes the recovery of Dunhuang relics as an issue that Chinese intellectuals cannot leave behind. Chinese intellectuals are very concerned about the repatriation of Dunhuang relics but not optimistic, as they believe that the present possessors are still very covetous towards those objects and are not aware of the wrongs done by their ancestors to other cultures.[88] In the eyes of Feng Jicai, cultural relics belong to their original lands, as they are the spirit of the lands for witnessing and continuing the history. Only when cultural relics are linked to their authentic lands are they given lives and endowed with cultural value. Each culture has its own integrity; to separate cultural objects from a culture is to encroach on its integrity. To return the Dunhuang cultural relics to Dunhuang, as well as to return other cultural objects to their culture, is to show respect to cultures created by our ancestors.[89]

Likewise, at the one hundred fiftieth anniversary of the ransacking of the Old Summer Palace, it was claimed that the cultural relics from the Old Summer Palace are the yardstick to test the degree of human civilization (civilized).[90] As stated in the report, the wound caused in the sacking of the Old Summer Palace is still bleeding. But the theme of the memorial event (of the destruction of the Old Summer Palace) is peace, cooperation and harmony. This reflects that the Chinese people are trying to heal the wound. Remembering history is not to continue the enmity, but for rational reexamination.[91] It is said the objects looted from the Old Summer Palace are far more than material treasures. Some say only when the location of these looted objects is determined in accordance with humanity and morality can this wound be healed.[92] As an Indian scholar expressed it, 'The

[86]Ibid., at 842.

[87]Feng, J., 'For the Sake of Dignity of Civilization: Regarding Return of Dunhuang Cultural Relics', *Zhongguo Wenhua,* (2001), no. 17–18, pp. 63–65.

[88]Ibid.

[89]Ibid.

[90]Lin (2010).

[91]Ibid.

[92]Ibid.

Garden cannot be restored but we can restore the broken trust between the civilizations which was damaged. The message China should send to the West and the whole world on this one hundred fiftieth anniversary is about global peace and harmony among the different civilizations.'[93] In brief, the return of he Chinese lost cultural relics carries meanings of respecting Chinese culture and repairing the broken trust between peoples by addressing the unfortunate past.

Just as Feng Jicai indicates, the issue of the Dunhuang manuscripts is an issue of respect of a culture. Also the issue of the Old Summer Palace relics is symbolic of wound and disrespect. It has been discussed above that the Chinese view the modern Chinese history as a century of humiliation. The memories of the encroachment on the Chinese sovereignty, the unequal treaty system, the Japanese aggression during WWII have shaped the Chinese thinking of international politics: China would not be treated as an equal if China is a weak country. The issue of the repatriation of lost Chinese cultural relics is a matter of national dignity and the respect of Chinese cultural identity.

The non-recognition of Chinese culture the Chinese have felt in the past has resulted in a sense of inferiority of culture for many Chinese, and this sense of inferiority has caused destructiveness and violence in the Chinese society, known as the Cultural Revolution. A statement by Liang Sicheng is quoted very often. 'China's repeated defeat from the mid-nineteenth century made Chinese intellectuals and ruling class lose faith in Chinese traditional culture. It has distorted their aesthetic and moral standards because of the lack of orientation: they abandon their traditional standard while they know nothing about the Western standard.'[94] There is an appeal for cultural awareness and cultural confidence in today's China. The thesis of cultural confidence calls upon the young Chinese to have confidence in their native culture and rid themselves of the sense of cultural inferiority. It stresses the key role of traditional Chinese culture in the construction of present Chinese cultural identity.[95]

---

[93]Binod Singh, 'History of the Old Summer Palace Will Teach Us a Lesson', *China Daily*, October 19, 2010, viewed June 13, 2014, http://www.chinadaily.com.cn/opinion/2010-10/19/content_11431079.htm.

[94]Quoted from Jin Yongbing, 'Cultural Confidence and Value of National culture' (in Chinese), *Wenyibao,* December, 9, 2011, viewed May 4, 2014, http://www.cflac.org.cn/wywzt/2012/liangsicheng/201202/t20120215_128705.html. Tu Wei-ming shares a similar view. On one hand, Chinese intellectuals have inseparable contacts with Chinese tradition, but on the other hand, they have to admit that Western culture has some advantages over traditional Chinese culture. However, they are repelled by the Western imperialism and colonization in history. Chinese nationalism and patriotism were stimulated to salvage China from subjugation, and at the same time Confucianism was marginalized. The marginalization of Chinese tradition has caused cultural identity crisis for many Chinese intellectuals. See Tu Wei-ming, 'Literates traditionally represented Heaven, but now they are experiencing crises of cultural identity' (in Chinese), June 7, 2013, viewed September 4, 2013, cul.qq.com/a/20130607/021501.htm.

[95]Jin, Y. ibid.; Li Lin 'A Review of the Call for the Young Generation's Cultural Confidence', (in Chinese), *Renmin Ribao,* May 27, 2014, viewed Junne 12, 2014, http://www.chinanews.com/cul/2014/05-27/6214253.shtml.

The repatriation of the elite Chinese art might have other merits for the Chinese. It has been put forward that 'art is therapy'.[96] As De Botton and Armstrong argue, 'art is ultimately a therapeutic medium, just like music. It, too, is a vehicle through which we can do such things as recover hope, dignify suffering, develop empathy, laugh, wonder, nurture a sense of communion with others and regain a sense of justice and political idealism'.[97] Access to the greatest Chinese art might help Chinese to leave behind the resentment, destruction, and old grudges formed in the past. But this view is going to be unfolded when more light shed to this issue.

6.4 Conclusion

Cultural relics have been appreciated for a long time in Chinese society. They symbolize and decode Chinese history, as well as represent traditional Chinese culture. Since history and traditional culture are integral elements in the construction and maintenance of Chinese cultural identity, cultural relics are regarded instrumental to Chinese cultural identity. The loss of cultural relics in modern Chinese still haunts many Chinese until today, and they regard it as a national cultural tragedy. However, the discussion of repatriation of the lost Chinese relics is a complex issue. Sentimentally, the Chinese grieve at the loss of cultural relics in modern Chinese history, but the Chinese did destroy Chinese cultural treasures themselves in some periods, and these destructive activities discredit their claims for the repatriation of the lost cultural relics. From the perspective of cultural identity, history and culture provide significant sources for Chinese self-definition, and due to the close interconnection with Chinese history and culture, cultural relics are regarded as instruments to Chinese cultural identity. Today cultural relics are appreciated and protected in China. For some Chinese, lost cultural relics have become a symbol of national stigma; these objects remind them of the subjugation, weakness, and non-recognition in modern Chinese history, during which Chinese nationalism was developed to salvage China from its weakness and defeat. In essence, repatriation of the lost cultural objects means respect to their cultural identity and acknowledgment of the unfair treatment in the former relationship with foreign powers. Repatriation of some most wanted cultural objects might not erase all the frictions between Chinese and others, but it is indeed a gesture of reconciliation and respect.

---

[96]de Botton and Armstrong (2013), Kramer (2000).

[97]Ibid.; A. de Botton, 'Alain de Botton's guide to art as therapy', *The Guardian*, January 2, 2014, viewed June 12, 2014, http://www.theguardian.com/artanddesign/2014/jan/02/alain-de-botton-guide-art-therapy.

Chapter 7
Conclusions and Recommendations

This book sets out to explore legal, cultural and ethical issues concerning repatriation of cultural objects to countries of origin or cultural groups by looking into the repatriation claims of China. The analysis of the previous chapters manifests that repatriation of cultural objects is an extremely difficult and complicated issue. As a legal issue, repatriation of some cultural objects is difficult because they were deprived from their original owners or trafficked in a distant past when the rules were not crystallized. Due to the lapse of time, seeking legal remedies is almost impossible. However, as a cultural and ethical issue, the increasing awareness of protection of cultural identity and the right to cultural heritage provided in various legal instruments make some repatriation claims reasonable and persuasive, even though some scholars criticize the notion of cultural identity. In a sense, the protection of property rights and the protection of cultural rights conflicts with each other in some cases.

To come back to the first research question of this book, I come to conclude that there is no sufficient legal protection of cultural objects that were looted, stolen, or illegally exported before the 1954 Hague Convention and the 1970 UNESCO Convention. As reflected in Chaps. 3 and 4, it is almost impossible for original owners or their rightful successors to obtain legal remedies to recover cultural objects which were removed a long time ago. Respecting international adjudication, the first obstacle would be the jurisdictional issue, as most tribunals require mutual consent of parties in contentious proceedings. Apart from that, the international conventions protecting cultural objects are of no retroactive effect. With regards to confiscation of cultural objects during war times, although today it is universally recognized that looted cultural objects should be restituted, there is no such defining moment since when these rules have become international customary law, considering that looting went hand in hand with war throughout human history. Pursuant to the doctrine of inter-temporal law, it is very difficult to determine customary international law to cases before the crystallization of the rules. Even if the illegality of the confiscation of cultural objects is indisputable in some cases, like the Japanese pillage during WWII, it does not necessarily guarantee the result

Z. Liu, *The Case for Repatriating China's Cultural Objects*,
DOI 10.1007/978-981-10-0597-8_7

that looted cultural objects will be restituted to their rightful owners. In some cases, the post-war settlement makes the repatriation claims more difficult. For instance, the waiver of right to war reparations in the Joint Communique by the Chinese government makes the repatriation claims for Japanese looted cultural objects during WWII from China at a disadvantage, even though today's customary law recognizes that cultural objects shall not be retained as war reparation. The principle of extinctive prescription in international law is another important element that might make the cases inadmissible. Respecting seeking remedies through international civil litigation, an original owner or a rightful successor would probably get a similar adjudication, even though jurisdiction of civil litigation is not based on mutual consent. Through civil litigation, a claimant needs to prove at least three issues to obtain legal remedies successfully: (1) He had acquired a valid title to the disputed objects; (2) The original deprivation did not transfer a valid title to a third party; (3) His rights have not been extinguished by the lapse of time due to limitation law or rules of prescription. In the case study of the Dunhuang manuscripts, even though pursuant to English conflict of laws, the Chinese law governs the first two issues if public interest is not invoked, an English court would rule against the claimant as the old English limitation rules had extinguished the original owners' right. In most cases of restitution of cultural objects stolen long ago, it is highly likely that the rights of the original owner or the rightful successor has been extinguished because of the limitation law or rules of prescription of national legislation of another country.

Regarding the second research question of this study, I note that cultural objects are regarded as instruments of people's cultural identity, and repatriation of cultural objects in some cases has implications of recognition of people's cultural identity. By situating the repatriation claims in political theories of recognition of cultural identity and contrasting it with the idea of cosmopolitanism, I conclude that to deprive people of their most valued cultural heritage against their will is a form of misrecognizing people's cultural identity, as well as to display or auction such cultural heritage. The politics of recognition share with cosmopolitanism the common root of egalitarianism, whereas to defend the collections of illegal provenance with disregard for objections from other people goes against the good philosophical foundation of universal museums. In the cases of colonial cultural heritage, the issue of repatriation of cultural objects carries meaning of recognition and respect of cultural identity of the people who were victimized of colonization. Some cultural objects, such as the Old Summer Palace relics, have become the marks of national tragedy for some people, which cast long-lasting misunderstanding, resentment, and hatred between different countries and peoples. The result of the application of these criterions will be different from case to case.

In the previous research by other scholars, e.g., Merryman's cultural property internationalism, some considerations have been made regarding the reallocation of cultural objects, including preservation, integrity and distribution. Along with that, I may suggest taking into account how cultural objects have been deprived and what the objects mean to people's cultural life and their cultural identity. In effect, the former issue regarding the way of deprivation concerns the legality of removal, while the latter concerns the intangible meanings of cultural objects to people. Regarding the legality issue, I have shown that the rules contemporaneous with the removal in some cases were not crystallized as they are today. Imagine the scenario that the sacking of the Old Summer Palace just took place recently. The applicable rules and the attitudes towards repatriation claims would be different. It is also a truism that we cannot go back indefinitely into the past and correct all the wrongs done in the past. But we should note that the legacies of some historical events are still haunting people until today, which has become a matter a dignity and respect. The large scale of depriving people of their valued cultural heritage in periods of colonization or wars is one of these matters, and I think it deserves more attention in our society as the 'identity' issue has become such an important issue in the changing world we are living. Besides, it also deals with historical injustice. I have not come up with a general criterion regarding what cultural heritage is integral to people's cultural identity. But clearly, the legal and cultural implications of such issues continue to resonate in the contemporary world.

This study contributes to the ongoing debate of the reallocation of disputed cultural heritage in various ways. In general, first of all, it provides a concrete answer to the first research question as whether there is sufficient legal protection of cultural objects that were removed before the adoption of today's international conventions protecting cultural objects. Secondly, it builds a normative framework for future research on this topic, which combines many fields together: public international law, private international law, transnational civil litigation, national legislation regarding property and cultural heritage, political theories. Thirdly, it communicates ideas between different cultures by telling the Chinese stories in the West, and it builds bridges of understandings on an important international issue. To be more specific, this study has explored the Chinese legal regime concerning the protection of cultural heritage before the foundation of PRC. Much research has been done to explore the contemporary Chinese legal framework on protecting cultural relics, but it is not known to many people whether there was law to protect cultural heritage in China before the 1980s. This book has briefly outlined the legislations concerning cultural objects in the late Qing and republic periods in China. Along with that, it looks into the Chinese participation in the two Hague Peace Conferences and how China entered into the relevant international conventions. Notably, this fact has been frequently ignored by many Chinese lawyers, and in practice, it is usually proclaimed that no international conventions apply to the cases. This study analyzes the applicability of the 1899 Hague Convention (II) and 1907 Hague Convention (IV) to the cases identified in this study. Another important observation of this study regards the effects of the Chinese government's waiver of war indemnity during the normalization of the diplomatic relationship between China and Japan. Also this study discusses the legal questions which might affect seeking remedies through international adjudication and civil litigation, such as jurisdiction, the determination of inter-temporal law, post-war settlement, waiver of claims, principle of extinctive prescription in public international law, conflict of laws, good faith acquisition, limitation of actions, acquisitive prescription and etc.

This book has put forward several questions that deserve more attention, in particular the interconnection between cultural objects and cultural identity, and implication of repatriation as recognizing people's cultural identity. It looks into the existing understanding of cultural heritage as instrument to cultural identity. Indeed, cultural identity is a controversial topic, as some people are not convinced of the theories and arguments regarding cultural identity, even though cultural identity has been reiterated in some international instruments and in the repatriation claims. This study is in favor of the argumentation that cultural heritage is instrumental to cultural identity, and links it with the politics of recognition and post-colonial thinking. It shares the view of 'peoplehood' put forward by Carpenter et al. (2009), by looking into the importance of the authenticity of cultural heritage, the interconnections between cultures and states, and those between cultural objects and countries of origin. These theories are applied to the Chinese cultural context. The Chinese conception of their culture, history and cultural relics, together with the vicissitudes of Chinese society and its participation in globalization and modernization, might introduce fresh elements to the issues concerning cultural identity. This study also reflects the huge gap on understanding of this issue. Many Chinese regard the loss of Chinese cultural heritage as a national tragedy of the decline of China in its modern history, part of their national humiliation. On the contrary, some people consider this issue as an ideological one that some Chinese portray themselves as victims of imperialistic aggression, and that the CPC utilizes it to justify its legitimacy of ruling in China. There are some factors that might account for the disfavor of China's repatriation claim: Chinese minority problems, the destructive Cultural Revolution, and the deep fear of communism in the West.

Even though this study yields fresh findings from China's perspective on an important international issue, they should be considered against several limitations, and these limitations raise a number of questions of value for future research. One of these questions is the lack of a specialized international tribunal with compulsory jurisdiction to settle cultural heritage disputes. In view of the European national committees on restitution of Nazi looted art, the possibility and design of legal procedures to deal with disputes over cultural heritage is of research and policy value for the international community.

Also, it is not clear to what extent post-war settlements influence the restitution or return of cultural objects confiscated in the event of armed conflicts. As described in the case between China and Japan during the normalization of diplomatic relations of the two states, the Chinese government's waiver of right to undefined war compensation has left many problems unsolved. If there is no specific provision, are cultural objects separated from the general course of war indemnity? Can a government—without a law- waive the right to cultural heritage for its citizens or cultural communities? More research needs to be done on the legal effects on the post-war settlements.

This book analyzes the applicability of the resolutions adopted by UN and UNESCO in the situation of international adjudication, but it does not answer the questions whether these resolutions have become international customary law, and whether they can be exception to the principle of inter-temporal law. I would suggest research on the international soft law making on restitution and return of cultural objects and the existence of international customary law.

Moreover, this study only deals with repatriation claims made by countries of origin or cultural groups, the historical background of which concerns occupation, colonization, and imperialism. As such, the conceptions explored in this study are not generalized beyond this context. Along with that, even as to two cases that occurred in the same period, each case should be discussed in its own cultural and historical context. For instance, the sacking of the Old Summer Palace relics and the looting of Benin bronzes both took place during the European punitive expeditions in the second half of the nineteenth century. However, it is possible that because Chinese perceptions of history and culture differ from that of Nigerians, the Nigerians' attitudes toward the Benin bronzes would be different from that of the Chinese towards their lost cultural relics. In other words, some findings of this study, especially the part on cultural identity and cultural objects, are not tested to discover whether they can be extended to other disputes over cultural heritage. More qualitative research from different perspectives is suggested to attest the contemporary conceptual framework concerning the repatriation of cultural heritage.

Last but not least, this study simplifies the interests in cultural heritage of various potential stakeholders. A comprehensive analysis from different perspectives might pull threads together, such as propriety interests of original owners and their rightful successors, propriety interests of present possessors, the display interests of cultural objects in museums, the religious/cultural interests attached on cultural objects by cultural groups, and intellectual property rights. In the balance of interest of various stakeholders, elements as such have to be taken into consideration. Apart from that, the question of how to create the balance between cultural identity of a cultural group and its contact with the outside world has not been elaborated on in this book. On the one hand, terrorism is threatening the security of our world in the present stage; some propose that terrorism is motivated by a cultural identity strongly based in collectivism and in fundamentalist adherence to religious or cultural principles. On the other hand, some are asking for the recognition of their cultural identity, which provides them with sources of pride, solidarity and dignity. In what ways should cultural identity be properly protected but not abused? To quote an old Chinese saying, this study just 'throws a brick in order to get a gem'; I expect to see more research to clarify this issue in the future.

Bibliography

J. Ai, 'Two Sides of One Coin: the Party's Attitude toward Confucianism in Contemporary China', *Journal of Contemporary China* 18 (2009), no. 61, pp. 689-701.

T. Alfred, 'Wasáse: Indigenous Resurgences', in: J.T. Levy (ed.), *Colonialism and its Legacies*, Lanham: Lexington Books 2011, pp. 79-96.

T. Alfred, *Wasáse: Indigenous Pathways of Action and Freedom*, Peterborough: Broadview Press 2005.

G.S. Alitto, *The Last Confucian: Liang Shu-ming and the Chinese Dilemma of Modernity,* (2nd ed.), Berkeley-London: University of California Press 1986.

M. Amaladoss, 'Global Homogenization: Can Local Cultures Survive?', *East Asian Pastoral Review* 36 (1999), no. 4.

B. Anderson, *Imagined Communities: Reflections on the Origin and Spread of Nationalism*, (rev. ed.), London-New York: Verso 2006.

K.A. Appiah, *Cosmopolitanism: Ethics in a World of Strangers*, New York: Norton Paperback 2007.

K.A. Appiah, *The Ethics of Identity*, Princeton: Princeton University Press 2005.

G.J. Ashworth, B.J. Graham & J.E. Tunbridge, *Pluralising Pasts: Heritage, Identity and Place in Multicultural Societies*, London: Pluto 2007.

D.A. Bell, 'From Marx to Confucius: Changing Discourses on China's Political Future', *Dissent* 54 (2007), no. 2, pp. 20-28.

R. Benedict, *Patterns of Culture*, New York: The New American Library 1960.

W. Benjamin, *The Work of Art in the Age of Mechanical Reproduction* (transl. J.A. Underwood), London: Penguin 2008.

U. Bresciani, *Reinventing Confucianism: The New Confucian Movement*, Taipei: Ricci Institute for Chinese Studies 2001.

G. Brockington (ed.), *Internationalism and the Arts in Britain and Europe at the* Fin de Siècle, Bern: Peter Lang 2009.

M.F. Brown, *Who Owns Native Culture?*, Cambridge: Harvard University Press 2003.

T.Burns & S. Thompson, *Global Justice and the Politics of Recognition,* Hampshire: Palgrave Macmillan 2013.

W.A. Callahan, 'National Insecurities: Humiliation, Salvation, and Chinese Nationalism', *Alternatives* 29 (2004), no. 2, pp. 199-218.

W.A. Callahan, 'History, Identity, and Security: Producing and Consuming Nationalism in China', *Critical Asian Studies*, 38 (2006), no.2, pp. 179-208.

K.A. Carpenter, S.K. Katyal & A.R. Riley, 'In Defense of Property', *Yale Law Journal*, 118 (2009), no. 6, pp. 1022-1125.

M. Castells, *The Power of Identity: The Information Age: Economy, Society and Culture* (2nd ed.), Malden: Wiley- Blackwell 2010.

M. Cheng, 'Globalization, Global History, and Chinese History' (transl. by H. Chan), *Chinese Studies in History* 42 (2009), no. 3, pp. 51-56.

Z. Liu, *The Case for Repatriating China's Cultural Objects*,
DOI 10.1007/978-981-10-0597-8

J. Clifford, *The Predicament of Culture: Twentieth Century Ethnography, Literature, and Art*, Cambridge: Harvard University Press1988.

A.Colás, 'Taking Sides: Cosmopolitanism, Internationalism and 'Complex Solidarity' in the Work of Fred Halliday', *International Affairs* 87 (2011), no. 5, pp. 1052-1065.

R.J. Coombe, 'The Properties of Culture and the Politics of Possessing Identity: Native Claims in the Cultural Appropriation Controversy', *Canadian Journal of Law and Jurisprudence, Vol.*6, No.2, (1993), pp. 249-285.

J.B. Cuno, *Who Owns Antiquity? Museums and the Battle over Our Ancient Heritage*, Princeton: Princeton University Press 2008.

J.B. Cuno, 'Ownership and Protection of Heritage: Cultural Property Rights for the 21st Century: U.S. Art Museums and Cultural Property', *Connecticut Journal of International Law* 16 (2001), no. 2, pp. 189-196.

N.G.W. Curtis, 'A Continuous Process of Reinterpretation: The Challenge of the Universal and Rational Museum', *Public Archeology* 4 (2005), no. 1, pp. 50-56.

A. de Botton & J. Armstrong, *Art as Therapy*, London: Phaidon Press 2013.

A.V. Dicey, J.H.C. Morris, L.A. Collins & A. Briggs, *Dicey, Morris and Collins on the Conflict of Laws* (15th ed.), London: Sweet and Maxwell 2012.

T. Doctoroff, *What Chinese Want: Culture, Communism and the Modern Chinese Consumer,* New York: Palgrave Macmillan 2012.

R. Esner, 'Art Knows no Fatherland: Internationalism and the Reception of German Art in France in the Early Third Republic', in: M.H. Geyer & J. Paulmann (eds), *The Mechanics of Internationalism: Culture, Society and Politics from the 1840s to the First World War*, Oxford: Oxford University Press 2001, pp. 357-373.

X. Fei, 'Plurality and Unity in the Configuration of the Chinese People', *The Tanner Lecture on Human Values*, delivered at The Chinese University of Hong Kong, November 15-17, 1988.

W.C. Fong, 'Why Chinese Painting is History', *The Art Bulletin* 85 (2003), no. 2, pp.258-280.

W.C. Fong, 'Chinese Art and Cross-Cultural Understanding', in: W.C. Fong & J.C.Y. Watt (eds), *Possessing the Past: Treasures from the National Palace Museum, Taipei*, New York: Metropolitan Museum of Art 1996.

W.C. Fong, *Beyond Representation: Chinese Painting and Calligraphy, 8th-14thCentury*, New York: Metropolitan Museums of Art 1992.

F. Francioni, 'Plurality and Interaction of Legal Orders in the Enforcement of Cultural Hertiage Law', in F. Franioni & J. Gordley (eds), *Enforcing International Cultural Heritage Law*, Oxford: Oxford University Press 2013, pp. 10-22.

F. Francioni, 'Public and Private in the International Protection of Global Cultural Goods', *The European Journal of International Law,* 23(2012), no.3, pp.719-730.

F. Francioni, 'The Human Dimension of International Cultural Heritage law: An Introduction', *The European Journal of International Law,* 22(2011), no.1, pp.9-16.

F. Franioni & J. Gordley (eds), *Enforcing International Cultural Heritage Law*, Oxford: Oxford University Press 2013.

N. Fraser & A. Honneth, *Redistribution or Recognition? A Political-Philosophical Exchange*, London, New York: Verso, 2003.

J. Friedman, 'The Past in the Future: History and the Politics of Identity', *American Anthropologist* 94 (1992), no. 4, pp. 837-859.

Y. Fung, *A History of Chinese Philosophy*, London: Macmillan 1948.

B.T. Hoffman (ed.), *Art and Cultural Heritage: Law, Policy and Practice,* Cambridge: Cambridge University Press 2006.

Ge Jianxiong, 'Why Traditional China had the Tradition of Respecting History' (in Chinese), *Exploration and Free Views,* (2008), no.9, pp. 11-13.

E. Gellner & A.D. Smith, 'The Nation: Real or Imagined? The Warwick Debates on Nationalism', *Nations and Nationalism* 2 (1996), no. 3, pp. 357-370.

E. Gellner, *Nations and Nationalism*, Ithaca: Cornell University Press 1983.

P. Gerstenblith, 'Identity and Cultural Property: The Protection of Cultural Property in the United States', *Boston University Law Review* 75 (1995), no. 3, pp. 559-688.

K.F. Gibbon (ed.), *Who Owns the Past? Cultural Policy, Cultural Property, and the Law,* New Brunswick: Rutgers University Press 2005.

A. Gillespie, *A History of the Laws of War: The Customs and the Laws of War with Regards to Civilians in Times of Conflict, Vol. 2*, Oxford: Hart 2011.

B. Graham & P. Howard (eds), *The Ashgate Research Companion to Heritage and Identity*, Aldershot: Ashgate 2008.

B. Graham, G.J. Ashworth & J.E. Tunbridge, *A Geography of Heritage: Power, Culture and Economy*, London: Arnold 2000.

S. Gruber, 'Protecting China's Cultural Heritage Sites in Times of Rapid Change: Current Developments, Practice and Law', *Asia Pacific Journal of Environmental Law* 10 (2007), no. 3-4, pp. 253-301.

M. Halbwachs, *On Collective Memory* (ed., transl., introd. by L.A. Coser), Chicago: University of Chicago Press 1992.

R. Hallman, 'Museums and Cultural Property: A Retreat from the Internationalist Approach', *International Journal of Cultural Property* 12 (2005), no. 12, pp. 201-223.

R. Handler, '*Is 'Identity' a useful Cross-Cultural Concept*?', in: J.R. Gillis (ed.), *Commemorations: The Politics of National Identity*, Princeton: Princeton University Press 1994.

R. Harris, 'China and the World', *International Affairs* 35 (1959), no. 2, pp. 68-69.

J. Harrison, *Modern Chinese Nationalism*, New York: Hunter College of the City of New York 1969.

J. Hay, 'The Functions of Chinese Painting, Toward a Unified Field Theory', in: M. Westermann (ed.), *Anthropologies of Art* (proceedings of the Clark Conference at the Sterling and Francine Clark Art Institute 2003), Williamstown: Sterling and Francine Clark Art Institute 2005, pp. 111-123.

James Hevia, 'Looting and Its Discontents: Moral Discourse and the Plunder of Beijing, 1900 −1901', in: R. Bickers & R.G. Tiedemann (eds), *The Boxers, China, and the World*, New York: Rowman & Littlefield 2007, pp.93-114.

K. Hill, 'Collecting on Campaign, British Soldiers in China during the Opium Wars', *Journal of the History of Collections* 2012, pp. 1-26.

P. Hopkirk, *Foreign Devils on the Silk Road: the Search for the Lost Cities and Treasures of Chinese Central Asia*, London: John Murray 1980.

P. Hopper, *Understanding Cultural Globalization*, Cambridge: Polity Press 2007.

M.J. Hornsey, 'Social Identity Theory and Self-categorization Theory: A Historical Review', *Social and Personality Compass* 2 (2008), no. 1, pp. 204-222.

A.W. Hummel, 'The New-Culture Movement in China', *Annals of the American Academy of Political and Social Science* 152 (1930), pp. 55-62.

I.C.Y. Hsu, *The Rise of Modern China* (6th ed.), Oxford: Oxford University Press 2000.

I.C.Y. Hsu, *China without Mao: The Search for a New Order,* Oxford: Oxford University Press 1990.

S. Image, 'Cosmopolitan Art. A Friendly Dispute between Mr Selwyn Image and Mr Lewis F. Day', *The Art-Journal* 18 (1902), pp. 374-375.

A. Iriye, *Cultural Internationalism and World Order*, Baltimore: John Hopkins University Press 1997.

A.A. Kaufman, 'The "Century of Humiliation", Then and Now: Chinese Perceptions of the International Order', *Pacific Focus* 25 (2010), no.1, pp. 1-33.

H. Kissinger, *On China*, New York: Penguin 2011.

N. Knight, 'Reflecting on the Paradox of Globalisation: China's Search for Cultural Identity and Coherence', *China:An International Journal* 4 (2006), no. 1, pp. 1-31.

W.W. Kowalski, 'Types of Claim for Recovery of Lost Cultural Property', *Museum International* 57 (2005), no. 4, pp. 85-102.

E. Kramer, *Art as Therapy: Collected Papers*, London: Jessica Kingsley 2000.

P.C. Kraus, 'The Repatriation of Plundered Chinese Art', *The China Quarterly*, Vol. 199, (2009), 837-842.

W. Kymlicka, *States, Nations and Cultures*, Assen: Van Gorcum 1997.

W. Kymlicka, *Multicultural Citizenship: A Liberal Theory of Minority Rights*, Oxford: Clarendon Press (1995a).

W. Kymlicka (ed.), *The Rights of Minority Cultures*, Oxford: Oxford University Press 1995.

J.R. Levenson, *Confucian China and its Modern Fate: A Trilogy,Vol. 1*, Berkeley: University of California Press 1968.

L. Zhaojie (James Li), 'The Impact of International Law on the Transformation of China's Perception of the World: A Lesson from History', *Maryland Journal of International Law* 27 (2012), no. 1.

Liang Shuming, *Eastern and Western Cultures and their Philosophies* (in Chinese, first published in 1921), Shanghai: *Shanghai Renmin Chubanshe* 2006.

Liang Shuming, *The Substance of Chinese Culture* (in Chinese, first published in 1949), Shanghai: *Shanghai Renmin Chubanshe* 2005.

Lin Mingjie, 'Relics from Yuangming Yuan Test Degree of Civilized' (in Chinese), *Xinmin Wanbao,* October 21, 2010, viewed May 7, 2014, http://news.xinhuanet.com/shuhua/2010-10/21/c_12683026.htm

L.H. Liu, *The Clash of Empires: The Invention of China in Modern World Making,* Cambridge: Harvard University Press 2004.

T.T. Liu & D. Faure (eds), *Unity and Diversity: Local Cultures and Identities in China,* Hong Kong: Hong Kong University Press 1996.

L. Lourme, 'How to Justify Institutional Cosmopolitanism?', May 5, 2014, viewed May 21, 2014, academia.edu/6985803/How_to_justify_institutional_cosmopolitanism.

D. Lowenthal, *Possessed by the Past: The Heritage Crusade and the Spoils of History*, Cambridge: Cambridge University Press 1988.

D. Lowenthal, *The Past is a Foreign Country*, Cambridge: Cambridge University Press 1985.

M. Lu & R. Dellios, 'One Culture Two Systems: A Cultural Approach to Inter-Chinese Politics', *Culture Mandala: The Bulletin of the Centre for East-West Cultural and Economic Studies* 3 (1998), no. 1, pp. 18-40.

N. MacGregor & J. Williams, 'The Encyclopedic Museum: Enlightenment Ideals, Contemporary Realities', *Public Archeology* 4 (2005), no. 1, pp. 50-59.

J. Makeham, *Lost Soul: 'Confucianism' in Contemporary Chinese Academic Discourse*, Cambridge: Harvard University Press 2008.

F.F. Mansvelt Beck, 'Liberalism, Minorities and Politics of Social Differentiaton', *2nd Pavia Graduate Conference in Political Philosophy* 2004.

C. McAndrew, *The Role of Art & Antique Dealers: An Added Value*, London: Publications UK 2011.

S. McCausland (ed.), *Gu Kaizhi and the Admonitions Scroll*, London: The British Museum Press 2003.

S.E. Mead, 'History and Identity', *Studies in Religion* 51 (1971), no. 1, pp. 1-14.

Mei Haofang, Zhou Liangkai & Tang Yian, *Objects, Heritage and Cultural Identity* (in Chinese), Nantou: Taiwan Wenxian Guan 2009.

J.H. Merryman (ed.), *Imperialism, Art and Restitution*, Cambridge: Cambridge University Press 2009.

J.H. Merryman, 'Cultural Property, International Trade and Human Rights', *Cardozo Arts & Entertainment Law Journal* 51 (2001), pp. 51-68.

J.H. Merryman & A.E. Elsen (eds), *Law, Ethics and the Visual Arts* (3rd ed.), Alphen a/d Rijn: Kluwer Law International 1998.

J.H. Merryman, 'Two Ways of Thinking about Cultural Property', *American Journal of International Law* 80 (1986), no. 4, pp. 831-853.

J.H. Merryman, 'Thinking about the Elgin Marbles', *Michigan Law Review* 83 (1985), no. 8, pp. 1881-1923.

N. Mezey, 'The Paradoxes of Cultural Property', *Columbia Law Review* 107 (2007), pp. 2004-2046.

V. Mishra, 'Multiculturalism', *Year's Work in Critical and Cultural Theory* 21 (2004), pp. 1-22.

J.A.R. Nafziger & R.K. Paterson (eds), *Handbook on the Law of Cultural Heritage and International Trade*, The Lypiatts: Edward Elgar Publishing Limited 2014

J.A.R. Nafziger & A.M. Nicgorski (eds), *Cultural Heritage Issues: The Legacy of Conquest, Colonization, and Commerce*, Leiden: Nijhoff 2009.

J.A.R. Nafziger, 'Protection of Cultural Property', in: M. Cherif Bassiouni (ed.), *International Criminal Law: Vol. 1: Sources, Subjects, and Contents* (3rd ed.), Leiden: Nijhoff 2008, pp. 977-1035.

Andrew J. Nathan, 'Is Chinese Culture Distinctive-A Review Article', *The Journal of Asian Studies,* Vol.52, (1993),no.4, pp. 923-936.

N. Niedzielski-Eichner, 'Art Historians and Cultural Property Internationalism', *International Journal of Cultural Property* 12 (2005), no. 2, pp. 183-200.

K. Nielsen, 'Cultural Nationalism, Neither Ethnic Nor Civic', in: R.S. Beiner (ed.), *Theorizing Nationalism*, Albany: State University of New York Press 1999, pp. 119-130.

P.J. O'Keefe & L.V. Prott (eds), *Cultural Heritage Conventions and Other Instruments, A Compendium with Commentaries,* Crickadarn: Institute of Art and Law 2011.

P.J. O'Keefe, 'A Comparison of the Washington and Vilnius Principles and Resolution 1205', in: L.V. Prott (ed.), *Witnesses to History: A Compendium of Documents and Writings on the Return of Cultural Objects*, Paris: UNESCO 2009, pp. 158-162.

P.J. O'Keefe, *Commentary on the UNESCO 1970 Convention on Illicit Traffic,* Leicester: Institute of Art and Law, 2000.

P.J. O'Keefe, 'Codes of Ethics: Form and Function in Cultural Heritage Management', *International Cultural Property Society* 7 (1998), no. 1, pp. 32-51.

P.J. O'Keefe, *Feasibility of an International Code of Ethics for Dealers in Cultural Property for the Purpose of More Effective Control of Traffic in Cultural Property* (Report for UNESCO), Paris: UNESCO 15 May 1994.

R. O' Keefe, *The Protection of Cultural Property in Armed Conflict*, Cambridge: Cambridge University Press, 2006.

B.O. Okere, 'International Regulation of the Return and Restitution of Cultural Property', *Revue Hellénique de Droit International* 40/41 (1987/88), pp. 141-156.

M. O'Neill, 'Enlightenment Museums: Universal or merely Global', *Museum and Society* 2 (2004), no. 3, pp. 190-202.

N. Palmer (ed.) *The Recovery of Stolen Art: A Collection of Essays,* London: Kluwer Law International 1998.

B.C. Parekh, *Rethinking Multiculturalism: Cultural Diversity and Political Theory*, Basingstoke: Palgrave MacMillan 2000.

Peng Lei, *A Research on Legal History of Return of Relics* (in Chinese), Nanjing: Yilin Publishing 2012.

E.A. Posner, 'The International Protection of Cultural Property: Some Skeptical Observations', *Chicago Journal of International Law* 8 (2007), no. 1, pp. 213-231.

L.V. Prott, 'UNESCO International Framework for the Protection of Cultural Heritage', in J.A.R. Nafziger & A.M. Nicgorski (eds), *Cultural Heritage Issues: The Legacy of Conquest, Colonization, and Commerce*, Leiden: Nijhoff 2009, pp. 257-285.

L.V. Prott, 'UNESCO and Unidroit A Partnership against Trafficking in Cultural Objects', *Uniform Law Review* 1 (1996), pp. 59-71.

L.V. Prott & P.J. O'Keefe, *Law and the Cultural Heritage: Vol. 3: Movement*, London: Butterworths 1989.

L. V. Prott & P. J. O'Keefe, "Cultural Heritage' or 'Cultural Property", *International Journal of Cultural Property,* no. 2 (1992), 307-320.

J.A.G. Roberts, *A History of China*, New York: Macmillan 1999.

Rong Xinjiang, *Eighteen Lectures on Dunhuang* (transl. by I. Galambos), Leiden: Koninklijke Brill 2013.

Rong Xinjiang, 'Chinese Dunhuang Studies and International Horizon',(in Chinese) *Lishi Yanjiu* 2005, no.

Rong Xinjiang, 'The Nature of the Dunhuang Library Cave and the Reasons for Its Sealing' (transl. by V. Hansen), *Cahier d'Extrême-Asie* 11 (1999-2000), pp. 247-275.

E.W. Said, *Orientalism*, New York: Vintage Books 1994.

W. Sandholtz, 'Plunder, Restitution, and International Law', *International Journal of Cultural Property* 17 (2010), pp. 147-176.

W. Sandholtz, *Prohibiting Plunder: How Norms Change*, Oxford: Oxford University Press 2007.

B.I. Schwartz, 'Culture, Modernity, and Nationalism-Further Reflections', in: W. Tu (ed.), *China in Transformation*, Cambridge: Harvard University Press 1993.

A. Sen, *Identity and Violence: The Illusion of Destiny*, New York: Norton 2007.

H. Seton-Watson, *States and Nations: An Inquiry into the Origins of Nations and the Politics of Nationalism*, London: Methuen 1977.

F. Shaheed, *Report of the Independent Expert in the Field of Cultural Rights*, UN Doc A/HRC/17/38, March 21, 2011.

E. Simpson (ed.), *The Spoils of War II and its Aftermath: The Loss, Reappearance, and Recovery of Cultural Property*, New York: Harry N. Abrams 1997.

A.D. Smith, *Myths and Memories of the Nation*, Oxford: Oxford University Press 1999.

L. Smith, *Archaeological Theory and the Politics of Cultural Heritage*, London: Routledge 2004.

M.A. Stein, *Innermost Asia: Detailed Report of Explorations in Central Asia, Kan-su, and Eastern Iran,* Oxford: Clarendon Press 1928.

M.A. Stein, *Serindia: Detailed Report of Explorations in Central Asia and Westernmost China,* Oxford: Clarendon Press 1921.

C.M. Taylor, *Sources of the Self: The Making of the Modern Identity*, Cambridge: Harvard University Press 1989.

R.L. Thorp & R.E. Vinograd, *Chinese Art & Culture*, Upper Saddle River: Prentice Hall 2006.

E. Tourme-Jouannet, 'The International Law of Recogntion', *The European Journal of International Law'* 24, no. 2, 667-690.

J. Townsend, 'Chinese Nationalism', *The Australian Journal of Chinese Affairs* 1992, no. 27, pp. 97-130.

Tu Wei-ming, 'Cultural China: The Periphery as the Center', *Daedalus* 134 (2005), no. 4, pp. 145-167.

A.F. Vrdoljak, *International Law, Museums and the Returns of Cultural Objects*, Cambridge: Cambridge University Press 2006.

A. Waldersee, 'Plundering Peking', *The Living Age* 317, no. 4118 (June 9, 1923), pp. 563-569.

D. Wang, 'The Discourse of Unequal Treaties in Modern China', *Pacific Affairs* 76 (2003), no. 3, pp. 399-425.

Wang Yunxia & Huang Shuqing, 'Stance of Cultural Heritage Law: Nationalism or Internationalism' (in Chinese,), *Jurists Review* 5 (2008), pp. 41-47.

Wang Yunxia, 'Legal Issues concerning the Restitution of Looted Cultural Objects from WWII' (in Chinese), *Liaoning Daxue Xuebao,* (2007), no. 4, pp. 140-145.

Wang Zheng, *Never Forget National Humiliation: Historical Memory in Chinese Politics and Foreign Relations*, New York: Columbia University Press 2012.

P. Weil, 'Towards Relative Normativity in International Law', *The American Journal of International Law* 77 (1983), pp. 413-442.

Annette Weiner, 'Inalienable Wealth', *American Ethnologist*, Vol. 12, Iss. 2, (1985), pp.210-227.

Annette Weiner, *Inalienable Possessions: The Paradox of Keeping While Giving*, Berkeley: University of California Press, 1992.

P.H. Welsh, 'The Power of Possessions: The Case Against Property', *Museum Anthropology* 21 (1997), no. 3, pp. 12-18.

Y. Wong, *A paradise Lost: The Imperial Garden Yuanming Yuan*, Honolulu: University of Hawai'i Press 2011.

D.Y. Wu, 'The Construction of Chinese and Non-Chinese Identities', *Daedalus* 120 (1991), no. 2, pp. 159-179.

Wu Mei & Guo Zhenzhi, 'Globalization, National Culture and the Search for Identity: A Chinese Dilemma', *Media Development* (Special Issue on UNESCO's Convention of Cultural Diversity). No. 1, pp. 11-16.

L. Xi, 'The Dialogical Consciousness of Third Generation Neo-Confucianism', *Dialogue and Universalism* 2 (2011), no. 2, pp. 23-32.

Xu Weiping and others (ed.), *Chinese History in Cultural Relics* (in Chinese) Beijing: People's Publishing 2011.

O. Yasuaki, 'Japanese War Guilt and Postwar Responsibilities of Japan', *Berkeley Journal of International Law* 20 (2003), no. 3, pp. 600-620.

Zang, Z. 'The Destruction of the Old Summer Palace was the Fatal Blow on Eastern Culture' (in Chinese), *Chinese Academy of Social Sciences Review* 12 November 2010.

Zhao Suisheng, *Nation-State by Construction: Dynamics of Modern Chinese Nationalism,* Stanford: Stanford University Press 2004.

Zhao Suisheng, 'Chinese Nationalism and Its International Orientations', *Political Science Quarterly* 115 (2000), no. 1, pp. 1-33.

Zhang Zhigang, 'Chinese Cultural Resources in Building a Harmonious World - A Review on the Exploring Achievements made by Chinese Senior Scholars', *Procedia-Social and Behavioral Sciences* 2013, no. 11., pp. 214-226.

Zhu Changqiao, 'Cultural Relics: Objects of Cultural Identity with the Dimensions of Time and Space' (in Chinese), *Sichuan Wenwu* 2007, no. 3, pp. 81-85.

MIX
Papier aus verantwortungsvollen Quellen
Paper from responsible sources
FSC® C105338

If you have any concerns about our products,
you can contact us on
ProductSafety@springernature.com

In case Publisher is established outside the EU,
the EU authorized representative is:
Springer Nature Customer Service Center GmbH
Europaplatz 3, 69115 Heidelberg, Germany

Printed by Libri Plureos GmbH
in Hamburg, Germany